TRUTH DECAY

DEFENDING
CHRISTIANITY AGAINST
THE CHALLENGES OF
POSTMODERNISM

DOUGLAS
GROOTHUIS

InterVarsity Press
Downers Grove, Illinois
Leicester, England

InterVarsity Press
P.O. Box 1400, Downers Grove, IL 60515
World Wide Web: www.ivpress.com
E-mail: mail@ivpress.com

Inter-Varsity Press, England
38 De Montfort Street
Leicester LE1 7GP, England

InterVarsity Press® is the book-publishing division of InterVarsity Christian Fellowship/USA®, a student
movement active on campus at hundreds of universities, colleges and schools of nursing in the United
States of America, and a member movement of the International Fellowship of Evangelical Students. For
information about local and regional activities, write Public Relations Dept., InterVarsity Christian
Fellowship/USA, 6400 Schroeder Rd., P.O. Box 7895, Madison, WI 53707-7895.

Inter-Varsity Press, England, is the book-publishing division of the Universities and Colleges Christian
Fellowship (formerly the Inter-Varsity Fellowship), a student movement linking Christian Unions in
universities and colleges throughout the United Kingdom and the Republic of Ireland, and a member of the
International Fellowship of Evangelical Students. For information about local and national activities write
to UCCF, 38 De Montfort Street, Leicester LE1 7GP.

All Scripture quotations, unless otherwise indicated, are taken from the British edition of the Holy Bible,
New International Version®. NIV®. Copyright ©1973, 1978, 1984 by International Bible Society,
Inclusive Language Version ©1995, 1996, and published in Great Britain by Hodder and Stoughton Ltd.
Distributed in North America by permission of Zondervan Publishing House. All rights reserved.

Cover illustration: Zefa Germany/The Stock Market

USA ISBN 0-8308-2228-3
UK ISBN 0-85111-524-1

Printed in the United States of America ∞

Library of Congress Cataloging-in-Publication Data

Groothuis, Douglas R., 1957-
    Truth decay: defending Christianity against the challenges of postmodernism/Douglas Groothuis.
        p. cm.
    Includes bibliographical references and index.
    ISBN 0-8308-2228-3 (pbk.: alk. paper)
    1. Truth (Christian theology) 2. Postmodernism—Religious aspects—Christianity. I.
Title.
BT50.G66 2000
230'.01—dc21

                                                                                    00-021471

British Library Cataloguing in Publication Data

A catalogue record for this book is available from the British Library.

20	18	17	16	15	14	13	12	11	10	9	8	7	6	5	4	3	2	1
15	14	13	12	11	10	09	08	07	06	05	04	03	02	01	00			

"There is no shortage today of evangelicals calling for a reaffirmation of objective truth in the face of postmodern relativism. However, a clear and helpful analysis on the nature of such truth seems to be rare. *Truth Decay* is such a book. Groothuis not only points out the problems with the denial of objective truth—by far the easier task—but he also constructs a sound understanding of truth and shows how it undergirds Christian concerns such as apologetics or ethics. He does so in a flowing style of argumentation which will make his ideas accessible to newcomers to philosophical writing and yet challenging to the academy. Any Christian with a passion for truth ought to study this book."

WINFRIED CORDUAN
Professor of Philosophy and Religion, Taylor University

"In *Truth Decay* Professor Groothuis has deftly woven together a vast array of crucial topics to produce a timely and engaging volume. Groothuis is clearly at home with the technical issues necessary to treat the issue with care, yet he has managed to communicate them in an accessible way that avoids being simplistic. In thirty years of evangelistic and apologetic ministry I have seen firsthand the emerging postmodernist gloom *Truth Decay* seeks to dispel, and I have witnessed how postmodernism inevitably shrivels the flourishing of humanity. It used to be that I could assume an audience knew what truth was, and my task was to help my listeners come to see Christianity as true. But that assumption has now been buried, and some of its gravediggers are Christian scholars, however well-intentioned they may be. In this regard *Truth Decay* is a must-read for all those concerned with the care of souls, not only because it clarifies the issues and critiques false and harmful trends but also because it is a noncontentious call to action."

J. P. MORELAND
Professor of Philosophy, Talbot School of Theology,
Biola University, and coauthor of Body & Soul *(IVP)*

"This is a clear-sighted, sure-footed guide across the soggy and treacherous swamps of the postmodern world. Along the way Groothuis gives us a vigorous defense of truth and helpful ideas about its application in a world in which the very idea of truth has become strange."

DAVID F. WELLS
Andrew Mutch Distinguished Professor of Historical and
Systematic Theology, Gordon-Conwell Theological Seminary

TO

FRANCIS SCHAEFFER (1912-1984)

AND CARL F. H. HENRY,

INTELLECTUAL MENTORS

WHO TAUGHT ME TO LOVE THE TRUTH

AND UNDERSTAND THE TIMES.

Contents

Introduction: The Problem of Truth & Integrity

Aristotle began his great work *Metaphysics* by writing that "man by nature desires to know." Centuries later the poet and playwright T. S. Eliot noted, "Humankind cannot bear very much reality."[1] Strangely, both are right. Out of this all-too-human tension and polarity is borne the perennially paradoxical quest for, and escape from, the truth. Truth is a daunting, difficult thing; it is also the greatest thing in the world. Yet we are chronically ambivalent toward it. We seek it . . . and we fear it. Our better side wants to pursue truth wherever it leads; our darker side balks when the truth begins to lead us anywhere we do not want to go. Let the truth be damned if the truth would damn us! We want both to serve the truth and to be served by it. Such is our uneasy lot, east of Eden. The apostle Paul knew this well. In the book of Romans he speaks of our inescapable knowledge of God's truth and our natural aversion to it:

> The wrath of God is being revealed from heaven against all the godless-
> ness and wickedness of those who suppress the truth by their wickedness,
> since what may be known about God is plain to them, because God has
> made it plain to them. For since the creation of the world God's invisible
> qualities—his eternal power and divine nature—have been clearly seen,
> being understood from what has been made, so that they are without
> excuse. (Rom 1:18-20)

Elemental to this deep division in our beings, this civil war within, is

---

[1]T. S. Eliot, *Murder in the Cathedral* (New York: Harcourt, Brace & World, 1963), p. 69.

not simply the question of what things we take to be true or false—"Am I
a good man or a bad man?"—but what we take the nature of truth to be. Is
the truth indissolubly connected to objective reality, or is it something
more malleable, fungible and adaptable to circumstance? Do we construct
truth—whether individually or as a culture—or do we receive truth as a
gift, however unnerving it may be? Can language capture realities outside
of itself or can it only refer to itself in a kind of linguistic solitaire?

Truth and Integrity

These are not philosophical games reserved for intellectuals or the otherwise bored. They are matters of personal rectitude and integrity. How
ought I to orient myself to truth? Can I find the truth and live within its
domain? Can I abide by its demands and delight in its benefits? We
ought to be haunted by the words of Ludwig Wittgenstein:

> No one can speak the truth; if he has still not mastered himself. He *cannot*
> speak it;—but not because he is not clever enough yet.
>   The truth can be spoken only by someone who is already at home in it;
> not by someone who still lives in falsehood and reaches out from false-
> hood towards truth on just one occasion.[2]

The philosopher does not here tell us just what truth is, but he underscores its inestimable value for those who desire integrity, to speak and
live truly.[3] Therefore, if the proper understanding of truth is undergoing
decay, we should be alarmed, as well as animated to reverse it.

In his journals, the young Søren Kierkegaard, then a university student, famously pondered his relationship to truth, wondering what his
calling under God might be:

> There is something missing in my life, and it has to do with my need to under-
> stand *what I must do*, not what I must know—except, of course, that a certain
> amount of knowledge is presupposed in every action. I need to understand my
> purpose in life, to see what God wants me to do, and this means that I must find a

---

[2]Ludwig Wittgenstein, *Culture and Value*, trans. Peter Winch (Chicago: University of
Chicago Press, 1984), p. 35e. The unorthodox punctuation of the first sentence is
found in the original translation.
[3]Wittgenstein's views of truth probably changed over time, and just what his final
view was is a matter of rather intense intellectual debate, which we will not address.

truth which is true for me, that I must find *that Idea for which I can live and die*.[4]

Kierkegaard later found the truth to which he would dedicate his short and productive life: the explanation and application of Christian faith through a vast outpouring of sophisticated literature. He took the idea of "truth as true for him" to mean what engaged him at the deepest levels of his heart, not in the sense that he could customize truth to fit his whims. He sought and eventually found "something which reaches to the deepest roots of my existence and wherein I am connected into the divine and held fast to it, even though the whole world falls apart."[5] Should we not aspire to do the same? Should we not be like David, who "served God's purpose in his own generation" (Acts 13:36)?

Over one hundred fifty years after young Søren's ruminations, some claim that the whole modernist world has fallen apart and that we are held fast by nothing certain, nothing objective, nothing absolute, nothing universal. There is no finally fixed point of reference, no immovable anchor for the soul. We have entered post-modernity; the modernist ways of thinking about truth are impossible. Postmodernism, broadly understood, has dispensed with Truth and has replaced it with truths. Some take this as liberating, even for Christian endeavors. I take it to be very bad news—philosophically, ethically, apologetically and theologically. The burden of this book is to show why.

Truth, Passion and Humility

I do not engage this topic dispassionately. Since I converted to the Christian faith in 1976 after my first year in college, I have been intensely concerned about the defense of Christian truth in contemporary culture. As a college student, a campus minister, a writer and a philosophy professor, I have labored to the best of my abilities to under-

[4]Søren Kierkegaard, "An Entry from the Journal of the Young Kierkegaard," in Louis Pojman, *Classics of Philosophy*, vol. 11, *Modern and Contemporary* (New York: Oxford University Press, 1998), p. 902; emphasis in the original. For an in-depth, sympathetic treatment of Kierkegaard's views on faith and reason, see C. Stephen Evans, *Faith Beyond Reason: A Kierkegaardian Account* (Grand Rapids, Mich.: Eerdmans, 1998). Some critical comments on Kierkegaard's apologetic are made in chapter seven.
[5]Kierkegaard, "Entry from the Journal" p. 902.

stand the rationality and implications of Christianity and to make those
known to the church and to the unbelieving world. Therefore, I have
taken a keen interest in postmodernism, a philosophy—or, better, a
cluster of philosophies—that seeks radically to reconceptualize traditional notions of truth and rationality.

Postmodernists fret mightily about arrogance and dogmatism, but to
avoid them they typically rebound into the equal and opposite errors of
cheap tolerance and relativism. However, a belief in the objectivity of
truth and its importance for all of life does not entail an arrogant attitude or an unbending, irrational dogmatism. Despite the strong convictions that drive this book, I want briefly to distinguish two claims, lest I
be misunderstood. It is one thing to claim that objective, absolute and
universal truth exists. It is quite another to claim that one has mastered
these objective, absolute and universal truths or that one has nothing
more to learn and is in no need of correction. I will argue strenuously for
the former claim but (not being omniscient) make no pretense to the latter. In fact, it is precisely belief in a truth beyond one's own thoughts and
culture that allows one to be rebuffed and reconstructed by reality. We
can, therefore, be realigned by the truth and with the truth. This nonnegotiable distinction should engender humility, not arrogance; a quest for
reasonable certainty through dialogue, not dogmatism through mindless affirmation and denunciation. Richard John Neuhaus's comments
ought to serve as a tonic for the Christian thinker, myself included, who
may be tempted by visions of intellectual grandiosity.

> Few things have contributed so powerfully to the unbelief of the modern
> and postmodern world as the pretension of Christians to know more than
> we do. . . . If Christians exhibited more intellectual patience, modesty, curi-
> osity, and sense of adventure, there would be few atheists in the world, both
> of the rationalist and postmodern varieties.[6]

Blaise Pascal, a true genius and extraordinary apologist, echoes this

---

[6]Richard John Neuhaus, "Encountered by the Truth," *First Things*, October 1998, p.
83. James Sire pointed out this quotation to me. For more on humility and apologetics, see Douglas Groothuis, "Apologetics, Truth, and Humility," in *Christianity That
Counts: Being a Christian in a Non-Christian World* (Grand Rapids, Mich.: Baker, 1994),
pp. 63-65.

concern about holding the truth wrongly:

> We make an idol of truth itself, for truth apart from charity is not God, but his image and an idol that we must not love or worship. Still less must we love or worship its opposite, which is falsehood.[7]

With these exhortations in mind let us investigate the conditions of truth decay in the postmodern world.

Truth Decay: A Preview

Truth Decay is written by a Christian primarily for Christians, but it should be of interest to anyone who is concerned about the nature of truth and its implications in postmodernity. Although I write from a Christian worldview, my critique of postmodernism is not simply a matter of citing biblical proof texts. Rather, my aim is to fairly present postmodernist ideas in relation to what I take to be a biblical and logical perspective. I hope that many non-Christians will read and profit from this book. Since some Christian thinkers are favorably disposed to post-modernism and some non-Christian thinkers are not so disposed, I hope to spark rational debate on both (1) the value of postmodernism for Christians and (2) the truth of Christianity in relation to its opponents, both modernist and postmodernist.

Chapter one discusses how postmodernism seeks to transform radically—and so jeopardize—the biblical understanding of truth. This is illustrated from many aspects of our culture. Chapter two considers the crucial distinctions between premodernity, modernity and postmodernity as cultural and historical conditions as well as the differences between modernism and postmodernism as philosophies. Chapter three addresses the basic biblical view of truth in relation to postmodernist objections, giving its eight defining features that are often ignored or downplayed today. Chapter four presents a philosophical argument for what is called "the correspondence view of truth"—the claim that a true statement is one that agrees with or matches the reality it describes—against postmodernist alternatives. Although this chapter

---

[7]Blaise Pascal, *Pensees*, ed. Alban Krailsheimer (New York: Penguin, 1966), 926/582; p. 318.

is probably the most philosophically demanding in the book, I encourage all readers to give it close attention, because so much rides on the outcome. Chapter five considers how postmodernist ideas have affected Christian theology—particularly in the work of Alister McGrath and Stanley Grenz—and what needs to be done to counteract the postmodernist influence in order to present a biblically accurate account of our faith. In chapter six, I assess the strategies of William Willimon, Philip Kenneson and Lesslie Newbigin—apologists who have, I believe, unwisely incorporated postmodernist themes into their defenses of the Christian faith. I provide what I believe to be a more solid and full-orbed approach to apologetics in chapter seven, arguing that there is a wealth of intellectual resources available for the defense of Christianity as both true and rational (even in postmodern times).

Chapter eight critiques various versions of postmodernists ethics, particularly those of Richard Rorty and Michel Foucault, and finds them seriously flawed, especially in comparison with Christian ethics. Ethics without a knowledge of objective reality is not achievable. Although postmodernists often claim that their philosophy is the best way to overcome racial and gender stereotypes that are grounded in modernist assumptions, I dispute this in chapter nine and present a Christian alternative that honors all people as made in the image of God and capable of redemption. Chapter ten disputes the postmodernist belief that art cannot be objectively evaluated; it further makes the case that art—both Christian and non-Christian—can convey objective beauty that is a gift from a good God. Chapter eleven offers a Pascalian reflection on "the fixed-point in the postmodern world," in which I exhort the reader to incarnate truth in the postmodern context through intellectual integrity, loving confrontation, sound teaching and preaching, truthful worship, astute evangelism and a rediscovery of the biblical doctrine of calling. The appendix, "Television: Agent of Truth Decay," argues that the very form of television reinforces central themes in postmodernism and that television should, therefore, be resisted by those troubled by truth decay.

My thanks go to David Werther, James Sire and Andy LePeau for their insightful and astute comments on the entire manuscript. Special thanks go to Rebecca Merrill Groothuis, my wife, for her invaluable contributions to every chapter. She has an uncanny knack for clarifying and correcting both my thinking and my writing. Of course, any errors or infelicities that remain should be credited to me, not them. I must also credit T-Bone Burnett for the witty phrase "truth decay," which was the title of one of his musical recordings.

1

TRUTH IN JEOPARDY

A venerable old Russian proverb claims that "one word of truth outweighs the world." Russian writer Aleksandr Solzhenitsyn mounted a decades-long, suffering-ridden campaign for truth on the basis of this proverb, believing that an entire communist regime would not forever resist, repress or refute the stubborn realities that witnessed against it. Having found God in the Gulag, and against all odds, Solzhenitsyn staked his life on the hope that the truth would prevail and that his calling would be vindicated—even in the face of entrenched ideology, massive propaganda, systematic oppression and pure terror. Though the history books be rewritten, the dissidents silenced and the masses misled, the truth itself would stand firm and upright. It could not be beaten into submission to falsehood. And Solzhenitsyn, under God, would be its prophet.

On July 4, 1776, the authors of the Declaration of Independence, voicing "the unanimous Declaration of the Thirteen United States of America," proclaimed, "We hold these Truths to be self-evident: that all Men are created equal; that they are endowed by their Creator with certain inalienable Rights: that among these are Life, Liberty, and the pursuit of Happiness."

Thomas Jefferson, the principle author of the Declaration, along with John Hancock and the other signatories, argued their case by presupposing that truth was objective and knowable, that it rested on "the laws of nature and nature's God," and that it supported their position against the British. For the founders, truth was not something to be manipulated for the sake of political gain. "Self-evident" truths must be recognized, respected and obeyed; they are not created nor can they be dissolved by any political power or military might. These truths alone provided a firm basis for asserting an independent national identity.

Nearly two hundred years after the founding of the United States of America, a moral reformer called his country to be true to its constituting ideals. On August 28, 1963, before over two hundred thousand people gathered between the Washington Monument and the Lincoln Memorial, Martin Luther King Jr. explained the purpose of this historic gathering:

> In a sense we have come to our nation's capital to cash a check. When the architects of our republic wrote the magnificent words of the Constitution and the Declaration of Independence, they were signing a promissory note to which every American was to fall heir. This note was a promise that all men would be guaranteed the inalienable rights of life, liberty, and the pursuit of happiness.[1]

But, King lamented, it "is obvious today that America has defaulted on this promissory note insofar as her citizens of color are concerned." Nevertheless, the civil rights leader passionately intoned, "I have a dream that one day this nation will rise up and live out the true meaning of its creed: 'we hold these truths to be self evident; that all men are created equal,'"[2] and that one day "all of God's children, black men and white men, Jews and Gentiles, Protestants and Catholics, will be able to join hands and sing in the words of the old Negro spiritual, 'free at last!

---

[1]Martin Luther King Jr., "I Have a Dream," in *The Book of Virtues: A Treasury of Great Moral Stories*, ed. William J. Bennett (New York: Simon & Schuster, 1993), p. 573.
[2]Ibid.

free at last! thank God almighty, we are free at last!' "[3]

King's flair for oratory should not obscure the philosophical assumptions on which his earnest and articulate outcry was founded. His moral appeal flowed from his conviction that America's deepest ideals, though imperfectly implemented, were true to a moral reality larger than America itself. His hope was animated by his belief that a greater measure of justice was attainable through the struggles of the oppressed, the repentance of the oppressors, and the providence of God Almighty. Truth would win out in the end—despite the snarling police dogs, the gushing fire hoses, the bombed black churches and the political damage control of an establishment unwilling to grant full personhood and the rights thereof to African-American citizens.

For millennia, a resolute confidence about truth has summoned philosophers, prophets, reformers and even a few politicians to defy convention and resist illicit authority, whether secular or ecclesiastical. When Professor Martin Luther affirmed at the Diet of Worms in 1521 the newly rediscovered doctrine of justification by faith alone—a truth that would galvanize and energize the Reformation—he confronted both state and church power by saying, "Here I stand. I can do no other. God help me."

The very phrase, "speaking truth to power," so often invoked by idealists and activists of many stripes, rests on the assurance that truth is owned by no one, is rejected at one's peril and contains a dynamic greater than any error. Whether we find Socrates suffering death at the hand of the state rather than recant his teachings, or envision Gandhi standing unarmed for Indian independence against the British imperial forces, or remember our American suffragists fighting for the right of women to vote in a male-dominated society, heroes have heretofore been defined and esteemed by their adherence to truth and their willingness to suffer all on its behalf.

Truth in Decay
Surrounded by such a great cloud of witnesses, American philosopher

---

[3]Ibid., p. 576.

Richard Rorty sounds a different tone. Following his hero, John Dewey, he asserts that truth is what one's peers let one get away with.[4] Rorty and a raft of other academics in philosophy, history, psychology, law, sociology, anthropology and even theology have abandoned the classical and commonsensical view of truth that lies at the heart of the examples given above and have instead embraced a concept of truth that undermines any sense of absolute, objective and universal verity. The idea of truth as objective, we are told, must be abandoned with the demise of modernism, which is regarded as the misguided attempt of the Enlightenment to attain objective certitude on matters of philosophical, scientific and moral concern. We are postmodern now and have left behind such grandiose endeavors for the sake of more modest aims.

For these postmodernist thinkers, the very idea of truth has decayed and disintegrated. It is no longer something knowable by anyone who engages in the proper forms of investigation and study. Truth is not over and above us, something that can be conveyed across cultures and over time. It is inseparable from our cultural conditioning, our psychology, our race and our gender. At the end of the day, truth is simply what we, as individuals and as communities, make it to be—and nothing more. Truth dissolves into a host of disconnected "truths," all equal to each other but unrelated to one another; there is no overall, rational scheme of things. One chronicler of postmodernism, Walter Truett Anderson, explains it this way:

> Postmodernity challenges the view that the truth is—as Isaiah Berlin put it—one and undivided, the same for all men everywhere at all times. The newer view regards any truth as socially constructed, contingent, inseparable from the peculiar needs and preferences of certain people in a certain time and place. This notion has many implications—it leaves no value, custom, belief, or eternal verity totally untouched.[5]

[4]Richard Rorty, *Philosophy and the Mirror of Nature* (New York: Princeton University Press, 1979), p. 176; see also Stephen Louthan, "On Religion: A Discussion with Richard Rorty, Alvin Plantinga and Nicholas Wolterstorff," *Christian Scholars Review* 26, no. 2 (1996): 177-83.
[5]Walter Truett Anderson, *The Future of the Self: Inventing the Postmodern Person* (New York: Jeremy P. Tarcher/Putnam, 1997), p. 27.

As a bumper sticker has it, "I've given up on reality. Now I'm looking for a good fantasy." Or consider the often-heard refrain concerning
matters of religious belief or moral decision: "Whatever . . ." Apathy,
rather than angst, often accompanies truth decay today.

But truth decay is not occurring only in the halls of the academy,
where isolated and idiosyncratic professors advance strange theories
before their curious colleagues and captive students. It is everywhere in
postmodern culture, often more assumed than argued for, more in the
air than on the mind. Truth decay dominates MTV (and most television
programs), the cinema, best-selling books and popular songs.

Truth decay insinuates itself even into churches, seminaries and
Christian colleges. During a somewhat heated debate on the nature of
truth at a conference on postmodernism at which I had spoken, a man
who teaches philosophy at a Christian college told me that objective
knowledge is impossible and that he rejects the claim that our ideas can
correspond to an external reality. When I asked him if the law of gravity
would be true if no one were on earth at the time, he replied, "No. Truth
is limited to our language." Philip Kenneson, another professor at a
Christian college, also propounds the notion that "there is no such thing
as objective truth, and it's a good thing, too."[6] Author and chaplain William Willimon stated in an article in *Christianity Today* that "Christians
who argue for the 'objective' truth of Jesus are making a tactical error,"
because "Jesus did not arrive among us enunciating a set of propositions that we are to affirm."[7]

Some church-growth advocates advise that churches tone down any
emphasis on the objective truth of Christian doctrine because postmoderns have short attention spans and are only interested in their
own felt needs. Many counsel that Generation Xers can be reached only

---

[6]Philip Kenneson, "There Is No Such Thing as Objective Truth, and It's a Good Thing
Too," in *Christian Apologetics in the Postmodern World*, ed. Timothy R. Phillips and
Dennis L. Okholm (Downers Grove, Ill.: InterVarsity Press, 1995), p. 155-72. Kenne-
son's view will be critiqued in chapter six.

[7]William H. Willimon, "Jesus' Peculiar Truth," *Christianity Today,* March 4, 1996, p. 21.
Willimon would not consider himself a postmodernist but a postliberal. Nevertheless, his views agree substantially with postmodernist themes, as will be taken up in
chapter six.

by a relational and largely noncognitive approach. One author counsels that since for Generation Xers "the linear method is no longer the primary method of study," Bible studies must de-emphasize the "inductive method with its progression of observation, interpretation and application." While this writer does not hold a postmodernist view of truth, he capitulates to the postmodern sensibilities of intellectual impatience and crass pragmatism that help contribute to truth decay in the churches.[8]

Such decay is evident in the fact that various polls have shown that high percentages of self-proclaimed evangelicals do not believe in absolute truth or the supremacy of Christ, or have a kingdom orientation to life. A recent study claimed that over half of evangelicals agreed with this statement: "The purpose of life is enjoyment and personal fulfillment."[9] A woman I know startled a table of Christian women at a luncheon by saying that her mission in life was to discover the truth and apply it to life. It was, apparently, a new thought for them.

Understanding Truth Decay

Truth decay is a cultural condition in which the very idea of absolute, objective and universal truth is considered implausible, held in open contempt or not even seriously considered. The reasons for truth decay are both philosophical and sociological, rooted in the intellectual world of ideas as well the cultural world of everyday experience. These two worlds reinforce one another. Postmodern culture—with its increasing pluralism, relativism, information overload, heightened mobility, identity confusions, consumerism and so forth—makes postmodernist philosophy seem more plausible. However, merely living in this cultural context does not mean that one must become a postmodernist on matters of truth, however tempting that may be to some.

The truth itself does not decay. In the words of the prophet Isaiah, "The grass withers and the flowers fall, but the word of our God stands

---

[8]Jimmy Long, *Generating Hope: A Strategy for Reaching the Postmodern Generation* (Downers Grove, Ill.: InterVarsity Press, 1997), p. 150.
[9]George Barna, cited in Jimmy Long, *Generating Hope: A Strategy for Reaching the Postmodern Generation* (Downers Grove, Ill.: InterVarsity Press, 1997), p. 21.

forever" (Is 40:8). Likewise, Jesus affirmed that "heaven and earth will pass away, but my words will never pass away" (Mt 24:35). Yet the human grasp of truth in a fallen world may loosen or slip. "Truth has stumbled in the streets," Isaiah lamented (Is 59:14). Jeremiah also declared to an apostate Israel, "Truth has perished; it has vanished from their lips" (Jer 7:28). Solzhenitsyn warned in his prophetic 1978 Harvard commencement address, "Truth eludes us as soon as our concentration begins to flag, all the while leaving the illusion that we are continuing to pursue it."[10] Or, as the Proverbs exhort, "Buy the truth and do not sell it" (Prov 23:23).

When Pontius Pilate interrogated Jesus before his crucifixion, Jesus proclaimed, "Everyone on the side of truth listens to me." (Jn 18:37). To this Pilate replied, "What is truth?" and immediately left Jesus to address the Jews who wanted Christ crucified (v. 38). As philosopher Francis Bacon wrote, "'What is truth?' said jesting Pilate; and would not stay for an answer."[11] Although we have no record of any reply by Jesus, Christians affirm that Pilate was staring Truth in the face, for Jesus had stated earlier to Thomas, "I am the way and the truth and the life" (Jn 14:6).

This raises the perennial question of the nature of truth. What does it mean for a statement, a belief, a philosophy or a religion to be true? This has been the subject of much debate in postmodernist circles, where the traditional view of truth as objective and knowable is no longer accepted. Even outside of academic discussions, people may be as cynical about truth as was Pilate. "What is truth?" they smirk, without waiting for an answer. Unless we are clear about what it means for something to be true, any religious or moral claim to truth—Christian or otherwise—will perplex more than enlighten. Before attempting to determine which claims are true, we need to understand the nature of truth itself. Or as Francis Schaeffer put it, we need to distinguish the *content* of truth (what statements are true) from the *concept* of truth (what truth is), because our view

---

[10]Aleksandr I. Solzhenitsyn, *A World Split Apart* (New York: Harper & Row, 1978), p. 1.
[11]Francis Bacon, "Of Truth," in *Francis Bacon: A Selection of His Works*, ed. Sidney Warhaft (Indianapolis: Bobbs-Merrill, 1965), p. 47.

of truth itself shapes everything about us.[12] Evangelical theologian, Carl
F. H. Henry captures the essence of the problem:

> Few times in history has revealed religion been forced to contend with
> such serious problems of truth and word, and never in the past have the
> role of words and the nature of truth been as misty and undefined as now.
> Only if we recognize that the truth of truth . . . is today in doubt, and that
> this uncertainty stifles the word as a carrier of God's truth and moral
> judgment, do we fathom the depth of the present crisis. When truth and
> word remain as the accepted universe of discourse, then all aberrations
> can be challenged in the name of truth. Today, however, the nature of
> truth and even the role of words is in dispute.[13]

The problem with postmoderns is that they have made peace with a
poisonous view of truth, an untrue view of truth. It is one kind of problem to believe an untruth, to take as fact something that in reality is a
falsehood, yet still believe that truth exists and can be known. If one believes, for instance, that Jesus never claimed to be God incarnate, historical evidence can be marshaled to refute this claim. However, it is
another kind of problem to believe that truth itself is merely a matter of
personal belief and social custom, so that the truth about Jesus depends
on who you take him to be; in this case, no amount of evidence or argument about particular matters of fact will change one's belief. The argument must instead be shifted to the very nature of truth itself.

Even though "the need of truth is more sacred than any other need,"[14]
as Simone Weil put it, this nutrient for the soul is often abandoned and
usurped by a desire for lesser goods. C. S. Lewis captured this problem a
generation ago in the *Screwtape Letters*, where a senior demon, Screwtape,
instructs a lower-ranking demon, Wormwood, in the art of deception.
His insights are a warning of things to come. Instead of using logical arguments to keep someone from following Christ, Wormwood is advised
keep the Christian's mind off the very idea of sound reasoning leading to
true conclusions. After all, Screwtape observes,

---

[12]Francis A. Schaeffer, *The God Who Is There*, 30th anniv. ed. (Downers Grove, Ill.:
InterVarsity Press, 1998), p. 175.
[13]Carl F. H. Henry, *God, Revelation, and Authority* (Waco, Tex.: Word, 1976), 1:24..
[14]Simone Weil, *The Need for Roots* (Boston: Beacon, 1953), p. 37.

Your man has been accustomed, ever since he was a boy, to have a dozen incompatible philosophies dancing about together inside his head. He doesn't think of doctrines as primarily "true" or "false," but as "academic" or "practical," "outworn" or "contemporary," "conventional" or "ruthless." Jargon, not argument, is your best ally in keeping him from the Church.[15]

Argument shifts the man's thoughts "onto the Enemy's own ground," and by "the very act of arguing, you awake the patient's reason; and once it is awake, who can foresee the result?" Wormwood must see to it that his man avoids the "fatal habit of attending to universal issues and withdrawing his attention from the stream of immediate sense experiences."[16] Attending to "universal issues"—to matters of objective and eternal verity—is just too dangerous, from the demonic perspective. Being concerned with "real life," meaning the unreflective immersion in the immediate, is far safer—and much more postmodern. But just don't think too much about what "real" actually means.[17]

Truth decay has ramifications for all religious truth claims, including those of Christianity, because traditional schemas of the sacred claim to represent ultimate reality, whether it be the Tao, Brahman, Nirvana, Allah or the Trinity.[18] But truth decay also affects every other area of life, from politics to art to law to history. If the idea of objective truth falls into disrepute, politics devolves into nothing but image manipulation and power mongering. As Robert Bork says, "Intellect loses its virtue when it ceases to seek truth and turns to the pursuit of political ends."[19] Social consensus and the duties of shared citizenship become irrelevant and impossible as various subsets of the population—differentiated by race, ethnicity and sexual orientation—grasp for power by claiming unimpeachable authority on the basis of their cultural particularities: "It's

---

[15]C. S. Lewis, *The Screwtape Letters*, rev. ed. (New York: Macmillan, 1961), p. 8.
[16]Ibid.
[17]Ibid.
[18]On the differences between major world religions, see Harold A. Netland, *Dissonant Voices: Religious Pluralism and the Question of Truth* (Grand Rapids, Mich.: Eerdmans, 1991; Vancouver, B.C.: Regent College Publishing, 1997).
[19]Robert Bork, *Slouching Towards Gomorrah: Modern Liberalism and American Decline* (New York: HarperCollins, 1996), p. 259.

a black thing; you wouldn't understand" or "It's a woman's thing; men just don't get it." If law is not grounded in a moral order that transcends any criminal code or constitution, it becomes a set of malleable and ultimately arbitrary edicts. If no objective facts can be discerned from the past, a novel cannot be distinguished from history, nor mythology differentiated from biography. History becomes a tool for special interest groups who rewrite the past on the basis of their predilections, without the possibility of rational critique from outside the group. If there is no beauty beyond the eye of the beholder, art becomes merely a tool for social influence, political power and personal expression; the category of obscenity is as obsolete as the ideal of beauty.

These interrelated elements of truth decay energize the culture wars that besiege our postmodern times. Just as warfare between nations breaks out after the breakdown of diplomacy, and civil wars break out after the breakdown of agreed-upon legal norms, so culture wars break out after the break down of a consensual understanding of truth as objective and knowable through rational investigation and persuasion. When reasonable debate serves no purpose in achieving a knowledge of truth, all that remains are the machinations of power—whether the cause be racial, sexual or religious. Citizens become tribespeople with little sense of the public good. The maxim of "speaking truth to power" is transformed into "mobilizing our power to overcome the other's power."

The Acids of Truth Decay

But what factors motivate truth decay? Why do people embrace a postmodernist viewpoint that radically redefines truth? People do not decide to jettison an ancient and venerable tradition for no reason. The following are some of the salient beliefs leading to truth decay. These issues will be addressed throughout the rest of the book.

1. The Enlightenment vision of unleashing reason's powers in pursuit of universal knowledge and technical mastery of the world has failed. The ideology of progress did not make good on its promises. Modernism has been eclipsed by postmodernism, which, according to Jean-Francois Lyotard, is characterized by "incredulity toward meta-

narratives,"[20] whether they be Marxist, democratic, religious or scientific attempts to definitively explain and master reality. The metanarrative must give way to the local narratives, the situational perspectives and contingencies of encultured existence. Cosmic pretense should be shunned, as should the naive hope in progress through technology or ideal forms of government.

According to architectural critic Charles Jencks, modernism was blown to bits in St. Louis on July 15, 1972, at 3:32 p.m., when the Pruitt-Igoe housing project was destroyed by dynamite. This was no terrorist ploy but a deliberate deed, symbolizing the failure of a grand vision. The huge housing project had been an attempt to create a functionally perfect living situation through rational planning. However, it became the target of incessant vandalism, and eventually was declared unlivable.[21] For Jencks and others, the razing of this housing project, along with the blasting of numerous other modernist buildings in the 1970s, served as a parable of the demise of modernism and an invitation to postmodernism, in both philosophy and architecture. "The 'death' of modern architecture and its ideology of progress, which offered technical solutions to social problems, was seen by everyone in a vivid way."[22]

2. The social situation of people in a cosmopolitan, media-saturated environment makes a unified worldview untenable. The notion of finding objective truth in the midst of the information/Internet age is a utopian illusion and should be dropped. Although he is not a post-modernist, critic Neil Postman has described the postmodern situation well:

> The tie between information and human purpose has been severed, i.e., information appears indiscriminately, directed at no one in particular, in enormous volume and at high speeds, and disconnected from theory, meaning, or purpose.[23]

---

[20]Jean François Lyotard, *The Postmodern Condition* (Minneapolis: University of Minnesota Press, 1979), p. xxiv.

[21]Steven Connor, *Postmodern Culture*, 2nd ed. (Cambridge, Mass.: Blackwell, 1997), p. 78.

[22]Charles Jencks, *What is Post-Modernism?* 4th ed. (Langham, Mass.: National Book Network, 1996), p. 30.

[23]Neil Postman, *Technopoly: The Surrender of Culture to Technology* (New York: Knopf, 1992), p. 70.

In such close conditions of information density, how can anyone hope to sort the true from the false, the trivial from the pivotal, and construct a justifiable metanarrative?

3. The diversity of religious and philosophical perspectives available to people today makes the notion of one absolutely true religion or philosophy unacceptable. There are many ways of knowing and many perspectives to be embraced. Traditional religions should, therefore, loosen their dogmatic grip and give way to a plethora of spiritualities, some of which are pastiches of several religious traditions. A cover story in *Utne Reader*, entitled "God with a Million Faces," surveyed the postmodern religious landscape in America and concluded that synthesizing one's own religion may be the best way to handle religious diversity and one's individual needs. The author cited Christian pollster George Barna's assessment that there is a "new perception of religion: a personalized, customized form of faith views which meet personal needs, minimize rules and absolutes, and bear little resemble to the 'pure' form of any of the world's major religions."[24] In a tolerant age, one is free to create a faith of one's own, because "a personal quest is a creative act, and thus just as authentic in what it says about innate human yearnings and desires" as are established religions.[25] Spirituality becomes more of a consumer item than a matter of facts, arguments and truth.

Postmodern pluralism also sparks religious challenges for the increasing number of interreligious marriages occurring in the United States.[26] On an airplane flight, I spoke at some length with a man who told me that he and his Hindu wife from East India had participated in two wedding ceremonies—a Hindu ceremony for her and a Methodist ceremony for him. The matter of how to train their two young children in religion had not yet been settled, although the husband hoped that some combination of the two faiths could be achieved.

4. Our cosmopolitan and pluralistic environments do not allow for a fixed sense of personal identity, or one best way of life. Identity should be fluid and flexible, in order to adjust to the kaleidoscopic features of

---

[24]Jeremiah Creedon, "God with a Million Faces," *Utne Reader,* July-August 1998, p. 46.
[25]Ibid., p. 48.
[26]Jerry Adler, "A Matter of Faith," *Newsweek*, December 15, 1997, pp. 49-54.

postmodern culture. There is no final truth of how humans ought to be, argues Walter Truett Anderson; we must simply experiment, adapt and adjust.[27] Consider the pop icon Madonna, who has made image make-overs a way of life—and a very lucrative life—for fifteen years. As theologian David Wells notes, "She is, in many ways, a perfect personification of the post-modern reality: . . . a self-created persona undergoing perpetual change for its own sake. In her world, everything is fluid and open. All boundaries and taboos are gone" because for her "there are no structures of meaning that transcend personal preferences"—or, we could add, that transcend marketing strategies.[28]

5. Language is ultimately a contingent creation of human beings. It cannot represent any objectively knowable reality. Our signifiers cannot be known to connect with the signified reality outside of them. Besides, language creates our sense of reality; it cannot describe a reality independent of itself. Truth is absorbed into various irreconcilable "language games," in Ludwig Wittgenstein's terminology, with no higher authority available. We may take language to have the potential to deliver reality, at least some of the time, but postmodernists want to disabuse us of our pretensions. Friedrich Nietzsche, who predated postmodernity, was nevertheless a kind of early postmodernist with respect to his views on truth and power. In an essay he said:

> What then is truth? a mobile army of metaphors, metonyms, and anthropo-morphisms—in short, a sum of human relations, which have been enhanced, transposed, and embellished poetically and rhetorically, and which after long use seem firm, canonical, and obligatory to a people: truths are illusions about which one has forgotten that this is what they are; metaphors which are worn out and without sensuous power; coins which have lost their pictures and now matter only as metal, no longer as coins.[29]

6. Written texts do not have a determinate, singular, knowable meaning or truth value. Human documents resist definitive interpretation

---

[27]See Anderson, *Future of the Self.*

[28]David Wells, *God in the Wasteland: The Reality of Truth in a World of Fading Dreams* (Grand Rapids, Mich.: Eerdmans, 1994), p. 48.

[29]Friedrich Nietzsche, "Truth and the Extra-moral Sense," in *The Portable Nietzsche*, ed. Walter Kauffman (New York: Viking, 1968), pp. 46-47.

and must be freed from the prison of objectivity. As founding decon-structionist Jacques Derrida famously said, "There is nothing outside of the text," and any text may be deconstructed to reveal its ultimately ambiguous nature.[30] An author's intended meaning does not limit the meanings of any given text. There are as many meanings as there are readers, and no reader is more justified in his or her interpretation than any other. Whether the deconstructionists themselves want to be read in this way is another matter.

7. Following up on themes in Nietzsche's work, Michel Foucault and his followers argue that what is defined as "truth" is a function not of verifiable evidence or sound logic but of power-relationships that masquerade as neutral means of enforcing order. Impartiality and objectivity are impossible in science, politics or any other endeavor. All claims to knowledge mask a subtle system of omnipresent power-relationships and transactions. As Foucault said in an interview:

> I think that, instead of trying to find out what truth, as opposed to error, is, it might be more interesting to take up the program posed by Nietzsche: how is it that, in our societies, 'the truth' has been given this value, thus placing us absolutely under its thrall.[31]

Modernist philosopher Francis Bacon claimed that "knowledge is power." By this he meant that one's awareness of the truths of nature will lead to a mastery of nature. Foucault, by contrast, takes knowledge to be essentially a function of power and inseparable from it. Whereas Bacon believed that knowledge leads to power, Foucault reverses the order: power creates forms of knowledge, and power ultimately explains the nature of supposed knowledge.[32]

This is sometimes taken to mean that dominant cultures must al-

---

[30]Jacques Derrida, *Of Grammatology* (Baltimore: Johns Hopkins University Press, 1976), p. 158.

[31]Michel Foucault, "Strategies of Power," in *The Truth About Truth: De-confusing and Re-constructing the Postmodern World*, ed. Walter Truett Anderson (New York: G. P. Putnam's Sons, 1995), p. 45.

[32]For a study of Bacon's ideas of nature in relation to those of Blaise Pascal, see Douglas Groothuis, "Bacon and Pascal on Mastery over Nature," *Research in Philosophy and Technology* 14 (1994): 191-203.

ways give way to oppressed cultures, that the powerless must be heard without criticism because they have been unfairly marginalized. John Leo reports that although Nobel Prize winner Rigoberta Menchu's 1983 book, *I, Rigoberta Menchu*, has been found to be filled with falsehoods and dubious material, some academics have ignored the criticisms, since the book champions the rights of indigenous and generally powerless peoples in the Third World. Leo comments: "The oppressed are never supposed to be analyzed or criticized by professors representing the oppressor culture of the West." He concludes:

> Our campus culture puts more emphasis on voice, narrative, and story than it does on truth. A growing number of professors accept the postmodernist notion that there is no such thing as truth, only rhetoric. The result is the blurring of distinctions between history and literature, fact and fiction, honesty and dishonesty.[33]

All of the seven claims given above contain some truthful insights. For instance, social and personal power relationships do tend to define what people take to be true and false; they do not, however, determine what is true or false with respect to objective reality. Nevertheless, the conclusions that postmodernists draw from these claims are not only hostile to the Christian notion of truth but are seriously intellectually flawed, as I will endeavor to establish in the chapters that follow.

---

[33]John Leo, "Nobel Prize for Fiction?" *U.S. News and World Report*, January 25, 1999, p. 17. Leo is reviewing the responses to David Stoll, *Rigoberta Menchu and the Story of All Poor Guatemalans* (Boulder, Colo.: Westview, 1999).

2

FROM MODERNISM TO POSTMODERNISM

A great deal of ink has been spilled in discussion of the differences between modernism and postmodernism, when postmodernism was born, whether it should be called postmodernism or ultramodernism or supermodernism or antimodernism, and the like. Instead of trying to canvass all of these disputes—which would take a (rather boring) book in itself—this chapter will chart the basic differences between modernism and postmodernism as philosophical approaches, and between modernity and postmodernity as social conditions. Since many have argued that Christians lag behind the times by continuing to fight a modernist foe that no longer exists (or is near extinction), we also need to discern just how pervasive postmodernism is if we are to engage unbelievers on the appropriate terms. Both modernism and postmodernism have contributed to truth decay in our times, but each in its own way.

It is vital to distinguish social conditions from philosophies or worldviews, despite the fact that they always overlap and influence one other. Some have argued that since we are clearly in the postmodern

era, we must embrace postmodernism. This is an over simplification
that often leads to errors. To cut our way through the philosophical and
cultural thicket, some basic terms need to be defined, clarified and illustrated. Historians and sociologists sometimes divide cultures into three
broad types: the premodern, the modern and the postmodern. These
can be understood as historical periods arranged in a chronological se-
quence or, to complicate matters a bit, they can refer to extant cultures.
We will explore these three periods and then look at some of the cultural conditions of postmodernity.

The Premodern Era

An aboriginal tribeswoman in the Australian outback in the year 2000
who has no access to electricity, cannot read, suffers no sense of identity
confusion and does not question her religious beliefs is living in a premodern culture (if such a person still exists).[1] Premodern cultures typically have little or no cultural or religious diversity, minimal or no
social change, have not been affected by secularization and are presci-
entific. A premodern society is culturally coherent, social roles are prescribed, and there is little exposure to aliens or foreigners who would
endanger its way of life. Walter Truett Anderson describes people in
premodern societies as being "relatively free from the 'culture shock'
experiences of coming into contact with other people with entirely different values and beliefs—the kind of experience that, in contemporary
urban life, you're likely to have a couple of times before lunch."[2] This
description can refer to our tribeswoman, or, in a different sense, to
medieval Europe before the Renaissance took hold.

The era of Christendom in Western culture is considered the grand
example of premodern existence. Society was generally united under
one religion, which prescribed rules and roles and beliefs. Unbelievers
and members of other religions—such as Jews and Moslems—were
marginal to its life and often persecuted. Religion, the state and culture

---

[1]I leave it up to the anthropologists to reach a firm conclusion on this, but it seems
that premodern peoples of some stripe still do exist in vanishingly small numbers.
[2]Walter Truett Anderson, "Introduction: What's Going On Here?" in *The Truth About
Truth*, ed. Walter Truett Anderson (New York: Putnam, 1995), p. 5.

were deeply enmeshed, if not fused institutionally. Theism was taken for granted. When Thomas Aquinas wrote his massive treatise *Summa Contra Gentiles* (or *Treatise Against the Unbelievers*), he may never have met an unbeliever.[3] This does not mean that Christendom was perfectly biblical or that there was uniform agreement on doctrine, ethics or practice. Pagan mythology and occultism, as well as non-Christian philosophical thought, were present as well. Nevertheless, the premodern medieval period was characterized by a fairly stable sense of cultural authority.[4]

This relative stability was shaken by the Renaissance and later by the Reformation. The Renaissance contained Christian and non-Christian elements, but its thrust challenged established theological and cultural opinions and explored pre-Christian, Greek thought for neglected insights. During this period humanism developed a double-edged sword that attempted to restore the human world of nature and the body to its rightful dignity yet also tended toward philosophical autonomy in philosophy and the arts. This means that thinkers began to develop their thinking outside of, and independent from, a biblical framework. The medieval synthesis of Christian and Greek thought had started to unravel.[5]

The Reformation challenged the authority of the Roman Catholic Church on the basis of the primacy of Scripture. Although Martin Luther never intended to found a new church, he was placed in this role when his efforts to bring about reform within the church were rejected. He and other Reformers called for a biblically based religion that emphasized the primacy of Scripture, faith and grace. The social effect of this theological reform, however, was a further destabilization of Christendom, such that it was split into two mutually opposed camps. European nations, once united by a Roman Catholic faith, now had to

[3]I owe this observation to a lecture by Os Guinness.
[4]It is true that the introduction of some of Aristotle's works in the twelfth and thirteenth centuries had a destabilizing effect concerning questions of the church's authority. I owe this insight to David Werther.
[5]On this, see Francis A. Schaeffer, *How Shall We Then Live?* (Old Tappan, N.J.: Revell, 1976), pp. 57-78.

choose allegiances, and the sad story of the wars of religion had begun.

The Modern Era

The period of the Enlightenment—which followed the Reformation—is typically regarded as the beachhead of modernism. To speak very generally, many philosophers of this period began questioning not merely certain Roman Catholic doctrines—such as papal authority and indulgences—but Christianity itself and the idea of divine revelation as a source of authority. Immanuel Kant (1724-1804) may have captured the spirit of the Enlightenment in his essay, "What is Enlightenment?" where he said its motto was "dare to know." This spirit of criticism sparked philosophers to question all received beliefs in the name of rationality. The goal of the "Enlightenment project," as Alasdair MacIntyre and others have dubbed it, was to free humanity from superstition and found a philosophy and civilization on rational inquiry, empirical evidence and scientific discovery.[6] The term "modernism" is often identified with this overall project. The modernist vision presupposed the power of rationality to discover objective truth. They desired a rational, scientific worldview over the perceived irrationality and acrimony stemming from religion, and the possibility of progress through humanity's emancipation from received dogma and superstition. Some Enlightenment thinkers did not entirely reject belief in God but replaced Christian theism with deism—belief in a Creator without revelation or providence or incarnation—but this evisceration of theism naturally led to naturalism. God readily went from being once removed to being absent entirely.[7]

It all gets a bit confusing, though, because "modernism" can also refer to schools of painting, architecture, literature, theology and so on.[8] However, when modernism is discussed in relation to postmodernism,

---

[6]Alasdair MacIntryre, *After Virtue: A Study in Moral Theory*, 2nd ed. (Notre Dame, Ind.: University of Notre Dame Press, 1984).

[7]For an understanding of this progression, see James W. Sire, *The Universe Next Door*, 3rd ed. (Downer Grove, Ill.: InterVarsity Press, 1997), chaps. 1-4.

[8]For a thorough historical treatment of modernism in its various dimensions, see Norman F. Cantor, *The American Century: Varieties of Culture in Modern Times* (New York: HarperCollins, 1997), pp. 43-166.

it typically refers to the concepts of universal rationality, objectivity, the development of science and goal of historical progress through these newfound human powers.

Jacques Derrida condemns modernism as being "logocentric," or focused on logic as the means of determining truth. Those so ensnared think their own view of reality is correct and rational. In his essay "White Mythology," Derrida derides "the metaphysical naiveté of the wretched peripatetic" who fails to see that his worldview is just mythology:

> A white mythology which assembles and reflects Western culture: the white man takes his own mythology (that is, Indo-European mythology), his *logos*—that is the *mythos* of his idiom, for the universal form of that which it is still his inescapable desire to call Reason.[9]

In other words, reason is a mere reification of white male prejudices, which must be deconstructed to be revealed as the sham that it really is.[10]

David Harvey summarizes a less judgmental and often heard description of the modernist endeavor:

> The Enlightenment project . . . took as axiomatic that there was only one possible answer to any question. From this it followed that the world could be controlled and rationally ordered if we could only picture and represent it rightly. But this presumed that there existed a single correct mode of representation which, if we could uncover it (and this was what scientific and mathematical endeavours were all about), would provide the means to Enlightenment ends. This was a way of thinking that writers as diverse as Voltaire, d'Alembert, Diderot, Condorcet, Hume, Adam Smith, Saint-Simon, August Comte, Matthew Arnold, Jeremy Bentham and John Stuart Mill all had in common.[11]

---

[9]Jacques Derrida, "White Mythology: Metaphor in the Text of Philosophy," *New Literary History* 6, no. 1 (autumn 1974): 11; cited in Gertrude Himmelfarb, *On Looking into the Abyss: Untimely Thoughts on Culture and Society* (New York: Vintage, 1994), pp. 14-15. The idiosyncratic punctuation is in the original.

[10]Derrida must presuppose basic logical principles even to state this charge. White mythology must be rejected as false, but this assumes the law of contradiction, which is part of white mythology. So he refutes himself.

[11]David Harvey, *The Conditions of Postmodernity: An Inquiry into the Origins of Cultural Change* (Cambridge, Mass.: Basil Blackwell, 1990), pp. 27-28.

Although it is an oversimplification, this description—shared by most postmodernists and other analysts of the Enlightenment's philosophical agenda—is generally correct.

It is difficult to identify one philosopher who marks the transition from modernism to postmodernism, but Friedrich Nietzsche (1844-1900) is probably the top candidate. His thinking will be explored in the chapters that follow, but suffice to say here that Nietzsche saw "the death of God" as having profound consequences for every area of thought and culture. He had little patience with Enlightenment philosophers who removed God from their belief systems yet retained belief in Christian moral principles and an orderly, rational universe. The end of theism brought with it the end of objective value, meaning and significance; altruism had no basis in a universal moral law; the will to power was the essential fact in the struggle to thrive, and only a few specimens of humanity were worthy of existence. In his famous parable "The Madman," Nietzsche poetically described the results of God's demise in a series of arresting questions uttered by an atheistic prophet:

> Who gave us the sponge to wipe away the entire horizon? What did we do when we unchained this earth from its sun? Whither is it moving now? Whither are we moving now? Away from all suns? Are we not plunging continually? Backward, sideward, forward, in all directions? Is there any up or down left? Are we not straying as through an infinite nothing? Do we not feel the breath of empty space? Has it not become colder? Is not night and more night coming on all the while?[12]

Nietzsche hails this "deicide" as the greatest of all deeds, but he knew—before many of his time—what the philosophical consequences would be. All sense of objective orientation, of fixed meaning, of divine illumination, of providential destiny would be irretrievably lost. Cosmic vertigo would result—and abide. Nietzsche is often viewed as an existentialist—and for some good reasons—since he attempted to carve out subjective meaning in a world of objective meaninglessness. But his emphasis on power relations over objective rationality and his aban-

---

[12]Friedrich Nietzsche, "The Gay Science," 125, in *The Portable Nietzsche*, trans. Walter Kaufmann (New York: Viking, 1968), p. 95.

donment of objective truth in favor of incomparable perspectives place him in the postmodernist camp as well. Michel Foucault, for example, was greatly influenced by Nietzsche's thinking with respect to nature of knowledge and social institutions, as we will see later in this book.

The Postmodern Era

Postmodernism rejects certain key aspects of modernism, yet it retains certain affinities with it as well. Both modernism and postmodernism are largely nontheistic; both either reject theism overtly or affirm agnosticism. None of the leading postmodernist thinkers—whether Rorty, Derrida, Foucault, Lyotard or Baudrillard—affirm belief in a personal deity. This matches the later forms of modernism that abandoned even deism in favor of atheism or agnosticism. Modernists and postmodernists are united in their philosophical naturalism. They deny the objective existence of God and the supernatural, and take the material universe to be all there is. Modernists defend this worldview through what they consider to be rational arguments that indicate objective reality, namely, that all is reducible to material processes. Postmodernists, such as Richard Rorty, reject the modernist view of universal human reason and objective truth but still (inconsistently) claim to be atheists or naturalists. Their worldview, however, ends up being more of a preference or prejudice than a philosophically argued position in the classical sense, given the postmodernist disparaging of reason as a way to ascertain objective reality.

Although earlier modernist philosophers attempted to retain some sense of objective moral values or crosscultural ethical standards, later modernists and postmodernists are moral relativists of one stripe or another. Postmodernists, however, tend to call themselves constructivists or contextualists rather than relativists.[13] For instance, Anderson, an able popularizer of postmodernist themes, argues that while "radical relativism" is "definitely part of the postmodern scene," constructivism is somewhat different. Although "human reality does not equate with objective, ultimate reality . . . we are not being asked to believe that any

---

[13]Richard Rorty denies being a relativist, a claim I dispute in chapter eight.

old reality will do." Having abandoned what he calls "metaphysical realism" (the teaching that there is an objective reality that we can
know),[14] Anderson can only deny radical relativism by saying that "stories and reality structures" can be evaluated pragmatically.[15] Not all
views work, so not all are equal. However, this begs the question of
what *ought* to "work" and what constitutes "working" in the first place.
Many people are very skilled in achieving evil ends (such as developing pornography empires); their programs "work." But this does not
make them good. Some noble efforts (such as outlawing partial birth
abortions) don't work (as yet). But this does not make them bad. So
Anderson's attempt to rescue constructivism from "radical relativism"—and most postmodernists fail even to try—founders in the end.
We can construct anything, really, if we are not bound by objective values and other fixed states of affairs such as human nature.

One point of difference between the older modernist project and
postmodernism comes in the depth of relativity postmodernists embrace and promote. Modernism began with the attempt to discern objective reality without recourse to divine revelation or religious
tradition, which it dismissed as merely culturally contingent and ultimately superstitious (except where religious belief overlapped with
moral claims that could be established by reason alone). Anthropologist
Ernest Gellner explains that the Enlightenment vision "does not believe
in the availability of a substantive, final, world-transcending *Revelation*," but "does believe in the existence of knowledge which transcends
culture."[16] Unlike postmodernists, Gellner is not a relativist about
knowledge in general; yet he does deny—a priori and without argument—the possibility of knowledge mediated through divine revelation. Gellner's rejection of revelation is a prejudice without proof; it
simply reflects an ingrained secular prejudice inherited from the En-

---

[14]Anderson might better have called this view "epistemological realism," since it is a
   claim about knowledge. I owe this observation to David Werther.
[15]Walter Truett Anderson, *Reality Isn't What It Used to Be* (New York: HarperSanFrancisco, 1990), p. 70. I address pragmatism in chapter four.
[16]Ernest Gellner, *Postmodernism, Reason, and Religion* (New York: Routledge, 1992), pp.
   75-76.

lightenment—a prejudice retained by postmodernists but with a different twist.

Postmodernists affirm relativism even at the level of language itself. Objective reality cannot be captured by the contingent human invention of language, whether it be language about God, the cosmos or human values. James Sire rightly calls this "linguistic relativism."[17] George Steiner speaks of the breaking of "the covenant between word and world," a covenant adhered to by even the most passionate skeptics until recently.[18] Whereas modernists such as Gellner still believe in the power of reason and empirical investigation to discover truth in the sciences and social sciences, postmodernists abandon this quest outright. Anderson summarizes the postmodernist approach by saying that "religious truth is a special kind of truth" that is not "an eternal and perfect representation of cosmic reality." In "moving beyond secular humanism," we must see that "the work of science" is "as yet another form of social construction and not a secret technique for taking objective photographs of the universe."[19] Although Anderson caricatures both religious and scientific beliefs, his denial of the possibility of objective knowledge in both realms is clear enough.[20]

Postmodernism: Modernism Gone to Seed

Postmodernism is so often presented as a radical departure from modernism that it is easy to miss the insight that postmodernism is, in many ways, modernism gone to seed, carried to its logical conclusion and inevitable demise.

Postmodernist thinking is, in part, a reaction against certain tenets of modernism, such as <u>scientism</u> (all truth must be scientifically proven), rationalism and the supposed myth of human progress. These tenets are based on concepts that are true: rationality and scientific inquiry are

---

[17]James W. Sire, *Chris Chrisman Goes to College* (Downers Grove, Ill.: InterVarsity Press, 1993), p. 65.

[18]George Steiner, *Real Presences* (Chicago: University of Chicago Press, 1989), p. 93. Steiner, however, understands the rupture of this covenant as part of modernity, not postmodernity.

[19]Anderson, *Reality Isn't*, p. 8.

[20]We will discuss in some depth the concept of truth in chapter four.

valid means of ascertaining objective truth, and progress is both possible and desirable. But modernism exaggerated these basic truths to the point of falsehood: it was believed that human reason could be completely objective, that scientific study defines the limits of knowledge (scientism), and that progress is inevitable when science and reason are our tools. Postmodernism has reacted by dismissing these modernist myths as cultural inventions of the powerful and the dominant. "Truth" is considered to be an empty concept but a powerful political tool, rationality is dismissed as mere logocentrism (a white male construct), science is deemed domineering and oppressive and unable to discern objective truth, and "progress" only describes whatever serves the interests and ideologies of the dominant culture.

But postmodernism is not only an overreaction to the true but exaggerated elements of modernism; it is also an exaggeration of the false elements in modernism. Modernism, especially in its later stages, is based on the worldview of naturalism, which paved the way for postmodernism by denying objective truth outside the natural realm. God and all other concepts having to do with values, morality, spirituality and supernatural/immaterial realities became *only* concepts. They are mere "linguistic signifiers" (or words, in common parlance) without objective referents. Modernist theology set the ball rolling with the assertion that the Bible is a collection of myths, as are religions in general. Since morality is grounded in religion, the next development was relativizing moral values. In the modern era, moral relativism was adopted primarily by the cultural elite, while common folk continued to hold on to a vestigial Christian morality. In the postmodern era, nearly everyone believes moral values are relative—that is, constructed by cultures, not ordained by God.

The implications of the postmodernist disjunct between the signifier (language) and the signified (reality), which developed first within modernist theology, are illuminated by Jean Baudrillard's words:

> All of Western faith and good faith was engaged in this wager on representation: that a sign could refer to the depth of meaning, that a sign could *exchange* for meaning and that something could guarantee this exchange—God, of course. But what if God himself can be simulated, that

is to say, reduced to the signs which attest his existence? Then the whole
system becomes weightless, it is no longer anything but a gigantic simulacrum—not unreal, but a simulacrum, never again exchanging for what
is real, but exchanging in itself, in an uninterrupted circuit without reference or circumference.[21]

Modern theological liberalism created just this sort of God—a God of
the imagination, whose reality is confined to the myths, signs and metaphors that human imaginations construct. When *ultimate* reality becomes circular and self-enclosed, as it did with modernism, then the
scientific enterprise that claims to discern objectively true *natural* reality
is left running on borrowed capital. With postmodernist philosophy,
the inevitable foreclosure has come.

Modernism laid the foundation for postmodernism not only in denying the objective reality of divine mind but also in denying that the
human mind is an immaterial, metaphysical entity apart from the physical brain. Naturalistic science deconstructs the mind such that it becomes
nothing more than biologically determined biochemical processes.[22]
Nature is mindless and purposeless, and nature is the only objective reality.[23] It is the closed-circuit futility entailed by this materialistic reductionism that postmodernists take to heart, without waffling or
sidestepping, as modernists tend to do. The conclusion is logical: human ideas are determined entirely by the biological and cultural forces
that shape us. The notion that with our minds we can transcend these
forces and discover the truth about a reality that exists apart from our
perception of it is, therefore, nonsense. If we have no immaterial mind
that exists independently of our material brains, and if natural reality is
all there is, then there is no basis for affirming or comprehending immaterial, abstract principles such as truth, beauty, goodness and meaning.
These must be deemed mere social reifications constructed by human
brains, as they are acted upon by various natural forces.

[21]Jean Baudrillard, "The Map Precedes the Territory," in *The Truth About the Truth*
(New York: Putnam, 1995), pp. 80-81.
[22]Phillip E. Johnson, *Reason in the Balance: The Case Against Naturalism in Science, Law
& Education* (Downers Grove, Ill.: InterVarsity Press, 1995), p. 64.
[23]Ibid., p. 38.

VALUE SUBJECTIVE
FACT   OBJECTIVE

The truth vacuum created by naturalism siphons out of objective existence not only religious concepts but philosophical and even scientific concepts as well. The modernist fact-value distinction, which rendered values objectively unreal (if subjectively compelling), now dissolves, as facts also become a quaint myth of Enlightenment thought. Both modernist science and postmodernist philosophy have arisen out of naturalistic premises. However, postmodernism ultimately annihilates the modernist belief in naturalistic science as an accurate method of ascertaining and describing objective, natural reality. In other words, naturalism leads to postmodernist epistemology, which in turn undermines the viability of naturalism—or any other worldview—as a philosophical basis for modern science.[24] Naturalism contains within it the philosophical seeds of its own destruction. Truth decay is hard at work here.[25]

Richard Rorty makes this decay clear when he admits that the Darwinian account of the evolution of life (naturalism's only available creation story) makes no room for truth, "one true account of nature":

> The idea that one species of organism is, unlike all the others, oriented not just toward its own increased prosperity but toward Truth, is as un-Darwinian as the idea that every human being has a built-in moral compass—a conscience that swings free of both social history and individual luck.[26]

Rorty, the naturalist, impales himself on his own assumption, however, since he is presupposing his knowledge of the *truth* of Darwinism in order to undermine the notion that human animals apprehend any *truth*, moral or otherwise. He cannot have it both ways and make his peace with logic. In the review just cited, Rorty accuses Paul Feyera-

---

[24]On the nature of science and its dependence on certain values not derived from scientific investigation itself, see J. P. Moreland, *Scaling the Secular City: A Defense of Christianity* (Grand Rapids, Mich.: Baker, 1987), pp. 185-224; and J. P. Moreland, *Christianity and the Nature of Science* (Grand Rapids, Mich.: Baker, 1989).

[25]The preceding seven paragraphs were written by Rebecca Merrill Groothuis.

[26]Richard Rorty, "Untruth and Consequences," review of Paul Feyerabend's autobiography, *Killing Time*, in *The New Republic*, July 31, 1995, p. 36.

bend of giving "slanted" accounts of the philosophy of science[27] and of being morally accountable for his service in the Nazi military.[28] Yet these charges assume the very objective view of truth that Rorty rejects, because nothing can be slanted unless compared with the straight (the factual), and moral responsibility is impossible without a moral ideal (objective moral value) to which one is accountable.

Today's Modernism against Postmodernism

Philosophical naturalists are at odds with themselves on postmodernism. Noted biologist and founder of sociobiology, Edward O. Wilson, wants to regain the Enlightenment vision for the unity of knowledge, or what Wilson calls "consilience." By this he means "literally a 'jumping together' or knowledge of the linking of facts and fact-based theories across disciplines to create a common groundwork of explanation."[29] In *Consilience* he argues against postmodernism and attempts to reinvigorate the attempt to fathom all of reality—at least in its basic elements—according to naturalistic principles discernible through science. He puts the contrast starkly but truly: "Enlightenment thinkers believe we can know everything, and radical postmodernists believe we can know nothing."[30] Wilson notes astutely that postmodernists claim we can know that multicultural tolerance is the mandated virtue, so we "agree to waive in this one instance the postmodernist prohibition against universal truth."[31]

Wilson rightly finds Derrida's deconstructionism to be self-refuting. Since "nothing of [any author's] true intention or anything else connected to objective reality can reliably be assigned to it, [the text] is open to fresh analysis and commentary issuing from the equally solipsistic world in the head of the reviewer,"[32] since "there is nothing outside the text" (in Derrida's famous phrase). This means that Derrida

---

[27]Ibid., p. 34.
[28]Ibid., p. 35.
[29]Edward O. Wilson, *Consilience: The Unity of Knowledge* (New York: Knopf, 1998), p. 8.
[30]Ibid., p. 40.
[31]Ibid., p. 41.
[32]Ibid.

and all the wannabe Derridas are themselves subject to deconstruction
ad infinitum. "If the radical postmodernist premise is correct, we can
never be sure that is what he or she meant. Conversely, if that is what
[Derrida] meant, it is not certain we are obligated to consider his argument further."[33] Wilson, who passionately believes objective truth is as-
certainable through scientific methods, dismisses Derrida's work as
"ornately obscurantist prose," and "the opposite of science, rendered in
fragments with the incoherence of a dream, at once banal and fantasti-
cal."[34]

Wilson also dismisses what he perceives as the "existential despair"
of Foucault, who pondered how to live without God, natural law or
transcendent Reason. To this Wilson replies, "It's not so bad." After we
recover from the "shock of discovering that the universe was not made
with us in mind," we can still find meaning and truth by "deciphering
the hereditary orderliness that has borne our species through geological
time and stamped it with the residues of deep history."[35] If the universe
was not made for us in mind, if there is no created "fit" between our
mind and our world, then there is no reason to trust our mind's apprehension of the universe. Nevertheless, optimistic modernism is still
alive and kicking, however weak its philosophical foundations may
be.[36]

Two leading modern philosophers have also penned spirited and
carefully reasoned defenses of the availability of objective truth as
knowable through philosophical and scientific methods. John Searle describes his book *Mind, Language, and Society* (1998) as "a modest contribution to the Enlightenment vision," arguing against postmodernist
perspectives on knowledge and rationality.[37] Similarly, Thomas Nagel's
The Last Word (1997) argues that we must be realists about logic, lan-

---

[33]Ibid.

[34]Ibid.

[35]Ibid., p. 43.

[36]On the case that naturalism leads to nihilism, see Sire, *Universe Next Door*, chaps. 4-
5; and Moreland, *Scaling the Secular City*, pp. 105-32.

[37]John Searle, *Mind, Language, and Society: Phillosophy in the Real World* (New York:
BasicBooks, 1998), p. 6. For a critique of Searle's secularism see Richard John Neuhaus, "Minding the Mind," *First Things*, November 1999, pp. 77-82.

guage and morality; we do not construct all of reality.[38] There is a real
world consisting of logical and moral truths that serves as "the last
word," and it cannot be dissolved into nature or culture. However, both
philosophers, as good secular modernists, reject theism out of hand
without spilling much ink.

Searle dismisses the notion of God in just a few pages without considering any substantive argument for theism. It seems beneath his contempt, despite the resurgence in Christian philosophy and the recent
development of more sophisticated versions of arguments for God's existence and the rationality of Christian belief.[39] Nagel considers the theistic account of moral and logical truth a bit more seriously, but rejects it
by making objective truths in logic and morality "brute facts" that need
no theistic support philosophically.[40]

The late Carl Sagan (d. 1997) exhibited animosity to postmodernism
as well from the perspective of a popular scientist and educator. The
great evangelist for science, Sagan was an avowed opponent of superstition and irrationalism, of which he thought religion was the chief ex-
ponent. His near worship of the cosmos, "all that is, was, or ever will
be,"[41] drove him to fathom its mysteries and to persuade others to adopt
scientism as a worldview. Sagan believed his beloved cosmos was
knowable through scientific procedures, however resistant it might be
to our fumbling probes. His metanarrative was philosophical material-
ism; his organizing principle was evolution. These were not in question.
The last of Sagan's books published during his lifetime, *The Demon-
Haunted World: Science as a Candle in the Darkness* (1996), challenged
readers to develop their "baloney detectors" in order to spurn supersti-

[38]Thomas Nagel, *The Last Word* (New York: Oxford University Press, 1997). For a
philosophical critique of Nagel's rejection of theism, see Douglas Groothuis, "Thomas Nagel's 'Last Word' on the Metaphysics of Rationality and Morality," *Philosophia
Christi*, series 2, vol. 1, no. 1 (1999): 115-20.
[39]Searle, *Mind, Language*, pp. 33-37. On Christians in philosophy and its significance
for the intellectual credibility of Christianity, see Kelly James Clark, ed., *Philosophers
Who Believe* (Downers Grove, Ill.: InterVarsity Press, 1993); and Thomas Morris, ed.,
God and the Philosophers (Oxford: Oxford University Press, 1994).
[40]Nagel, *Last Word*, especially pp. 127-43.
[41]Carl Sagan, *Cosmos* (New York: Random House, 1980), p. 4.

tion and fumigate the world of occult and theistic influences.[42]

Sadly, Sagan never used his "baloney detector" against the deficiencies in his own naturalistic worldview,[43] but he rejected a postmodernist orientation that would render the achievements of science mere "social constructions of reality." Sagan's tireless crusade for the cause of Western science and secular humanism has certainly had its effect. His public television series "Cosmos" (also made into a best-selling book) has been used in countless classrooms since 1980. His books have sold in the millions.

On a different modernist front, the philosophy of Ayn Rand (d. 1982), called Objectivism (no postmodernist ring there), has been experiencing a resurgence, although it never was welcomed by the academic community. Rand, whose chief enemies were religion, altruism, socialism and existentialism, advanced a forthright atheistic rationalism that affirmed objective and knowable reality as the starting point ("existence exists"), as well as the immorality of altruism and any form of collectivism. There is nothing relativistic about her view of language, truth, art or ethics. Rand's philosophy places primacy on the individual—not on race, class, gender or culture (as does postmodernism). Her heroic ideal is the rationally self-interested individualist who is motivated by "the virtue of selfishness" to stand against the herd and assert his unique identity.[44] She loved the modernist architecture (the international style) of the New York skyline, which symbolized to her the human triumph over nature.

Rand's published works, particularly her novels *The Fountainhead* and *Atlas Shrugged*, sell hundreds of thousands of copies per year. In January of 1998, fifty-five years after its publication, the freshman class of the University of California at Berkeley named *The Fountainhead* as its favorite novel. A feature-length documentary of Rand's life, "Ayn

---

[42]Carl Sagan, *The Demon-Haunted World: Science as a Candle in the Darkness* (New York: Random House, 1996).

[43]Ibid., pp. 205-20. Phillip Johnson discusses the "baloney" in Darwinism in his *Defeating Darwinism by Opening Minds* (Downers Grove, Ill.: InterVarsity Press, 1997), pp. 37-52.

[44]See Ayn Rand, *The Virtue of Selfishness* (New York: Penguin, 1964).

Rand: A Sense of Life," was nominated for a 1998 Academy Award, and her face recently appeared on a U.S. postage stamp. More than one hundred Objectivist clubs have been started on campuses across the country, while her disciples argue over who is the rightful heir of her philosophical legacy.[45] Rand's message is modernism with a vengeance, and she does not lack disciples today, postmodernist influence notwithstanding.[46]

Other modernists have attacked postmodernism, not in the name of Christian revelation, but in the name of logic. *Skeptical Inquirer* and *Free Inquiry*, both leading organs of skepticism, have published articles attacking postmodernism. George Englebretsen, writing in *Skeptical Inquirer*, laments that those who deny the law of noncontradiction dismiss science as merely "the handmaiden of technology" (Rorty's phrase), refuse to separate truth from falsehood, open the door to New Age nonsense, and make gender and racial differences so all-determining as to eliminate rational and moral common ground. "The natural result of such division is an intolerance, that, in the long run at least, tends to manifest itself in racism, nationalism, sexism, and the like."[47]

Lewis Vaughn, the editor of *Free Inquiry*, also writes against postmodernist relativism by arguing that it eliminates universal human rights, contributes to pseudoscience (the ultimate blasphemy for skeptics who find truth and great hope in science), undermines moral and rational discourse (by making whatever we believe "true"), makes communication between those of differing worldviews impossible, and so on.

Christians can find apologetic support against postmodernist irrationality in some of the works of the old-style modernists who, while still naturalists, prize rational testing as a means to determine objective

---

[45]See Marci McDonald, "Fighting over Ayn Rand: A Radical Individualist's Followers Can't Get Along," *U.S. News and World Report*, March 9, 1998, pp. 54-57.

[46]For a critique of Ayn Rand, see John Robbins, *Without a Prayer: Ayn Rand at the End of Her System* (Hobbs, N.M.: The Trinity Foundation, 1997).

[47]George Englebretsen, "Postmodernism and New Age Unreason," *Skeptical Inquirer*, May-June 1995, p. 53.

truth.[48] Of course, "the enemies of our enemies are not always our friends"; so Christians need to continue the apologetic work by addressing the counter-Christian claims of modernist unbelief as well. The very notion of available objective truth and a rationally comprehensible universe fits far better in a theistic worldview than in an undesigned and purposeless world. Nevertheless, modernists base their critique of postmodernism upon an aspect of God's creation and a gift of common grace, namely, human rationality and a knowable world.

Even as Christians reject the postmodernist view of truth and agree with modernists on their view of truth (but disagree as to what is, in fact, true), we can point modernists to postmodernism as an object lesson in the vanity of autonomous reason and the attempt to find objective meaning and universal truth apart from God.

Postmodernists realize that a naturalistic (i.e., nontheistic) worldview renders transcendence impossible. There is no "God's eye view" of anything, and all human eyes are hopelessly prejudiced. Truth dissolves into endless perspectives, which are accountable to nothing outside of themselves. Postmodernists deconstruct reason into nonrational elements and attempt to live somehow in the dispersed debris by taking it all lightly. But, as God's wisdom proclaims, "Whoever fails to find me harms himself; all who hate me love death" (Prov 8:36)—and even madness. In 1966, before many were speaking of postmodernism, Stephen Marcus reviewed Michel Foucault's book *Madness and Civilization* and noted that Foucault opposed "the authority of reason" and despaired of "the transcendent power of rational intellect."[49] He turned to those considered insane for their indictment on supposed sanity and reason. For Foucault, "madness is really a form of freedom."[50] Marcus notes that Foucault has captured part of

---

[48]One can also find some good arguments against New Age beliefs in the works of skeptical modernists as well, as I have in my research on the New Age over the years. See Douglas Groothuis, *Unmasking the New Age* (Downers Grove, Ill.: InterVarsity Press, 1986); Douglas Groothuis, *Confronting the New Age* (Downers Grove, Ill.: InterVarsity Press, 1988).

[49]Stephen Marcus, "In Praise of Folly," *New York Review of Books*, November 3, 1966, p. 10.

[50]Ibid., p. 8.

the intellectual spirit of "the present moment,"

> a moment that is coming to think of itself as post-everything, *post-modern*, post-history, post-sociology, post-psychology. . . . We are in the position of having rejected the nineteenth and twentieth century systems of thought, of having outworn them without having transcended them with new truth, or discovered anything of comparable magnitude to take their place.[51]

While Marcus thought Foucault's ideas revealed "not so much the desperate situation of the contemporary mind as the luxury of intellectual life,"[52] his insight that we are now "posteverything" was an advance warning of the postmodernist philosophical upheaval and value vertigo that would need to be faced honestly, and not just by intellectuals.

The Revenge of the Premodern Against the Modern

Despite the naturalism of leading postmodernist philosophers, the conditions of postmodernity involve an increasingly disorienting religious pluralism that tends to dilute claims to absolute truth and authority in any one religion. Postmodern pluralism has also combined with the postmodernist rejection of modernist rationalism to generate interest in non-Christian, premodern religious traditions that once were uniformly dismissed as irrational, superstitious or outmoded. These traditions are thus granted a kind of legitimacy not accorded them under modernist assumptions, even if any claim they may make to absolute and universal truth is still looked at askance.

This aspect of postmodernist tolerance is exemplified by Vine Deloria, a Native American writer who has written widely on the plight of his people and whose work has helped spark the American Indian renaissance and revolution. Deloria is hostile toward both secular science and Christianity, which he finds oppressive to native peoples. He employs the sociology of knowledge to debunk the notion that science is

---

[51]Ibid., p. 10, emphasis added. This review is cited in Francis A. Schaeffer, *Escape from Reason* (Downers Grove, Ill.: InterVarsity Press, 1968), pp. 69-70, which shows Schaeffer's prescience in recognizing the importance of Foucault before most other Christian thinkers did so.
[52]Marcus, "Praise of Folly," p. 10.

purely disinterested and objective. Scientists "search for, take captive, and protect the social and economic status of scientists. As many lies are told to protect scientific doctrine as were ever told to protect 'the church.'"[53]

The theme of Deloria's book *Red Earth, White Lies: Native Americans and the Myth of Scientific Fact* is that secular anthropology has dismissed the oral histories of native Americans as ignorant superstitions and that this ethnocentrism is wrongly motivated by an antireligious prejudice. "The Indian explanation is always cast aside as a superstition, precluding Indians from having an acceptable status as human beings, and reducing them in the eyes of educated people to a prehuman level of ignorance."[54] In a chapter called "Evolutionary Prejudice," Deloria argues that secular science is far less secure than it claims and that "'science' should drop the pretense of having absolute authority with regard to human origins and begin looking for some other kind of explanation that would include the traditions and memories of non-Western peoples."[55] In essence, Deloria is challenging secular modernism in the name of his own premodern people. Pluralistic postmodernity sets up the conditions for such an enterprise.

Christians can agree at some points with Deloria's critique of the secular critique of the spiritual as irrelevant to questions of human origins. Of course, the Christian critique is grounded ultimately in the authority of inspired Scripture understood in relation to general revelation, and not in either Western science or Native American traditions.[56]

Postmodernity also allows for the appropriation of ancient Gnostic ideas, as evidenced by Harold Bloom's wide-ranging and idiosyncratic book *Omens of Millennium: The Gnosis of Angels, Dreams, and Resurrection* (1996). Bloom, a best-selling literary critic, finds the Gnostic vision of uncreated greatness imprisoned in human flesh as inspiring and rele-

---

[53]Vine Deloria, *Red Earth, White Lies: Native Americans and the Myth of Scientific Fact* (Golden, Colo.: Fulcrum, 1997), p. 5.

[54]Ibid., p. 7.

[55]Ibid., p. 54.

[56]For an overview of Native American religion from a Christian perspective, see Winfried Corduan, *Neighboring Faiths: A Christian Introduction to World Religions* (Downers Grove, Ill.: InterVarsity Press, 1998), pp. 160-88.

vant for today. Although he does not accept these teachings at face value, he sees in them an antidote to both problematic Western religion and a secular viewpoint that eliminates the spiritual entirely. Bloom's attraction to gnosticism is more psychological and literary than historical or logical, since he gives no strong arguments against the factuality of Christianity in favor of gnosticism.[57]

Bloom captures the gnostic teaching in a chapter called "Not by Faith, Nor by the Angels: A Gnostic Sermon," where he states, "In the first place, the Gnosis makes us free because it is the knowledge of who we were, before the priestly Creation that was actually our Fall from divinity into division and splintering."[58] Bloom rejects Christian *faith* in favor of gnostic *knowledge,* he rejects worship in favor of self-discovery, and he rejects naturalistic reductionism in favor of transcendence. Instead of settling for the shifting shadows of postmodern externalities, Bloom endeavors to find a truer, deeper self that "was part of the fullness that was God, a more human God than any worshipped since."[59]

Postmodernity as a Social Condition

Having looked at modernism and postmodernism as philosophical systems of thought, we also need to distinguish modernity and postmodernity as social conditions.

Although many claim we live in postmodernity, a good case can be made that the social revolutions of modernity have not been entirely transcended. Postmodernity is really a hypertrophied condition of modernity itself. This means that the forces of modernity are amplified and extended in postmodernity. Modernity describes historical and cultural developments such as the emergence of capitalism in the fifteenth century, the movement from feudalism and monarchy to democratic arrangements in Europe and America over several centuries, the industrial revolution of the eighteenth century and the communications revo-

---

[57]For a critique of gnosticism, both and ancient and modern, see Douglas Groothuis, *Jesus in an Age of Controversy* (Eugene, Ore.: Harvest, 1996), pp. 77-118.
[58]Harold Bloom, *Omens of Millennium: The Gnosis of Angels, Dreams, and Resurrection* (New York: Riverhead Books, 1996), p. 257.
[59]Ibid., p. 183.

lution of the twentieth century.[60] The forces of modernity that persist today are international capitalism, the information revolution, international travel, democratic governance as an ideal, and pluralization
through freedom of religion and liberalized immigration laws. Postmodernity has not eclipsed these basic cultural realities. As Os Guinness
observes:

> Modernism as a set of ideas may well have collapsed and "postmodern"
> may therefore be legitimate to describe the set of ideas that succeeds it.
> But to be postmodern in the structural sense is as yet inconceivable. Thus
> to bandy about the term "postmodern," as if by definition it takes us
> beyond modernity, is a theoretical error with grave practical conse-
> quences. Modernity, in the deeper sense, is now a global force. What Max
> Weber pictured as an iron cage, Peter Berger as a gigantic steel hammer,
> and Anthony Giddens as a careening juggernaut cannot be checked
> merely by wafting the term postmodern.[61]

Postmodernity, as a recent development of modernity, can be typi-
fied by several cultural factors. A leading feature of postmodernity is
the breakdown of social and religious consensus, or rampant pluralism,
which tends to fray social cohesion. Modernity allowed or encouraged
pluralism, but usually within limits set by religion and history. The
motto of the United States is *e pluribus unum:* out of many, one. Many
today wonder what the *unum* might be, given the proliferation of new
religions, transplanted religions such as Islam and Hinduism, and self-
styled religious relativism in which people assemble a grab bag of beliefs to fit their own preferences or "what they are comfortable with."[62]
With no consensus of religious perspective and the decline of familial
influence on religion, we are faced with what Peter Berger calls "the heretical imperative." A heretic in premodern times chose a belief against
the well-entrenched cultural and religious majority. Today, in a sense,
everyone must be a heretic because we select our "religious preferences" from an array of options, none of which are mandated. What

---

[60]See Os Guinness, *The American Hour* (New York: Free Press, 1992), pp. 26-27.
[61]Ibid., p. 27.
[62]On this see Robert Bellah, *Habits of the Heart* (New York: Harper & Row, 1985).

was once reckoned a matter of life and death commitment is, under postmodern conditions, relegated to an option or preference or lifestyle, which is negotiable and often impermanent. Religious activities and experiments are juggled along with an ever-changing set of interests, curiosities and diversions.[63]

Postmodern social experience in general saturates the self with a welter of conflicting and confusing images and ideas, with little unity or coherence at hand. What Kenneth Gergen calls "technologies of social saturation"—radio, television, computers, movies, telephones, rapid transportation and so forth—tend to overwhelm our ability to rank our stimulations in order of importance.[64] Benjamin Barber marks the transition from modernity to postmodernity by the dominance of the image over the word. After citing the effects of movable type as a key engine in ushering Western culture into modernity and out of "the medieval world of status, hierarchy, and popular ignorance," he notes that "movable photographic frames (and, in time, scanning ion beams) have challenged the world of print, propelling us out of the modern and into the postmodern."[65] The cultural shift from emphasizing the word to focusing on the image—or what Jacques Ellul called "the humiliation of the word"[66]—retards abstract thinking, replaces the work of imagination with literal pictures, weakens community, which is bound together by words, and undermines "public goods, which demand the interactive deliberation of rational citizens armed with literacy."[67] Postmodernity has thus tended to subvert our sense of rational and moral coherence, the value of language and a shared objective world describable through words.

Postmodernity also tends to destabilize individuals' sense of fixed identity in favor of ever-shifting negotiations of personae in various sit-

---

[63]See Peter L. Berger, *The Heretical Imperative: Contemporary Possibilities of Religious Affirmation* (Garden City, N.Y.: Anchor, 1979), pp. 15-16.

[64]Kenneth Gergen, *The Saturated Self* (New York: HarperCollins, 1991), p. xi.

[65]Benjamin Barber, *Jihad vs. McWorld* (New York: Ballantine, 1996), p. 89.

[66]See Jacques Ellul, *The Humiliation of the Word* (Grand Rapids, Mich.: Eerdmans, 1985). The dominance of the image over the word with respect to television is discussed in the appendix, "Television: Agent of Truth Decay."

[67]Barber, *Jihad vs. McWorld*, p. 89.

uations. With the loss of "cultural authority,"[68] especially in the United States, almost everything seems weightless and up for grabs. As the saying goes: "We know the price of everything and the value of nothing." Commercial transactions provide the model for much of our social interaction, as people "sell themselves" and "buy into" ideas and, to avert boredom, "reinvent" themselves in some "new and improved version." As Baudrillard observes:

> The aura of our world is no longer sacred. We no longer have the sacred horizon of appearances, but that of the absolute commodity. Its essence is promotional. At the heart of our universe of signs there is an evil genius of advertising.[69]

James Twitchell argues that advertising culture (what he calls Adcult) has taken the role traditionally played by religion in that it now assigns meaning to objects—but not on the basis of their inner or objective nature (since most major brands are similar to their competitors) but by virtue of whatever marketing spin is being applied at the moment.[70] Today's advertising is not about providing relevant information, as in the nineteenth century, as much as it is "about creating an infotainment culture sufficiently alluring so that other messages—commercials—can get through."[71] In Adcult, truth is the first casualty, and consumers are often the last to know—or even care.[72]

The public space of settled communities is replaced by the giant, impersonal strip mall, which serves as a surrogate for the older ideal of a marketplace of ideas. But no ideas are present, because truth repeatedly succumbs to "the evil genius of advertising," in Baudrillard's phrase. The mall simulates everything—with high-tech glamour and promotion—and represents nothing, outside of consumerism and commodity.

---

[68]See Guinness, *American Hour,* for a sustained treatment of this crisis of cultural authority.
[69]Jean Baudrillard, *The Perfect Crime* (New York: Verso, 1996), pp. 73-74.
[70]James Twitchell, "'But First, a Word from Our Sponsor,'" in *Dumbing Down: Essays on the Strip-Mining of American Culture*, ed. Katherine Washburn and John Thorton (New York: W. W. Norton, 1996), p. 202.
[71]Ibid., p. 198.
[72]See also James Twitchell, *Adcult USA: The Triumph of Advertising in American Culture* (New York: Columbia University Press, 1996).

Truth decay happens easily and naturally in such intellectually and morally impoverished environs.

Much of postmodern architecture also betrays an "unreal America," where theme parks recreate situations that never existed, amusement parks amuse at the expense of real connections to nature and history, and historical restorations restore what never occurred. In this "America the Faux," nothing is authentic, and we like it that way. Instead of authentically representing previous historical styles for artistic purposes, postmodernist architecture haphazardly appropriates images from the past in order to promote itself commercially and without any real interest in history per se.[73] Ada Louise Huxtable nicely summarizes these trends:

> With reality voided and illusion preferred, almost anything [in postmodern architecture] can have uncritical acceptance. Trendy exhibitions strip away everything of meaning or relevance for a perverse, camp reading that mutilates art and design history. "Interpretations" rush in to fill the vacuum where knowledge fails; research that retrieves reality is of less interest than critical inventions that subvert it. For those without memory, nostalgia fills the void. For those without reference points, novelties are enough.[74]

Disney productions dispense unrealities for the millions to consume globally. As Barber quips, "Disney's creations . . . aspire not to truth but to verisimilitude: the metatruth of virtuality. The whole point of virtual reality is that it is just like the reality that it assiduously is not and cannot be."[75] When so much is simulated with such stunning effects and astronomical profits, it becomes difficult to retain even the notion of objective truths about history or geography or much of anything else.

Sociologist John O'Neil laments the loss of meaningful metanarratives that give direction to work, families and communities. He believes this loss results in an unfulfilled desire for immediate meaning, because all meaning is disconnected from anything outside of itself. Although he is not a Christian, O'Neil claims that the "rejection of Christ's mediation of

---

[73]See Ada Louise Huxtable, *The Unreal American: Architecture and Illusion* (New York: New Press, 1997), p. 88.
[74]Ibid.
[75]Barber, *Jihad vs. McWorld*, p. 136.

human history . . . has scattered all interpretation," leaving no central reference point, no authoritative and unified meaning to history. Instead, "we have reduced language and history to our own uses." There is no objective meaning anchored in a reality beyond ourselves; everything is unhinged; everything can mean anything, so everything means nothing. Style is all that remains; substance disappears. "In such contexts, the self loses its depth; everything becomes a surface—our mirrors reflect nothing but a glassy superficiality of looks, arrangement, decor, montage."[76]

When all that is available is surface, when the ocean is all wave and no bottom, anchorage is out of the question. To change metaphors, the ad hoc pastiche replaces the fixed pattern and is rearranged for no reason but whimsy and profit—and that is as good as it gets. What was once taken as abiding and fundamental—such as scientific progress, moral values, social order—has been destabilized. What was taken as contingently cultural—styles, appearances and so forth—is all that is left; it becomes, as it were, absolute.

Guinness summarizes the postmodern condition as well as anyone could:

> Under postmodern conditions, words lose their authority and become accessory to images. The past is no longer a heritage, but a debris-strewn ruin to be ransacked for a bric-a-brac of beliefs that is as incoherent as it is inconsequential. . . . The grand flirtation with the meaninglessness of modernity goes on, but in a party mood. Religion is no longer transcendent, but a recreational pursuit for the connoisseurs of "spirituality." Art, homes, life-styles, ideas, character, self-renewal, and even belief in God all become auxiliary to sales and the ceaseless consumption of styles.[77]

Part of postmodernism's unreality game encompasses the uncharted terrain of cyberspace. Although computers have many redeeming features, the vast proliferation of information, the speed at which it is transferred and the allure of engrossing but artificial realities all tend to reinforce a world removed from reality and far from truth. The flood of information becomes difficult to sort into the true and the false, the meaningful and the

---

[76]John O'Neil, *The Poverty of Modernism* (New York: Routledge, 1995), p. 19.
[77]Guinness, *American Hour*, pp. 129-30.

meaningless, the consequential and the trivial. The ability to produce words rapidly and have instant access to information tends to inhibit the reflection needed to discern reality. As Norman Cantor notes:

> The intensive thought, quiet reflection, and rational order that went into the old way of writing with pen and on typewriter, slow typesetting, and storage in and retrieval from a printed book is eroding. The quality of sensibility, the peace of insight, the perception offered by slow literature production is challenged by the new ways [of computers].[78]

Virtual realities—whether as pedestrian as chat rooms or as exotic as fantasy role-playing environments—create an alternative domain ruled by strange or no rules with little connection to life off-line. The anonymous character of much of cyberspace also allows people to construct various identities by pretending to be people they are not. Some postmodernist thinkers see this as a technological manifestation of the notion that the self is not a fixed, spiritual substance, but a fluid entity capable of almost infinite variation. In cyberspace, as elsewhere in postmodernity, choice—whether about products, education, religion or even personal identity—is the ultimate concern, albeit without objective criteria for making wise choices.[79]

Sorting Things Out

This chapter has covered much terrain conceptually, but all of it necessary for charting where we are. The broad lay of the land philosophically is that modernism and postmodernism both overlap and contradict one another. Modernism is not dead; postmodernism does not completely dominate the scene as a philosophy, although it affects some areas—such as literary criticism and cultural studies—much more

[78]Cantor, *American Century*, p. 496.
[79]For more on the postmodernist implications of cyberspace technologies and the philosophical implications of cyberspace in general, see Douglas Groothuis, *The Soul in Cyberspace* (Grand Rapids, Mich.: Baker, 1997; Eugene, Ore.: Wipf and Stock, 1999), particularly, pp. 23-36; Douglas Groothuis, "Christian Scholarship and the Philosophical Analysis of Cyberspace Technologies," *Journal of the Evangelical Theological Society* 41, no. 4 (1998): 631-40; and Douglas Groothuis, "Cyberspace, Critical Thinking, and the Return to Eloquent Realities," *Inquiry: Critical Thinking Across the Disciplines* 28, no. 4 (1999): 6-26.

than others. However, the postmodern social condition affects us all, whether we are modernists, Christians or postmodernists. Bearing witness to the truth of Christ and his gospel in postmodern times means being savvy to postmodern realities culturally. It does not mean capitulating to postmodernist unrealities philosophically or theologically. How this all sorts out is the concern of the rest of this book.

3

THE BIBLICAL
VIEW OF TRUTH

Although the Bible does not present a carefully nuanced philosophical discus-
sion of the nature of truth, it does offer a unified perspective on the matter of truth and falsity that flatly opposes the postmodernist orientation. It speaks authoritatively not only on what things are true but on
the nature of truth itself. The biblical view of the nature of truth was
common in the cultures for which it was originally written, but this
view can be rigorously defended before the postmodern world as well.
In this chapter we will discuss the biblical notion of truth and then, in
the next chapter, advance a more philosophical exposition and defense
of that view against postmodernist rejections of it.

Biblical Language and the Nature of Truth
The Scriptures use the Hebrew and Greek words for truth and their
derivatives repeatedly and without embarrassment. The meaning of the
Hebrew term *'emet*, which is at the root of the great majority of the
Hebrew words related to truth, involves the ideas of "support" and
"stability." From this root flows the twofold notion of truth as faithful-

ness and conformity to fact.[1]

God is true (or faithful) to his word and in his activities and attitudes; God is the God of truth. So, David prays, "Into your hands I commit my spirit; redeem me, O LORD, the God of truth" (Ps 31:5; see 2 Chron 15:3). Through Isaiah, God declares, "I, the LORD, speak the truth; I declare what is right" (Is 45:19). Likewise, people need to respond to the God of truth in truth: "The LORD is near to all who call on him, to all who call on him in truth" (Ps 145:18).

The Hebrew 'emet can also represent "that which is conformed to reality in contrast to anything which would be erroneous or deceitful."[2] In several passages "If it is true" means "If the charge is substantiated" (Deut 13:14; 17:4; Is 43:9). Many biblical texts include statements such as "speaking the truth" (see Prov 8:7; Jer 9:5) or "giving a true message" (see Dan 10:1) or a "true vision" (see Dan 8:26). After Elijah raised from the dead the son of Zarephath's widow, she exclaimed that "the word of the LORD from your mouth is the truth" (1 Kings 17:24). 'Emet can also connote "what is authentic, reliable, or simply 'right,'" such as "true justice" (Zech 7:9) or as in swearing in a "truthful, just and righteous way" (Jer 4:2) or "your law is true" (Ps 119:142).

Roger Nicole explains that faithfulness and conformity to fact are

> converging lines of meaning in the Old Testament. Neither is reducible to the other, yet they are not mutually conflicting. It is because truth is conformity to fact that confidence may be placed in it or in the one who asserts it, and it is because a person is faithful that he or she would be careful to make statements that are true.[3]

There is no indication that *truth* in the Hebrew Bible is another word for belief or mere social custom, since beliefs can be false and customs can be opposed to God's will. "The LORD detests lying lips, but he delights in those who are truthful" (Prov 12:22). Jeremiah attacked the falsehood and unfaithfulness of his people when he said, "How can you

---

[1]Roger Nicole, "The Biblical Concept of Truth," in *Scripture and Truth,* ed. D. A. Carson and John D. Woodbridge (Grand Rapids, Mich.: Zondervan, 1983), p. 290.
[2]Ibid.
[3]Ibid., p. 291.

say, 'We are wise, for we have the law of the LORD,' when actually the lying pen of the scribes has handled it falsely?" (Jer 8:8). When Elijah confronted the prophets of Baal on Mount Carmel, he drew a stark contrast between irreconcilable options: "How long will you waver between two opinions? If the LORD is God, follow him; but if Baal is God, follow him" (1 Kings 18:21). The ensuing power confrontation vindicated Elijah's God as the one who is the faithful and true God. After God sent fire to consume the sacrifice left unchanged by the pleas of Baal's frantic followers, the people "fell prostrate and cried, 'The LORD—he is God! The LORD—he is God!' " (1 Kings 18:39). Nicole notes that "the clear and insistent witness of the Old Testament in condemnation of all lies and deceit reinforces its strong commendation of '*emet* as faithfulness and veracity."[4]

Although some scholars have posited a great difference between the Hebrew and Greek notions of truth, the Greek New Testament's understanding of truth is consistent with that of the Hebrew Scriptures. The New Testament word *aletheia* and its derivations retain the Hebrew idea of "conformity to fact" expressed in '*emet*. To cite just one book of the New Testament, the Gospel of John employs *aletheia* ("truth") and related words very frequently in a variety of settings. "John uses truth vocabulary in its conventional sense of veracity/genuineness/opposite of false; but also develops his own particular meaning, where truth refers to the reality of God the Father revealed in Jesus the Son."[5] John's understanding of truth presupposes a correspondence view of truth, but it also builds this foundation theologically by adding specific content concerning the manifestation of truth in Jesus Christ (Jn 7:28; 8:16).[6]

The related idea of faithfulness is typically expressed by words in the family of *pistos*, which are translated "faithful, reliable or trustworthy."[7] The New Testament frequently combines the words "grace and truth,"

[4]Ibid., p. 292.
[5]D. M. Crump, "Truth," in *Dictionary of Jesus and the Gospels,* ed. Joel B. Green, Scott McKnight and I. Howard Marshall (Downers Grove, Ill.: InterVarsity Press, 1992), p. 859.
[6]See ibid., pp. 859-62, for more on this.
[7]Nicole, "Biblical Concept," p. 292.

which is reminiscent of the Hebrew phrase "mercy and truth." Jesus is "full of grace and truth" (Jn 1:14) and "grace and truth came through Jesus Christ" (Jn 1:17). Another fact that shows the continuity between the two Testaments' view of truth is the New Testament's use of the Hebrew "amen," which occurs 129 times.[8] This is typically translated as "truly" or "I tell you the truth," as when Jesus says, "I tell you the truth, no one can see the kingdom of God unless he is born again." In Revelation 3:14, the glorified Christ refers to himself as "the Amen, the faithful and true witness" (see also Is 63:16).

Each member of the Trinity is closely associated with truth in the New Testament. In praying for his disciples Jesus says, "Sanctify them by the truth; your word is truth" (Jn 17:17). The gospel is sometimes called "the truth of Christ" (2 Cor 11:10). The Holy Spirit is called "the Spirit of truth" (Jn 14:17; 15:26) or simply "the truth" (1 Jn 5:6).

According to Nicole, "The primary New Testament emphasis is clearly on truth as conformity to reality and opposition to lies and errors."[9] Both the Hebrew Scriptures and the New Testament draw a clear contrast between truth and error. John warns of distinguishing the "Spirit of truth and the spirit of falsehood" (1 Jn 4:6). Paul says that those who deny the reality of the God behind creation "suppress the truth by their wickedness" (Rom 1:18). Before Pilate, Jesus divided the field into truth and error: "For this reason I was born, and for this I came into the world, to testify to the truth. Everyone on the side of truth listens to me" (Jn 18:37). Pilate took the side of falsehood.

In another group of passages, mostly in John's writings, "the contrast is not so much between correct and false, but rather between complete and incomplete, definitive and provisional, full-orbed and partial."[10] For instance, "the law was given through Moses; grace and truth came through Jesus Christ" (Jn 1:17). Christ's truth completed what was anticipated in the law.[11]

New Testament scholar, Leon Morris points out that the apostle Paul

---

[8]Ibid., p. 293.
[9]Ibid.
[10]Ibid., p. 295.
[11]See also John 1:9; 6:32, 55; 15:1; Heb 8:2; 9:24.

often uses the noun *aletheia*, which Paul uses to mean "that truth is accuracy over against falsehood." Paul also refers "to speaking the truth" just as we commonly do (Eph 4:25; 1 Tim 2:7; etc.).[12] Paul develops this basic concept of accuracy in a rich and full way in his references to "the truth of God" (Rom 1:25; 3:7; 15:8) and "God's judgment" as "based on truth" (Rom 2:2). Morris comments that for Paul "human judgments might be biased according to class or creed, but with God truth is the only consideration."[13] Paul finds truth in the Old Testament Law (Rom 2:20), in God's creation (Rom 1:18-20) and supremely in Jesus Christ (Eph 2:21). This claim about Christ is that "the revelation of truth in Jesus is utterly reliable."[14] Paul also writes of the truth of the gospel (Gal 2:5; Eph 1:13; Col 1:15). As Morris notes:

> The truth that is so closely bound up with God finds its expression here on earth in the gospel, which sets out the ultimate truth of the love of God especially as shown in the cross, the sinfulness of the human race, and the provision God has made for salvation. The gospel and truth are closely connected. This is so also in the passage in which Paul speaks of God's will for people "to be saved and come to the knowledge of truth" (1 Tim 2:4).[15]

A survey of the biblical view of truth cannot do justice to the richness of the words employed in a wide diversity of contexts. Nevertheless, it should be clear that such a view of truth collides with postmodernist notions of the social construction of reality and the relativity of truth. Nicole concludes, "The biblical view of truth (*'emet-aletheia*) is like a rope with several intertwined strands"; it *"involves factuality, faithfulness, and completeness."*[16] The Bible does not present truth as a cultural creation of the ancient Jews or the early Christians. They received truth from the God who speaks truth to his creatures, and they were expected by this God to conform themselves to this truth.

---

[12]Leon Morris, "Truth," in *Dictionary of Paul and His Letters*, ed. Gerald F. Hawthorne, Ralph P. Martin, Daniel G. Reid (Downers Grove, Ill.: InterVarsity Press, 1993), p. 954.

[13]Ibid.

[14]Ibid.

[15]Nicole, "Biblical Concept," p. 296.

[16]Ibid.; emphasis in the original.

The Distinctives of the Biblical View of Truth

Before explaining and defending this basic biblical view of truth more philosophically in the next chapter, we need to amplify the character of the truth described above and draw some contrasts with postmodernist claims. There are several core aspects to a biblical view of truth, especially in regard to the great truths of God's redemptive program.[17] In explaining these crucial categories of the nature of biblical truth, I do not mean to imply that neither anyone else nor I have perfectly grasped the nature or extent of God's truth. We all err in many ways, not least of which in our thinking about the most important truth of all—God! However, I believe this discussion helps open up what Scripture claims about God's revelation.

1. Truth is revealed by God. It is not constructed or invented by individuals or communities. Various *beliefs* may be the result of human invention and group construction, but *truth* comes from the disclosure of a personal and moral God who makes himself known. Paul's letter to the Romans, for instance, tells us that God has made his existence known through both creation and human conscience, so that all people are without excuse before their Creator and Lawgiver (2:14-15). Those who suppressed this revealed truth crafted idols in wickedness (1:18) instead of worshiping God (1:21-25), but in so doing "they exchanged the truth of God for a lie" (1:25). Lies become idols, and every idol obscures the truth. This is because all idols are unrealities in deceptive dress, untruths and shabby social constructions of the supposed sacred.

Besides revealing himself generally through creation and conscience, God has revealed the particular truths of salvation through his mighty deeds in history, the incarnation and in the sixty-six books of holy Scripture. The writer of Hebrews declares the nature of God's revelation: "For the word of God is living and active. Sharper than any double-edged sword, it penetrates even to dividing soul and spirit, joints and marrow; it judges the thoughts and attitudes of the heart" (Heb 4:12). The word of God is a revelation from a transcendent, holy and

---

[17]I address some of the philosophical nuances on different kinds of truths—including subjective truths—in the following chapter.

communicative being, and so has an inner dynamism that rises above the psychology, sociology and politics of its readers, even though it is mediated through the particular cultural forms of its original context. For Paul, Scripture is divinely inspired: "All Scripture is God-breathed and is useful for teaching, rebuking, correcting and training in righteousness" (2 Tim 3:16). G. K. Chesterton captured the meaning of divine revelation, as opposed to human construction, when he affirmed this about the Christian faith: "I won't call it my philosophy; for I did not make it. God and humanity made it; and it made me."[18] This stress on God's authority and ownership of truth should give followers of Christ a deep sense of anchorage in a divine reality beyond themselves. Their faith is not a "religious preference" but has an indissoluble reference to revealed truths.

The Christian worldview, contra-postmodernism, understands language not as a self-referential, merely human and ultimately arbitrary system of signs that is reducible to contingent cultural factors, but as the gift of a rational God entrusted to beings made in his own image and likeness (Gen 1:26). "In the beginning was the Word [Logos], and the Word was with God and the Word was God" (Jn 1:1-2). Communication has eternally existed between all the members of the Trinity and continues as God speaks to us—through creation, conscience and Scripture—and as we speak truth to each other and to God. Human language has been wounded by the fall and fractured by the judgment at Babel (Gen 11), but it is not thrown down for the count.[19] Language is God's vehicle for conveying truth, although it may be clouded in much of our experience (as evidenced by the density and outright unintelligibility of much postmodernist writing.)[20]

God's disclosure of himself through revelation is not an existential experience devoid of rational, knowable content. God reveals objective

---

[18]G. K. Chesterton, *Orthodoxy* (1908; reprint, New York: Doubleday, 1990), p. 9.
[19]For more on the nature of language, see chapter four.
[20]For a humorous treatment of this, see Stephen Katz, "How to Speak and Write Postmodern," in *The Truth About Truth*, ed. Walter Truett Anderson (New York: Putnam's, 1995), pp. 92-95. See also John Leo, "Tower of Pomobabble," *U.S. News & World Report*, March 15, 1999, p. 16.

truth about himself. J. P. Moreland makes this point with respect to biblical revelation:

> The central biblical terms of revelation—*galah* (Hebrew), *apocalupto*, *paneroo* (Greek)—express the idea of revealing, disclosing, making manifest or known. When we affirm that the Bible is a revelation from God, we do not simply assert that God as a person is known in and through it. We also mean that God has revealed understandable, objectively true propositions. The Lord's Word is not only practically useful, it is also theoretically true (Jn 17:17). God has revealed truth to us and not just Himself.[21]

2. Objective truth exists and is knowable. The claim that God has revealed himself to us presupposes objective truth as the cognitive content of revelation. God is the source of objective truth about himself and his creation. Unlike a Platonic view that makes truth abstract and independent of God's being and revelation, the biblical view deems truth to be personal in that it ultimately issues from a personal God. But truth is also objective because God is the final court of appeal, the source of all truth, by virtue of his nature and his will. Objective truth is truth that is not dependent on any creature's subjective feelings, desires or beliefs. Paul makes this point when he discusses the unbelief of some Jews: "What if some did not have faith? Will their lack of faith nullify God's faithfulness? Not at all! Let God be true, and every person a liar" (Rom 3:3-4). God's truth is not dependent upon any individual's or group's experiences or interpretations, however strongly felt or culturally entrenched they may be.

George Barna claims that 80 percent of Americans "believe that the Bible includes the statement that 'God helps those who help themselves.' "[22] But the numbers say nothing concerning the facts of the matter because this folk belief is not based on any objective reality and woefully contradicts the biblical teaching on God's grace (Eph 2:8-9; Tit 3:3-8).

---

[21]J. P. Moreland, *Love Your God with All Your Mind* (Colorado Springs, Colo.: NavPress, 1997), p. 45. For an in-depth treatment of the biblical words for revelation and modern views of revelation, see Anthony Thiesleton, "Truth," in *The New International Dictionary of New Testament Theology,* ed. Colin Brown (Grand Rapids, Mich.: Zondervan, 1978), 3:309-39.

[22]George Barna, *Index of Leading Spiritual Indicators* (Waco, Tex.: Word, 1996), p. 80.

The biblical emphasis on objective truth does not minimize the imperative to make God's truth subjectively or existentially one's own; rather, it sharpens and deepens the need for authentic personal experience. Believing in objective truth does not mean one is neutral or detached concerning that truth. Truth matters mightily, particularly the saving and sanctifying truth of the gospel. Biblical faith involves assent to true doctrine (derived from biblical revelation) as a necessary element of saving faith and growth in Christ, but it also demands trust and commitment to the flaming truths to which one gives assent.[23] The objective truth must be subjectively appropriated. Deeper and more personal yet, a person should entrust himself or herself to the very God of truth, the one "to whom we must give account" (Heb 4:13). When Paul was laboring to persuade the Galatians not to follow the error of the Judaizers, he spoke to them as his "dear children, for whom I am again in the pains of childbirth until Christ is formed in you" (Gal 4:19). This highlights the need for biblical truth to stick to the soul and transform the whole person into greater Christlikeness. As David prayed, "Surely you desire truth in the inner parts; you teach me wisdom in the inmost place" (Ps 51:6).

Neither does the objectivity of God's truth diminish the reality of the church as an interactive and interdependent community of believers. Postmodernism has tended to stress communal norms and practices over the existence of objective truth, but biblically there should be no conflict between the two. The church, as the community of God, was born through truth and is constituted by the truth. Therefore, Paul calls the church "the pillar and foundation of the truth" (1 Tim 3:15). He also desires that the church mature to the degree that members are "speaking the truth in love" to one another (Eph 4:15). The worship, teaching, preaching, fellowship, outreach and service of the church must all be centered on revealed and objective truth as its unifying and impelling dynamic. The body of Christ, like Christ himself, must "bear witness to the truth" (Jn 18:36).

---

[23]I take the term "flaming truth" from Francis Schaeffer, *The Great Evangelical Disaster* (Westchester, Ill.: Crossway, 1984), pp. 81-83.

3. Christian truth is absolute in nature. This means that God's truth is invariant. It is true without exception or exemption. Neither is God's truth relative, shifting or revisable. The weather may change, but God will not. An example from physics helps illustrate the concept. According to Einstein's theory of relativity, the speed of light is an absolute limit in physics; nothing can travel faster. For this reason, Einstein almost called his model idea "the theory of invariance." He named it "the theory of relativity" not because everything is relative but because things are relative to what is invariant or absolute, namely, the speed of light.[24]

A classic text on the absoluteness of truth is Jesus' uncompromising statement, "I am the way and the truth and the life. No one comes to the Father except through me" (Jn 14:6). There is no exception or exemption from this claim: there is but one way to the Father—Jesus himself. Facing the pluralism of the ancient Mediterranean world, Paul was so bold as to say this in his discussion of food offered to idols:

> We know that an idol is nothing at all in the world, and that there is no God but one. For even if there are so-called gods, whether in heaven or on earth (as indeed there are many "gods" and many "lords"), yet for us there is but one God, the Father, from whom all things came and for whom we live; and there is but one Lord, Jesus Christ, through whom all things came and through whom we live. (1 Cor 8:4-6)

The truth of the gospel is not subject to any human veto or democratic procedures. Jesus was not elected Lord by humans but was chosen by God; nor can he be dethroned by any human effort or opinion or insurrection. Jesus declared, "For God so loved the world that he gave his one and only Son" (Jn 3:16). Jesus is an only child, without peer and beyond challenge.

The insistence on absolute truth is a massive and sharp stumbling block for postmoderns—given their absolute abhorrence of the absolute—but it cannot be softened or avoided if believers are to remain faithful to the truth of God. In George Barna's annual surveys he asks a

---

[24]On this see Paul Johnson, *Modern Times: The World from the Twenties to the Nineties*, rev. ed. (New York: HarperCollins, 1991), pp. 1-5.

random sample of adults their opinion on this statement: "There is no such thing as absolute truth; two people could define truth in totally conflicting ways, but both could still be correct." He found that between 1991 and 1994 the percentage of those who agree with this statement grew faster among Christians than non-Christians, with 62 percent of Christians rejecting absolute truth in 1994.[25] Charles Colson comments that "believers cannot present a credible defense of biblical truth when more than half don't even believe in real truth."[26]

The notion of absolute truth is sometimes misunderstood and rejected for false reasons. Consider, for instance, the following statement: "Jesus alone is Lord and provides the only way for anyone to be reconciled to God." There are several things this statement does *not* mean.

First, it does not mean that Christians claim to have unlimited or perfect knowledge about God or humanity—or anything else. It simply means that God has revealed his one way of salvation through Christ and made this known in history, as recorded in Scripture and as illuminated by the Holy Spirit. Those who know Jesus as Lord confess his absoluteness, not their own. Christ's supremacy means our dependency. We can know this truth and testify to it only in light of God's grace because it is only by grace that grace can be known.

Second, to confess the absolute truth of Christ does not entail that one must be able to prove it absolutely to anyone on command. The nature of truth and its verification are two different matters. For instance, a mathematical problem has only one correct answer, but the calculation of that answer may be quite long and involved. The defense of the Christian worldview (apologetics) involves many intellectual claims and counterclaims, but this does not detract from the absoluteness of the truth that is being defended.[27]

Holding to absolute truth does not remove one from the give-and-take of logical argument and the presentation of evidence. Sadly, many Christians confess Christ's absoluteness and then resolutely refuse to

---

[25]Reported in Charles Colson, "Apologetics for the Church: Why Christians Are Losing the Culture War," *Christian Research Journal*, summer 1996, p. 52.
[26]Ibid.
[27]I take this up in chapters six and seven.

engage in any apologetic discussion of the matter. This leads their ques-
tioners to conclude that Christian faith is not only absolutely unshakable but absolutely unconvincing. Yet a solid conviction of truth should
lead to intellectual satisfaction and contentment, as well as the willingness to dialogue. As Harry Blamires put it in his classic *The Christian
Mind*, "If one is conscious of drawing one's convictions from a solid,
deep-rooted tradition, one inevitably has a sense of quiet assurance in
one's beliefs and a feeling that is the reverse of touchy defensiveness."[28]

Third, to claim that the truth about God and God's ways with humanity is absolute is not to claim that Christians are inerrant in their
understanding about every aspect of their faith. The apostle Peter, a
personal disciple of Jesus Christ, stubbornly refused to believe that
Gentiles could be full participants in the new order of redemption revealed through Jesus until God gave him a vision to dispel his theological narrowness (Acts 10:9-48). Christians should be open to having their
theology corrected and deepened through prolonged intellectual engagement with fellow believers and non-Christians alike. If the core of
their faith is indeed absolutely true, there is nothing to fear—and much
to gain—from such a dialogue. J. Gresham Machen (1881-1937) was a
staunch and brilliant defender of the fundamentals of the faith against
those who would undermine it; yet he realized that our grasp of the
truth always needs to be refined and improved. Theology can progress
because our errors can be corrected by God's truth. Theology is

> a setting forth of those facts upon which experience is based. It is not
> indeed a complete setting forth of those facts, and therefore progress in
> theology becomes possible; it may be true so far as it goes; and only
> because there is that possibility of attaining truth and of setting it forth
> ever more completely can there be progress.[29]

More positively, though, the absolute truth of Jesus Christ frees erring and needy mortals from the confusion of a mass of conflicting religious claims. God is focused in Jesus and not spread all over the map.
There is one way out of the spiritual maze—if one looks up to the cross.

---

[28]Harry Blamires, *The Christian Mind* (New York: Seabury Press, 1963), pp. 120-21.
[29]J. Gresham Machen, *What is Faith?* (New York: Macmillan, 1927), pp. 32-33.

As Jesus said, "Just as Moses lifted up the snake in the desert, so the Son of Man must be lifted up, that everyone who believes in him may have eternal life" (Jn 3:15).[30]

4. *Truth is universal.* To be universal means to apply everywhere, to engage everything and to exclude nothing. The gospel message and the moral law of God are not circumscribed or restricted by cultural conditions. When Peter preached before the Jewish religious authorities, he was filled with the Holy Spirit and declared in clear terms concerning Jesus of Nazareth: "Salvation is found in no one else, for there is no other name under heaven given to people by which we must we saved" (Acts 4:12). This includes everyone and excludes no one. Salvation is offered to all humanity, not just a particular group of people. Paul further extends the universality of the gospel by affirming the supremacy of the risen Christ "not only in the present age, but also in the one to come. And God placed all things under his feet and appointed him to be head over everything for the church" (Eph 1:21-22). The scope of Christ's authority is unlimited. Paul further expands on this in his great christological hymn that declares that because Christ Jesus, though "being in very nature God," emptied himself to come to earth for our salvation, God the Father "exalted him to the highest place and gave him the name that is above every name." In light of this, "every knee should bow" and "every tongue confess that Jesus Christ is Lord" (Phil 2:6, 9-10). Evangelical theologian Carl F. H. Henry drives this home:

> Christianity contends that revelational truth is intelligible, expressible in valid propositions, and universally communicable. Christianity does not profess to communicate a meaning that is significant only within a particular community or culture. It expects men of all cultures and nations to comprehend its claims about God and insists that men everywhere ought to acknowledge and appropriate them.[31]

---

[30]On Christ's exclusivity, see R. Douglas Geivett, "Is Jesus the Only Way," in *Jesus Under Fire: Modern Scholarship Reinvents the Historical Jesus*, ed. Michael J. Wilkins and J. P. Moreland (Grand Rapids, Mich.: Zondervan, 1995), pp. 177-205; Ajith Fernando, *The Supremacy of Christ* (Wheaton, Ill.: Crossway, 1995); and Douglas Groothuis, *Jesus in an Age of Controversy* (Eugene, Ore.: Harvest House, 1996).
[31]Carl F. H. Henry, *God, Revelation, and Authority* (Waco, Tex.: Word, 1976), 1:229.

The universality of the gospel message is conceptually locked into the Great Commission. Jesus proclaims that he possesses *all* authority in the universe. On this basis, his disciples must disciple *all* the nations, baptizing converts in the name of the Trinity and teaching them *all* that Christ commanded. Those sent can take heart that Jesus will be with them *always*, even to the end of the age (Mt 28:18-20). Jesus' authority is universal, as is the field of mission, the scope of the teaching and the duration of Christ's fellowship.

The book of Revelation gives us a powerful picture of the universal effects of the Great Commission. While not all who are offered the gospel will believe it and receive it, the apostle John was privy to a heavenly vision of a vast and diverse multitude who accepted the truth of Jesus and worshiped him accordingly:

> I looked and there before me was a great multitude that no one could count, from every nation, tribe, people and language, standing before the throne and in front of the Lamb. They were wearing white robes and were holding palm branches in their hands. And they cried out in a loud voice:
>
> > "Salvation belongs to our God,
> > who sits on the throne,
> > and to the Lamb." (Rev 7:9-10; see also 5:9)

God's truth is not provincial, parochial or partial; it is universal in scope and application. Yet it also allows for unique cultural expression and the creative individuality of people made in the divine image and redeemed through the Lamb. The truth does not flatten us out into faceless conformity, but liberates each of us to be who we ought to be under the Lordship of Christ. Just as God provided for twelve different tribes in the Hebrew economy, Providence makes room for a diversity of gifts, personality types and callings in Christ. Yet all exist because of, and under, God's universal truth. As Jesus promised, "If you hold to my teaching, you are really my disciples. Then you will know the truth, and the truth will set you free" (Jn 8:31).

5. *The truth of God is eternally engaging and momentous, not trendy or superficial.* In postmodern times, our sensory environments are saturated with bright images, intrusive words and blaring sounds—all vy-

ing for our attention (and our funds). Fads, whether in advertising, politics or sports, come and go with increasing rapidity. It seems that nothing is settled or rooted or stable over time. In his book, *The Culture of Disbelief: How American Law and Politics Trivialize Religious Devotion* (1993), Stephen Carter laments that for many people (and the state), religion is little more than a hobby, something with which to amuse oneself, a kind of curiosity for when the mood strikes but not something to take all that seriously, especially in matters of legality.[32]

Yet beyond empty ephemeralities, there lies "the Rock of ages." Beyond the fragility of shifting tastes, hobby horses and market fluctuations stands the Word of the Lord, resolute and rooted in the eternal God of the universe. "The grass withers and the flower falls, but the word of God stands forever" (Is 40:8). "Your word, O LORD, is eternal; it stands firm in the heavens" (Ps 119:89). And as God declared to his rebellious people: "I the LORD do not change" (Mal 3:6; see also Heb 13:8). God remains faithful to his covenant with creation and to the community he summons forth. His word endures and is reliable, from age to age. James combines the eternal trustworthiness of God with divine goodness and truth:

> Every good and perfect gift is from above, coming down from the Father of the heavenly lights, who does not change like shifting shadows. He chose to give us birth through the word of truth, that we might be a kind of firstfruits of all he created (Jas 1:17-18).

God's truth is grounded in God's eternal being. It has no expiration date and needs no image makeovers. Moreover, it is a living, personal and dynamic truth—a truth that transcends the transient trivialities of our age and touches us at the deepest levels of our beings by including us in an eternal drama. This truth transforms us, as David knew well: "I have hidden your word in my heart that I might not sin against you" (Ps 119:11).

While postmodernists are enamored of stories and narratives, they demur when it comes to metanarratives, deeming them hopelessly

---

[32]Stephen Carter, *The Culture of Disbelief: How American Law and Politics Trivialize Religious Devotion* (New York: HarperCollins, 1993), pp. 23-43.

ideological and debunked by the failures of history. But God's eternal truth involves the metanarrative of divine Providence. Being a disciple of Jesus alerts us to the grand themes of God's story and the unfolding of his eternal plan of creation, fall and redemption. Christians live, as Kierkegaard put it, "under the audit of eternity" and within the vicissitudes of the divine drama.[33] Everything matters, when viewed under the eternal audit.

Far from being trivial, the truth of God made known to a rebellious planet is perennially engaging and continually controversial. Because of this, followers of Jesus are enlisted in the great debate for the hearts and minds of immortal beings. The stakes are infinite, the participants precious. The eternal God offers eternal life through "the blood of Christ" who "offered himself unblemished to God" to "cleanse our consciences from acts that lead to death, so that we may serve the living God" and "receive the promised eternal inheritance" (Heb 9:14-15). The truth is deathless, but the "second death" awaits those who reject God's saving truth (Rev 21:8). Because of its view of truth—the truth of Christ, of heaven and of hell—the Christian claim is the highest stakes proposition on earth. God's revelation of truth has eternal consequences for us all. As Os Guinness said, "Hell is nothing less than the truth known too late."[34]

6. *Truth is exclusive, specific and antithetical.* For every theological yes, there are a million no's. What is true excludes all that opposes it. This why God declares, "You shall have no other gods before me" (Ex 20:3). If there is but one God, all other claimants are impostors. The inexorable logic of antithesis is also behind Jesus' fearful utterance, "Enter through the narrow gate. For wide is the gate and broad is the road that leads to destruction, and many enter through it" (Mt 7:13). As R. J. Rushdoony commented, "Truth is exact and precise, and the slightest departure from the truth is the substitution of falsity for truth."[35] Exacti-

---

[33]On this, see Søren Kierkegaard, *Purity of Heart Is to Will One Thing* (New York: Harper & Row, 1948).

[34]Os Guinness, *The Dust of Death: The Sixties Counterculture and How It Changed America Forever*, rev. ed. (Wheaton, Ill.: Crossway, 1994), p. 358.

[35]R. J. Rushdoony, *Foundations of Social Order: Studies in the Creeds and Councils of the Early Church* (Fairfax, Va.: Thoburn Press, 1978), p. 118.

tude in truth should be our goal, even if it is never our perfect achievement.

While "all truth is God's truth," not all that claims to be true fits together logically and factually. Postmoderns find this hard to swallow, because of their taste for a smorgasbord of varying "truths" selected and combined according to whim, fashion, feeling or even frenzy. This was highlighted by a rather surreal exchange between Pastor Leith Anderson and a young man who asserted he believed in (1) Reformed theology, (2) the inerrancy of Scripture and (3) reincarnation—all without seeing the contradiction between believing in reincarnation and believing in a Bible and a theology that teaches resurrection! Because the young man did not think in terms of truth being exclusive (resurrection eliminates reincarnation), he held to both because he "liked" both.[36] One may like green peas and chocolate ice cream without pain of logical contradiction, but resurrection (the once-for-all uniting of the soul with one immortal body) cannot be squared with reincarnation (the recycling of the soul through different many bodies over time).[37]

The logic of truth is the logic of the law (or principle) of noncontradiction. First codified (but not invented) by Aristotle, this law states, "Nothing can both be and not be at the same time in the same respect." Nothing can possess incompatible properties; that is, nothing can be what it is not. For example, Jesus cannot be both sinless and sinful. Put another way, if one thing is true, the opposite thing cannot also be true in the same respect at the same time. If there is exactly one God, there cannot be more than one God. This logical principle is not the unique possession of Christianity; it is a truth of all creation. It is how God ordained us to think. Despite what some benighted theologians have claimed, Christian faith does not require that we somehow transcend this law of logic. Although God's ways are above our ways (Is 55:8-9),

---

[36]Reported in Gene Edward Veith, *Postmodern Times* (Wheaton, Ill.: Crossway, 1994), pp. 175-76.

[37]There are, in fact, various theories of reincarnation, some much more complex than this. However, all views of reincarnation—whether Buddhist or Hindu—are logically incompatible with the doctrine of resurrection. On this, see Douglas Groothuis, *Confronting the New Age* (Downers Grove, Ill.: InterVarsity Press, 1988), pp. 85-105.

God is consistent and cannot lie (Tit 1:2). God cannot deny himself or assert what is false; nor can he make something both true and false in the same way at the same time.[38]

Those who claim that this basic principle of thought is false must assert this principle in order to deny it. In so doing, they make a mockery out of all thought, language and the very notion of truth. Consider the statement: "The law of noncontradiction is false." For this statement itself to be true, it must contradict its opposite (that the law of noncontradiction is true). But in so doing, it must affirm the duality of truth and falsity—which is the very thing that the law of noncontradiction itself requires. As Francis Schaeffer tersely, but truly, put it: "When a man says that thinking in terms of an antithesis is wrong, what he is really doing is using the concept of antithesis to deny antithesis. That is the way God has made us and there is no other way to think."[39] Schaeffer, the great modern soldier for truth, was echoing Aristotle, Plato, all great philosophers—and Reality itself.[40]

The law of noncontradiction combined with the specificity of Christian truth and the high stakes involved in choosing whether to believe in Christ means that truth for the Christian is confrontational. The Christian cannot rest contented and happy in a world oozing with error. When Paul beheld the idolatry of Athens, he was "greatly dis-

---

[38]For the record, this is not a denial of God's omnipotence, because omnipotence concerns the ability to perform logically possible actions.

[39]Francis A. Schaeffer, *Escape from Reason* (Downers Grove, Ill.: InterVarsity Press, 1968), p. 35. For a good explanation of noncontradiction, see Ronald Nash, *Life's Ultimate Questions: An Introduction to Philosophy* (Grand Rapids, Mich.: Zondervan, 1999), pp. 193-208.

[40]Some think that modern physics has done away with the principle of noncontradiction because light behaves like both wave and particle. This is not true. The discovery of quantum electrodynamics (QED) near the turn of the century showed that "light is essentially made up of particles but that all elementary particles are capable of "wave-like" behavior. By showing in a logically consistent manner how light was capable of behaving like a wave on some occasions and a particle on others, this breakthrough produced one self-consistent paradigm that satisfactorily resolved the confounding puzzle of "wave-particle duality." Scott R. Burson and Jerry L. Walls, *C. S. Lewis and Francis Schaeffer: Lessons for a New Century from the Most Influential Apologists of Our Time* (Downers Grove, Ill.: InterVarsity Press, 1998), pp. 86-87. The authors cite as their source Richard P. Feyman, *QED: The Strange Theory of Light and Matter* (Princeton, N.J.: Princeton University Press, 1985), p. 37.

tressed" and "so he reasoned in the synagogue with the Jews and the God-fearing Greeks" (Acts 17:16-17), which led to his famous Mars Hill address. While the postmodern world beholds the great welter of life-styles, trends and facades and can only utter "whatever" with a smirk and a slouch, the followers of "*the* Way" (Acts 11:26) must lift their heads, take a few deep breaths, pray for courage and humility, and defend "the faith that was once for all entrusted to the saints" (Jude 3).

Anthropologist Ernest Gellner, who is a secular critic of postmodernism, pays tribute to monotheism when he notes that the Enlightenment emphasis on "the uniqueness of truth" and the hope of discovering nature's objective secrets is rooted in monotheism's avoidance of "the facile self-deception of universal relativism."[41] Gellner says:

> It was a jealous Jehovah who really taught mankind the Law of Excluded Middle: Greek formalization of logic (and geometry and grammar) probably would not have been sufficient on its own. Without a strong religious impulse toward a single orderly world, and the consequent avoidance of opportunist, manipulative incoherence, the cognitive miracle [of the Enlightenment] would probably not have occurred.[42]

The law (or principle) of excluded middle thus trades on the same essential insight as the law of noncontradiction by stating that any factual statement and its denial cannot both be true. Either Jehovah is Lord or he is not Lord. There is no middle option. Jesus assumes this principle when he warns, "No one can serve two masters. Either you will hate the one and love the other, or you will be devoted to the one and despise the other. You cannot serve both God and Money" (Mt 6:24). Although Gellner embraces the Enlightenment vision, which he deems more rational than Christianity, he respects monotheism for its insistence on a singular and knowable truth—against postmodernism's "opportunist, manipulative incoherence."[43]

The fires of theological antithesis are at work in the apostle Paul

---

[41]Ernest Gellner, *Postmodernism, Reason, and Religion* (New York: Routledge, 1992), p. 95.
[42]Ibid., pp. 95-96.
[43]Ibid., p. 96.

when he sharply warns the foolish Galatians not to embrace heretical teachings that opposed the gospel. Being "astonished" that the Galatians were "so quickly deserting the one who called [them] by the grace of Christ" and were "turning to a different gospel—which is really no gospel at all" (Gal 1:6-7), Paul drives home his point with passion and power in two passages:

> Evidently some people are throwing you into confusion and are trying to pervert the gospel of Christ. But even if we or an angel from heaven should preach a gospel other than the one we preached to you, let that person be eternally condemned. (Gal 1:7-8)

> I want you to know, brothers and sisters, that the gospel I preached is not of human origin. I did not receive it from any human source, nor was I taught it; rather, I received it by revelation from Jesus Christ. (Gal 1:11-12; cf. Acts 9)

The logic of Paul's appeal is simply the logic of antithesis and exclusion. He is unwilling and unable to synthesize or amalgamate the truth of the gospel with the error of the Judaizers, who were bewitching his beloved flock of believers (Gal 3:1). This truth is far too important to be compromised; the stakes are far too high for that, because only one gospel can deliver sinful people from eternal condemnation—the gospel of Jesus. Paul is not having a temper tantrum or throwing his apostolic weight around. No, he recognizes the terms of the debate and the eternal implications of truth and falsehood for the soul.

7. *Truth, Christianly understood, is systematic and unified.* Truth is one, as God is one. All truths cohere with one another as expressions of God's harmonious objective reality—of his being, his knowledge and his creation. Something cannot be true in religion and false in science (or vice versa), or true in philosophy but false in theology (or vice versa).[44] There is only one world, God's world; it is a uni-verse, not a multi-verse. Although not a Christian, philosopher Ludwig Wittgenstein understood this unity of truth well: "If a god creates a world in which certain propositions are true, he creates thereby also a world in

---

[44]On this see Mortimer Adler, *Truth in Religion: The Plurality of Religion and the Unity of Truth* (New York: Macmillan, 1990), pp. 10-39.

which all propositions consequent to them are true." This is because a "proposition asserts every proposition which follows from it."[45]

In an age content with fragmented knowledge and conflicting opinions, Christians must strive for a well-integrated perspective on life that rings true wherever it is articulated. Nietzsche anticipated the postmodern mood when he opined: "I mistrust all systematizers and I avoid them. The will to a system is a lack of integrity."[46] But Nietzsche was wrong. As Arthur Holmes put it, "In a universe subject to the rule of one creator-God . . . truth is seen as an interrelated and coherent whole."[47] All areas of thought and life should be brought under the cosmic lordship of Christ. Francis Schaeffer challenges us in this:

> It is no use saying He is the Alpha and Omega, the beginning and the end, the Lord of all things, if He is not the Lord of my whole unified intellectual life. I am false or confused if I sing about Christ's lordship and contrive to retain areas of my own life that are autonomous.[48]

In our finitude and fallenness, we often fail to see the harmony of God's orchestration of all truths, but we strive to know what we can and to rest content with the mysteries framed by our knowledge. A fragmented and incoherent worldview is never the goal of the truth-seeking Christian.

8. Christian truth is an end, not a means to any other end. It should be desired and obtained for its own value. This flies in the face of postmodernist pragmatism, which reduces truth to social function or personal preference. As Harry Blamires declared,

> There is no subtler perversion of Christian Faith than to treat it as a mere means to a worldly end, however admirable that end in itself may be. The

---

[45]Ludwig Wittgenstein, *Tractatus Logico-Philosophicus* (New York: Routledge, 1981), p. 107. Wittgenstein's understanding of the concatenation of propositional truth in the *Tractatus* was smaller than that which is implied in the Christian worldview, where all things (whether necessary or contingent truths) work together according to God's plan, but his essential insight concerning logical implications with respect to propositions still holds and is, I believe, instructive for Christian thinkers.

[46]Friedrich Nietzsche, "Twilight of the Idols," aphorism 26 in *The Portable Nietzsche*, ed. Walter Kauffman (New York: Penguin, 1976), p. 470.

[47]Arthur Holmes, *All Truth Is God's Truth* (Grand Rapids, Mich.: Eerdmans, 1977), p. 7.

[48]Schaeffer, *Escape from Reason*, p. 83.

Christian Faith is important because it is true. What it happens to achieve, in ourselves or in others, is another and, strictly speaking, secondary matter.[49]

Postmodernist spirituality deems truth as malleable and adaptable to one's perceived needs and style. One's "God-concept" or "personal spirituality" is formed irrespective of the idea of reality in and of itself. Truth, religious or otherwise, is what works—for me or for my social group. But Christian faith teaches that it works (or bears spiritual fruit) only because it is true.

The notion of spiritual truth as a means and not an end was hammered home to me by a college student who attended a lecture I gave on comparative religion, in which I attempted to argue that all religions cannot be one in essence since they make such radically different truth claims.[50] She claimed that both Buddhism and Christianity can be true since Buddhists are helped by their Buddhist meditations and Christians benefit from their Christian prayers. To this, I gave an example of a married couple where one partner is committing adultery. The innocent partner is oblivious and thinks they have a good marriage. The marriage seems to "work," but the reality is otherwise. Even if this scenario is somewhat unlikely, the illustration hit home, because the student then asked how we can ever know the truth at all. This skepticism ("What is the truth?") is better than pragmatism ("Truth is nothing but what works"), because it allows for the existence of a discoverable truth that means more than mere pragmatic results.

Returning to Truth

Without a thorough and deeply rooted understanding of the biblical view of truth as revealed, objective, absolute, universal, eternally engaging, antithetical and exclusive, unified and systematic, and as end in itself, the Christian response to postmodernism will be muted by the surrounding culture or will make illicit compromises with the truth-

---

[49]Blamires, *Christian Mind*, p. 104.
[50]See Douglas Groothuis, *Are All Religions One?* (Downers Grove, Ill.: InterVarsity Press, 1996).

impoverished spirit of the age. The good news is that truth is still truth, that it provides a backbone for witness and ministry in postmodern times, and that God's truth will never fail. As J. P. Moreland puts it:

> This is why truth is so powerful. *It allows us to cooperate with reality, whether spiritual or physical, and tap into its power.* As we learn to think correctly about God, specific scriptural teachings, the soul, or other important aspects of a Christian world view, we are placed in touch with God and those realities. And we thereby gain access to the power available to us to live in the kingdom of God.[51]

---

[51]Moreland, *Love Your God*, pp. 81-82; emphasis in the original.

4

THE TRUTH ABOUT TRUTH

The last chapter sketched out the biblical view of truth. At its heart is the claim that truth is what represents or corresponds to reality. Put differently, a true statement connects with the reality or facts it describes. Or so the Bible teaches. But what is the common consensus today about truth, and how well does it hold up philosophically?

Two Views of Truth
Postmodern culture presents two contradictory (but seemingly commonsensical) views of truth. A recent political event illustrates the coexistence of both views. During the House debate and Senate trial on the impeachment of Bill Clinton, opinion on whether he committed an impeachable offense generally split along party lines. Most Republicans said yes; most Democrats said no. This does not mean that the truth of the matter could not be known but that the handling of the question had little to do with ascertaining objective realities; it had much more to do with image control, propaganda and political posturing. The "truth" of the matter could be constructed according to the needs of the politi-

cians responsible for ascertaining the truth.

The statement "Clinton committed one or more impeachable of-
fenses" is either true or false. It cannot be neither true nor false. It cannot be both true and false. This presentation of the issue assumes a
certain view of truth. True statements accurately reflect or represent reality; false statements fail to do so. And a statement cannot be both true
and false in the same respect at the same time. The correspondence
view of truth is at work here, along with the notion of antithesis or either-or thinking.

At the same time, another view of truth was at work in the controversy, a view enlivened by matters of political expediency. Some argued
as though Clinton's objective guilt or innocence was not the issue. What
mattered was political victory and not disrupting a "good economy." It
behooved certain political agendas to redescribe the situation in ways
that obscured or neglected the actual facts of the matter in favor of
things deemed more important. When viewed from this angle, the stark
logic of correspondence and antithesis vanishes into the background or
is eliminated entirely with respect to his objective guilt or innocence.
One's opinion concerning the Clinton case becomes a matter of how
one constructs the discourse, how one interprets a situation given certain political and economic factors.

"Common sense" seems to be waging war with itself. On the one
hand, Clinton was guilty or innocent—either-or. On the other hand, it's
all a matter of how you see it. So, truth can be two very different kinds
of things. Or can it?

An anecdote furthers illustrates these irreconcilable but commonly
held views of truth. "I love Jesus," a middle-aged woman in the audience exclaimed, "but he never wanted anyone to worship him!" As I
looked at the group of about thirty people I saw nods of agreement and
heard rumblings of approval. A woman who was part of the panel discussion in which I was participating said, "I find the way of Jesus helpful, but I can't exclude anyone's spirituality outside of Christianity."
Another woman in the audience declared that Jesus was only a prophet
and that the Qur'an was more important than the New Testament because it was inspired by Allah.

These comments were offered during an event that brought together local authors for discussion among themselves and with an audience on the subject of "spirituality." Two of the other panelists were from a liberal seminary where Jesus is not acknowledged as Lord and the Bible is not respected as God's inspired Word. They were quick to distance themselves from my theologically conservative viewpoint. Another panelist was a New Ager who repeatedly said all religions teach that we are one with God. She said she accepted Jesus, but only as one way, not the only way.

The beliefs of those attending the event were all over the spiritual map. They perceived spirituality as a private concern not subject to the challenges of evidence and logic; it was rather like a hobby. One spirituality is as good as another—as long as you don't think your way is the only way. When I offered reasons why Jesus should be the center of everyone's spirituality, most in the audience bristled.

When it came to the nature of truth itself, I had much more in common with the Muslim woman in the audience than the two liberal Christian panelists or most of the other "spirituality" enthusiasts. This woman claimed that Islam was objectively true, a revelation from Allah. She offered a mini-apologetic for Mohammed's authenticity and the view that Jesus was a prophet but not God incarnate. To her, the affirmation, "Allah is God and Mohammed is his prophet" is not just a spiritually enriching concept or the linguistic practice of a certain community of religious believers. She takes it to be a representation of objective reality. Although we disagreed on what was *true* (I believe Jesus is Lord; she believes Allah is Lord), we agreed on the nature of truth (that which corresponds to reality). She upheld correspondence and antithesis with respect to religious truth, while most in the audience and the panel did not, however warmly they may have felt about Jesus and "Christian spirituality."

As Walter Truett Anderson observes, we find in these postmodern times "a strange and unfamiliar kind of ideological conflict: not merely conflict *between* beliefs, but conflict *about* belief itself."[1] The Muslim and

---

[1]Walter Truett Anderson, *Reality Isn't What It Used to Be* (New York: HarperSanFrancisco, 1990), p. 3.

I had a conflict between our respective beliefs. We each took our own view to be objectively true and to exclude the other. On the other hand, most in the audience did not care whether we deemed Jesus or Allah to be Lord, because they took belief itself to be subjective, pragmatic and personal—exempt from the demands of objectivity, antithesis and rational verification.

Defending the Correspondence View of Truth

Careful consideration of the view of truth as correspondence to reality reveals that only one of the two supposedly commonsensical notions of truth can itself be true. The issue at hand does not concern the ways of verifying or proving whether a statement is true but rather the definition or nature of truth itself.[2]

Human languages perform many different services in life. Many of our communications, whether writing, speaking or sign language, do not issue truth claims. For instance, when I found out I had been given a free ticket to a high-priced jazz concert featuring the Pat Metheny Group, I exclaimed, "Great!" When fans cheer or jeer at a baseball game, they are voicing their approval or disapproval with exclamatory words such as "Hurrah!" or "Boo!" However, if I claim the pitch that was called a strike by the umpire was really a ball, I am making a truth claim. The question "How many books has Alvin Plantinga written?" is not claiming or asserting anything about external reality but is inquiring into a state of affairs—the number of books he has authored. The *answer* to the question will be a truth claim. If a captive begs his captor to stop torturing him, he is entreating or beseeching someone, not stipulating a fact about some situation. When I pray, "Lord, make me an instrument of your peace," I petition God for various blessings and virtues. I am not stating overtly my theology, although I am assuming a theology in the petition itself, which involves beliefs about God's goodness and omniscience. When I say at a wedding ceremony, "I now pronounce you husband and wife," this is not a judgment of fact but a

---

[2]The matter of verification is addressed in chapter seven: "Apologetics for Post-moderns."

declaration or an enactment of a reality.[3] The sentence "You shall not commit adultery" makes no claim about who has or has not committed adultery, but rather it gives an imperative, a command or injunction about what one ought and ought not to do.

Why analyze these everyday kinds of utterances? We need to understand the truth-function of language in order to see what the truth about truth really is, and so avoid truth decay. My expression of joy at the prospect of seeing Pat Metheny in concert (for free) did not, in itself, claim anything about reality. However, the "Great!" I uttered was nested in a cluster of truth claims of various stripes. I take the statement "Pat Metheny is a world-class jazz guitarist" to be true. That's why I was excited. It is also true that my friend had been given two free tickets, one of which he offered to me.

Any language that states a truth claim—whether expressed in a sentence, an utterance or a belief—is called a proposition. A proposition is what a declarative sentence affirms or asserts. Another way to put it is that a proposition is what a declarative sentence *means*.[4] Questions, imperatives, exclamations and entreaties are not expressed in declarative or descriptive sentences, and so do not express propositions. Sentences about facts do express propositions. The imperative statement "Do not murder" does not *express* a proposition as it stands. It does, however, *presuppose* a proposition, namely, "murder is wrong," which makes a truth claim about the nature of (moral) reality. This proposition is true, because it reflects the commands of God, based on his eternal and objective character as good.[5] The sentence "My wife, Rebecca, has written two books on Christianity and gender" can be put into any number of languages, but the meaning or propositional content is the same in all languages, as is the fact that the statement is true. The proposition describes a state of affairs and does so by agreeing with—as opposed to

---

[3]Technically this is called a "performative utterance," a concept I will return to in chapter eight.

[4]For a philosophical discussion of meaning see Douglas Groothuis, "Meaning," in *The Encyclopedia of Empiricism* (Westport, Conn.: Greenwood Press, 1997), pp. 244-46.

[5]I will discuss this in more detail in chapter eight.

contradicting—objective reality. Propositions make truth claims; they stake out a chunk of reality linguistically.

Aristotle made a classic statement about the nature of propositions in his definition of truth and falsity:

> To say of what is that it is not, or of what is not that it is, is false, while to say of what is that it is, and of what is not that it is not, is true; so that he who says of anything that it is, or that it is not, will say either what is true or what is false.[6]

Propositions are true or false because they make truth claims, stipulations about "what is" and "what is not," as Aristotle states it. The correspondence view of truth, held by the vast majority of philosophers and theologians throughout history until recently, holds that any statement is true if and only if it corresponds to or agrees with factual reality. The statement "The desk in my study is brown" is true only if there is, in fact, a brown desk in my study. The statement "There is no brown desk in my study" is then false because it fails to correspond to any objective state of affairs (i.e., to the facts of the matter). As Christian philosopher Nicholas Wolterstorff succinctly states it,

> If I believe of something that it is a duck, that is true of it if and only if it is a duck. And if that is indeed true of it, it is not true of it relative to some conceptual scheme. It is just true, period. Thoughts are true or false of things, period—not relative to something or other.[7]

This commonsensical view presupposes some basic laws of logic, which we met briefly in the previous chapter. The law (or principle) of excluded middle affirms that "either A or non-A." Either there is a brown desk in my study or there is not; either there is a duck on the pond or there is not. There is no middle option. One more principle of logic teams up for further clarification. The law (or principle) of noncontradiction states that "A cannot be non-A in the same way and in the same respect at the same time." It cannot be true that there both is and

[6]Aristotle *Metaphysics* bk. 4, chap. 7.

[7]Nicholas Wolterstorff, in Stephen Louthan, "On Religion: A Discussion with Richard Rorty, Alvin Plantinga and Nicholas Wolterstorff," *Christian Scholars Review* 26, no. 2 (1996): 180.

is not a brown desk in my study. However, a brown desk can be in my study one day and be gone the next. There is no contradiction in this because of the change in time.

Propositions may be controversial ("Hell exists"), trivial ("Australia is south of Europe"), little-known ("John Coltrane had bad teeth"), well-known ("Bill Clinton was impeached"), humorous (you fill this one in), obscure ("Max Stirner's philosophy resembled Nietzsche's"), frightening ("Airbags may kill passengers"), offensive ("Jesus is the only way to heaven") or comforting ("God will wipe away every tear in the end"). These different qualities affect a proposition's *significance* to us but not its truth value. Further, what is controversial to one person may not be to the next; so there is some person-relativity with respect to our responses to various truths (and falsehoods). However, the truth or falsity of these propositions is not a matter of individual subjectivity, preference or taste.

Our beliefs and statements concern propositions about reality. We either assent to them, deny them or suspend judgment about them. Reality or actuality concerns objects or states of affairs, either real or imaginary. D. Elton Trueblood gives a helpful breakdown:

Minds may be knowing or ignorant.

Propositions may be true or false.

Objects may be real or imaginary.[8]

For a mind to know that something is true or false, it must necessarily hold a belief about a proposition that makes a truth claim concerning something's existence or nonexistence. For example, unicorns are imaginary *objects*; therefore, the *proposition* "Unicorns do not exist" is true, and when my *mind* assents to this proposition, I know it to be true.

Beliefs depend on minds for their existence. There can be no beliefs without minds to hold those beliefs (whether a human mind, an angelic mind or the divine Mind). However, what a belief is *about*, or what it *refers to*, is not dependent on our mind believing it. The truth value of a proposition's content is mind-independent. If I believe that Blaise Pascal was a great philosopher, the truth or falsity of my belief relates to

---

[8]D. Elton Trueblood, *General Philosophy* (New York: Harper & Row, 1963), p. 47.

the status of the proposition "Pascal was a great philosopher." The proposition is true or false not because of any quality of my belief concerning it, but by virtue of whether the belief accurately represents or corresponds to reality—in this case, the reality concerning Pascal's philosophical prowess.

As Bertrand Russell put it, "Although truth and falsehood are properties of beliefs, they are properties dependent upon the relations of the beliefs to other things, not upon any internal quality of the beliefs."[9] Therefore,

> the truth of a belief is something not involving beliefs, or (in general) any mind at all, but only the *objects* of belief. A mind, which believes, believes truly when there is a *corresponding* complex [of facts] not involving the mind, but only its objects. This correspondence ensures truth, and its absence entails falsehood. Hence we account simultaneously for the two facts that beliefs (*a*) depend on minds for their *existence*, (*b*) do not depend on minds for their *truth*.[10]

Russell speaks only of *beliefs* being true or false, but the issue of truth value applies to *propositions* as well. Beliefs concern propositions[11] and the relation of those propositions to reality.[12]

John Searle highlights Russell's insight by saying, "Facts don't need statements in order to exist, but statements need facts in order to be true."[13] Aristotle also noted that the existence of a man makes the statement about his existence true, but the statement itself does not make the

---

[9]Bertrand Russell, *The Problems of Philosophy* (1913; reprint, New York: Oxford University Press, 1959), p. 121.

[10]Ibid., p. 129. Russell was an atheist, so he did not factor in the reality of the divine mind, which knows all things (true propositions). Russell was speaking of human minds in relation to truth. In that case, his claims about beliefs follow logically on the relationship of propositions to God's mind; see Alvin Plantinga, "How to Be an Anti-Realist," *Proceedings of the American Philosophical Society* 56, no. 1 (1982): 47-50.

[11]The fact that beliefs relate to propositions involves what are called "propositional attitudes" in the philosophical literature.

[12]All propositions are held as beliefs by God, since God (unlike humans) has only true beliefs and since God (unlike humans) knows everything there is to know. Therefore, God believes all true propositions to be true and believes all false propositions (the denials of true propositions) to be false, without remainder.

[13]John Searle, *The Construction of Social Reality* (New York: Free Press, 1995), p. 218.

man exist.[14] In other words, the facts make a statement true, or alternately, the lack of correspondence to fact makes a statement false.

Even subjective or person-relative statements, such as "I feel a pain in my right knee," depend on facts for their truth or falsity. If I speak truthfully and am experiencing a pain in my right knee, the statement is true. The statement refers to an objective state of affairs—my state of being in pain. If I am not in pain, the statement is false because it does not correspond to an objective state of affairs. To use Searle's words, I may be in pain without uttering it ("facts don't need statements to exist"), but if I utter it, this does not in itself make it true ("statements need facts in order to be true").

Things become somewhat more tricky when we speak of the truth or falsity of statements made in the future tense, that is, when we make predictions about things that do not yet exist. In these cases we can't claim that a statement such as "Jesus will come again to judge the world" is true on the basis that it *now* corresponds to a present or past objective event, since the event of the second coming is future. This differs from the statement "Jesus rose from the dead" since that is a past event of objective history. Yet in the case of the second coming we can still apply the principle of the excluded middle to determine that either Jesus will come back or he won't. Only one of these antithetical realities will happen. So the statement is not exempted from the condition of being either true or false.[15] The particular truth value of the statement "Jesus will come again to judge the world" is still based on its correspondence to God's perfect knowledge and infallible plan for the world. In addition, the predictive statement will, at some unknown time in the future, correspond to the actual event of the second coming by being fulfilled in history.

The truth of logical principles corresponds to reality in a different way than do statements about empirical facts, but the truth of logical principles still depends on matching a reality outside of the statements that assert

---

[14]Aristotle *Categories* 14b.15-20.
[15]Some philosophers debate whether or not a statement about contingent truths concerning the future are true or false before the events they predict occur, but I will not take that up here. For a view that every statement is always true or false, see Richard Taylor, *Metaphysics*, 4th ed. (New York: Prentice Hall, 1992), pp. 54-67.

these principles. The law (or principle) of contradiction is true, not because it corresponds to any one slice of reality (such as my brown desk), but because it corresponds to all of reality. The fact that nothing can be itself and not itself in the same way and in the same respect (A is not non-A) is a universal condition or requirement of existence (and meaningful language). It is true at all times and at all places, and must be so. The truth of the law of noncontradiction further corresponds to the workings of God's mind. God is a God of truth and not of falsehood, a God of logic, not illogic (Is 1:18). God does not contradict himself (Tit 1:2; Heb 6:18) and cannot disown himself (2 Tim 2:13). He knows all things truly and knows that neither his being nor his creation can contain logical contradictions.

Moral statements are also true because they match reality. The statement "Adultery is morally wrong" is true not because it matches one particular item of reality but because the statement corresponds to the objective, universal and absolute moral law laid down by God. It therefore applies to all of reality, to all marriages. The wrongness of murder is not verified in the same way as an individual fact of history (such as the resurrection of Christ), but all statements about morality are true or false depending on whether they match God's moral law. The statement "Extramarital sex is morally allowable as long as both spouses agree to it" is false because it fails to correspond to the objective morality of marriage instituted by the Creator for our own good.

Although Sigmund Freud was a vehemently antireligious thinker, he nevertheless held to a Christian view of the nature of truth, and his view on truth makes a good summary of what I have argued for above. Freud was a modernist who sought a rational explanation of human nature that matched reality. He believed that science aims to

> arrive at correspondence with reality, that is to say with what exists outside of us and independently of us. . . . This correspondence with the real external world we call truth. It is the aim of scientific work, even when the practical value of that work does not interest us.[16]

---

[16]Cited in Mortimer Adler, "Truth," in *The Great Ideas Synopticon II*, ed. Mortimer J. Adler (Chicago: Encyclopedia Britannica, 1952), p. 917.

The Postmodernist View of Language and Truth

The classical distinctions between minds, beliefs and reality have been blurred by postmodernists who reject the correspondence view of truth as modernist fiction. They conflate these categories by claiming that truth is not established by anything outside of the mind or the culture that shapes beliefs. The word *truth* is simply a contingent creation of language, which has various uses in various cultures. It expresses certain purposes, customs, emotions and values, but it cannot be said to represent or mirror reality itself. Our access to the territory of reality is through our language, which acts as a map. But we cannot check the map against the territory, since we can know nothing outside our language. Thus, language becomes a kind of prison of signifiers that can never connect with the signified outside of itself. When language attempts to refer to anything outside language itself, it fails.[17] We should not even expect it to succeed. Richard Rorty makes this point:

> It is useless to ask whether one vocabulary rather than another is closer to reality. For different vocabularies serve different purposes, and there is no such thing as a purpose that is closer to reality than another purpose. . . . Nothing is conveyed in saying . . . that the vocabulary in which we predict the motion of a planet is more in touch with how things really are than the vocabulary in which we assign the planet an astrological influence.[18]

Rorty's view is absurd on the face of it. The purpose of astrology is to augur the meaning of life and to predict the future on the basis of the influence of the planets on one's personality and destiny. The theory is based on a refuted geocentric cosmology and has no predictive value scientifically. It is also condemned as false divinational religion in Scripture (see Deut 18:9-14). The truth claims expressed in the "vocabulary" of astrology are, therefore, false. Even though astrology serves a different purpose or has a different social function than modern astronomy, astrology still issues truth claims—claims that have been believed, but

---

[17]On this see Jim Leffel, "Our New Challenge: Postmodernism," in *The Death of Truth*, ed. Dennis MacCallum (Minneapolis: Bethany House, 1996), pp. 38-39.

[18]Richard Rorty, introduction to John P. Murphy's *Pragmatism: From Peirce to Davidson* (Boulder, Colo.: Westview, 1990); quoted in Stanley Grenz, *A Primer on Postmodernism* (Grand Rapids, Mich.: Eerdmans, 1996), p. 155.

claims that are false and falsifiable. The meanings of astrology and astronomy, contra-Rorty, are not exhausted by their respective social purposes or functions. Their effects on cultures are integrally related to the
claims they make about objective reality, either rightly or wrongly.

The sheer fact that finite, previously earthbound human beings
could construct manned space vehicles that travel to the moon and
back reveals that the sophisticated mathematical formulations required
for the successful navigation of space *corresponded* to the territory where
no one had gone before. The map was a proper guide to the territory
because it objectively fit the territory. In other words, the mathematical
equations and the language related to their implementation (the signifiers) connected to the objective realities of outer space (the signified).
Astrologers were not consulted for their insights into the navigational
requirements for space flight.

Postmodernists often argue that the semantics (word meanings) and
syntax (grammatical structure) of human languages are contingent and
ultimately arbitrary. They are mere constructions. Humans have many
differing languages, and translations between languages are often difficult. Moreover, the way people understand reality is, at least to a large
extent, supposedly dependent on the nature of their languages. These
observations have led postmodernists to take languages to be self-enclosed, self-referential systems.

However, as Searle has noted, this argument commits a basic fallacy.
Any number of words can be used to name a dog, a tree or a philosophy. In one sense, this is arbitrary; the semantics could be different.
There is nothing in the nature of what we call a dog that demands it be
called a dog (or any of the other English words for canines). This is true
as well for trees, philosophies, music and so forth. Yet this has no bearing on the effectiveness of the use of words in designating the reality to
which they refer. The words, however varied in different languages,
when used in propositions still have an irreducibly referential function;
they point to things outside of themselves. To put it another way, words
(or signifiers) in declarative sentences have an extralinguistic focus (the
signified). As Searle puts it, "From the fact that a *description* can only be
made relative to a set of linguistic categories, it does not follow that the

facts/states of affairs/, etc., described can only *exist* relative to a set of categories."[19] How we apply the terms *cat, kilogram, canyon* or whatever is contingent on various languages.

> We arbitrarily define the word "cat" in such and such a way; and only relative to such and such definitions can we say, "That's a cat." But once we have made the definitions and once we have applied the concepts relative to the system of definitions, whether or not something satisfies our definition is no longer arbitrary or relative. That we use the word "cat" the way we do is up to us; that there is an object that exists independently of that use, and satisfies that use, is a plain matter of (absolute, intrinsic, mind-independent) fact.[20]

Postmodernists have confused the relativity of term selection (semantic variation) with an inability of language to represent objective reality. This is like saying that because we can drive any number of different cars, trucks, bicycles or motorcycles, we can never arrive at the same destination. Semantic and syntactical differences do not annul the ability of language to refer to realities outside of itself, or to refer to its own objective realities successfully. We do not create different worlds through our languages as the postmodernists would have it, but we do use varying descriptions of the actual world, which either correspond or fail to correspond to the world that is there.[21]

Even though our use of particular sounds and markings for words is not dictated by the nature of the things they describe, semantics and syntax can connect us with reality. Consider an international scientific conference that draws on the leading thinkers in a discipline such as physics, chemistry or medicine. The experts speak different languages (with differing semantics and syntax), but attempt to describe the same realities within their disciplines. Translators aid the scientists in understanding what other scientists in their field are reporting. This sort of common enterprise—whether among scientists, politicians or religious leaders—would seem impossible given the postmodernist contention that lan-

---

[19]Searle, *Construction of Social*, p. 166; emphasis in the original.
[20]Ibid.
[21]Ibid.

guage cannot penetrate to reality and that it walls us off from others who use different languages, since languages are socially constructed in varying contexts. Yet it is not impossible; it happens often. Certainly, ever since the fall of the tower of Babel (Gen 11), communicating truth across languages has been difficult, but it is not hopeless. Language may penetrate to reality, and those of differing language may share truths.

Christian Missions as a Counterexample

Although the history of Christian missions may carry little argumentative weight for non-Christians, it is instructive for people of Christian faith. Implementing the Great Commission (Mt 28:18-20; Acts 1:8) requires that the communication set truths to people of cultures and languages other than the original cultures and languages of the Bible. Christian missionaries endeavor to present the timeless truths of the gospel to those who are immersed in other worldviews and who have had little or no contact with Christianity. They are not starting from nothing, because all humans are created in God's image and, through general revelation (Rom 1—2), have some knowledge of their Creator, the moral law and their own sin. The human mind, although varied in the semantics and syntax it employs in languages and thought patterns, has some structural constants, such as the laws of logic and the referential function of language. Minds and languages are not infinitely elastic, because all humans are made in the image and likeness of God (Gen 1:26). The success of missionary activities across cultures witnesses to this fact. In one sense, the miracle of Pentecost and its ongoing effects partially overcomes the linguistic fragmentation of Babel as the Holy Spirit makes saving truth known in various languages (Acts 2).[22] William Dyrness speaks of the effect Christianity has had on linguistics:

> No religion has had the effect of Christianity on linguistics. Wherever Christianity has gone, it has concerned itself with language and translation. Believing in the importance of the revealed Word of God, Christians have worked to make it as widely available as possible. Ulfilas, the apos-

---

[22]On this, see Gene Edward Veith Jr., *Postmodern Times: A Christian Guide to Contemporary Thought and Culture* (Wheaton, Ill.: Crossway, 1994), pp. 20-23.

tle to the Goths (ca 311-83), invented a special alphabet for the Gothic language and translated the Bible into it.[23]

Christians have taken the Christian message and translated it into the language of the people, even if that meant creating a written language to express the extant oral language. This testifies to the fact that peoples of greatly diverse cultures and languages can come to fathom the same message. The question of whether the Christian worldview corresponds to reality will be addressed in the chapters on apologetics, but the point here is that the expansion of Christianity through cross-cultural communication of the Christian worldview refutes the postmodernist claim that language is unable to communicate across cultures in a commonly understood fashion.

Logical Consistency and Truth

The logical consistency of the biblical worldview is a necessary condition of its truth, but it is not a sufficient condition. For any worldview to be true, its essential tenets must be consistent with one another logically, in accordance with the laws of noncontradiction and excluded middle. Yet some have tried to make logical consistency the *definition* of truth itself and have rejected correspondence with reality as the definition of truth. They claim that if a set of statements is consistent with another, that is enough to make it true. This is called the coherence theory of truth. Truth is simply coherence among various statements. Postmodernists who are more philosophically rigorous insist on this kind of internal coherence for the truth of worldviews.[24] Others think that even the requirement of logical coherence is just another sad example of modernist logocentrism.

The primary problem with coherence as the definition of truth is that we can imagine a worldview that may fail to contradict itself logically (because its core ideas cohere), but which contradicts another system of thought that also coheres within itself. Thus both worldviews cannot be

---

[23]William Dyrness, *Christian Apologetics in a World Community* (Downers Grove, Ill.: InterVarsity Press, 1983), pp. 80-81.

[24]It should be noted that some nonpostmodernist philosophers hold to the coherence view of truth as well.

true. Moreover, a worldview may be consistent itself but fail to correspond with external reality. For example, a legal trial could be rigged so
that every witness's testimony agrees that Jones killed Smith. It fits together. But the fact of the matter, despite the unified testimony, is that
Jones did not kill Smith. With respect to a worldview, it may be that Islam's central presuppositions do not contradict themselves.[25] Nonetheless, Islam denies the incarnation as a fact of history, since it deems
Jesus to be only a prophet of Allah and not of God the Son. Since the incarnation occurred, Islam's internal consistency is insufficient to entail
its final truth, that is, its correspondence with reality.[26]

The correspondence theory of truth declares that correspondence is
the *definition* and *nature* of truth and that coherence is one necessary
(but not sufficient) *test* of truth. If a worldview's core claims are logically inconsistent, that worldview is necessarily false. For instance, if
pantheism claims that (1) God is all that exists and there is no evil, but
also that that (2) karma metes out rewards and punishments based on
the evaluation of good and evil deeds, pantheism is inconsistent logically and therefore false. This is because it affirms both the existence of
evil and the nonexistence of evil—a situation that is logically and ontologically impossible.

Truth and Power Relationships

Another postmodernist criticism of the correspondence view of truth is
that "truth" is really just a function of power relationships of many
kinds. Ideologies, philosophies and moralities sanctioned as true in a
given culture really reflect only varying types of discourse, which are
shaped by social arrangements. These belief systems do not indicate
anything about reality itself but only how reality is contingently constructed under certain conditions. Michel Foucault (d. 1984) was probably the leading thinker in promoting this kind of view and has inspired

---

[25]I do not take this to be true, but I am granting it for the sake of argument. On the
logical problems with the Islamic worldview, see Norman Geisler and Abdul
Saleeb, *Answering Islam* (Grand Rapids, Mich.: Baker, 1993).

[26]See Sulia Mason, *The Correspondence and Coherence Theories of Truth* (Master's thesis,
Denver Seminary, 1998), chap. 3.

many others to develop these notions along similar lines. Foucault is difficult to interpret and did not present a unified perspective over his prolific career.[27] However, he tends to collapse the concept of truth into the concept of beliefs and to regard beliefs as a product of complex power relationships. This quote gives a flavor of how Foucault understands "truth":

> Truth isn't outside of power, or lacking in power; contrary to a myth, . . .
> truth isn't the reward of free spirits, the child of protracted solitude, nor
> the privilege of those who have succeeded in liberating themselves. Truth
> is a thing of this world: it is produced only by virtue of multiple forms of
> constraint. And it induces regular effects of power. Each society has its
> regime of truth, its "general politics" of truth: that is, the types of dis-
> course which it accepts and makes function as true.[28]

Although some think that Foucault left room in his thinking for some objective truths,[29] he seems not to distinguish between statements that explain the objective world and statements that describe certain so-cial customs that are negotiated by human agreement (amidst diverse power relationships). He controversially claims in *The Order of Things* that the idea of human nature was a recent invention of Western cul-ture.[30] But as Roger Scruton points out, the nature of fish or the nature of humans is not decided by consensus or power relationships. "Con-cepts like those of fish and man are aimed at reality; they are forensic concepts, tied to explanation. . . . Their application is determined by the world, not by us."[31] On the other hand, the concept of an ornament, for instance, is not a fact of nature in itself but a product of human culture.

---

[27]For a good summary of Foucault's thought, see Gary Gutting, "Foucault," in *Routledge Encyclopedia of Philosophy*, ed. Edward Craig (New York: Routledge, 1998), 3:708-13.
[28]Michel Foucault, "Truth and Power," in *The Foucault Reader*, ed. Paul Rabinow (New York: Pantheon, 1984), pp. 72-73.
[29]See Gutting, "Foucault," p. 711.
[30]Michel Foucault, *The Order of Things: An Archaeology of the Human Sciences* (New York: Random House-Pantheon, 1970), pp. 386-87; cited in Stanley Grenz, *A Primer on Postmodernism* (Grand Rapids, Mich.: Eerdmans, 1996), p. 129.
[31]See Roger Scruton, *An Intelligent Person's Guide to Philosophy* (New York: Penguin, 1998), p. 35.

Ornaments are made so by human choice and convention.

Foucault, in claiming that concepts such as human nature are cultural creations of contingent power relationships, puts human nature itself in the category of a social construction, such as an ornament. This is clearly an error, because the concept of human nature "identifies something which preceded its own invention, whose nature is given by laws. . . . In such a case, it is not the concept which creates the kind, but the kind which creates the concept."[32] At any rate, for Foucault's own theories of truth and power to be true, they must accurately describe the realities he addresses. Therefore, he cannot completely reduce truth to power relations and claim that his own views are true.

Truth and the Sociology of Knowledge

Properly speaking, Foucault's observations on truth and power say nothing about the nature of definition of *truth* but concern the sociology and psychology of *beliefs*. The origin, perpetuation and effects of beliefs in various settings are a different matter from the truth of beliefs. However, an awareness and analysis of the effects of social institutions, language and customs on how discourse is formed and how it functions to perpetuate ideas is extremely helpful in coming to terms with truth claims. More broadly conceived, the discipline of the sociology of knowledge concerns the social factors that influence beliefs.[33] As Peter Berger and Thomas Luckmann put it:

> The sociology of knowledge must concern itself with whatever passes for "knowledge" in a society, regardless of the ultimate validity or invalidity (by whatever criteria) of such "knowledge." And insofar as all human "knowledge" is developed, transmitted and maintained in social situations, the sociology of knowledge must seek to understand the processes by which this is done in such a way that a taken-for-granted "reality" congeals for the man in the street."[34]

---

[32]Ibid.

[33]The sociology of knowledge broadly overlaps with social epistemology. On the latter see Alvin I. Goldman, "Social Epistemology," in *Cambridge Dictionary of Philosophy*, ed. Robert Audi (New York: Cambridge University Press, 1995), p. 746.

[34]Peter L. Berger and Thomas Luckmann, *The Social Construction of Reality: A Treatise in the Sociology of Knowledge* (Garden City, N.Y.: Anchor Books, 1966), p. 3.

For these writers, the sociology of *knowledge* is really the sociology of *belief*, because such a study does not make any normative judgments on the veracity of various beliefs (noted by the quotation marks around the word *knowledge* in the citation). Many postmodernists take insights from this field of study and combine it with a worldview that renders truth impossible. However, this is not justified on the basis of the discipline itself, which does not attempt to make judgments about the truth and falsity of worldviews, but simply to describe accurately and *truthfully* social situations in relation to how they legitimize or stigmatize beliefs. Berger speaks of the "plausibility structures" in society that function to render some beliefs plausible and others implausible.[35] For instance, being a Muslim in Iraq is natural and easy because the social system encourages it at every level. This is their plausibility structure. Being a Baha'i in Iraq is unnatural and dangerous, given Islam's hostility to this "heresy." The powers in charge oppose freedom of religion. This, however, says nothing of the truth or falsity of Islam or the Baha'i faith, or even of their rationality. Based on a network of social inducements and inhibitions, certain ideas and practices are culturally available and attractive (or "plausible"), while others are not.

Social relationships—whether in civil government, the academy, politics, the media or the family—do affect how people view truth, what questions they ask, what they take for granted and about what ideas they are skeptical. Some truths have been suppressed by unjust structures over long periods of time. The American legal system was rigged to exclude and marginalize African Americans even decades after the Emancipation Proclamation. This was reflected in Jim Crow laws, in how blacks were portrayed in American cinema (always as servants or entertainers) until roughly the 1960s and in many other subtle and more obvious ways. But the truth of the matter—which slowly emerged through a long struggle—is that racial discrimination is unwarranted because the races are equal and ought to be treated as such. This truth still labors to be free and to gain all the ground it deserves, but a truth it

---

[35]Peter Berger, *A Rumor of Angels: Modern Society and the Rediscovery of the Supernatural*, exp. ed. (New York: Doubleday, 1990), pp. 38-42.

is, despite whatever patterns of bigotry and racism remain unexposed and uncorrected.

Similarly, the American scientific establishment is hard-wired to presuppose, defend and perpetuate some form of Darwinian evolution. This is the established orthodoxy, which is perpetuated by a tight and intolerant system of discourse. Dissenters are almost invariably labeled as "young earth, fundamentalist creationists" who fail to recognize the nature of science but simply defer to the Bible. Even sophisticated Christian critics of Darwinism who go to great lengths to refute this stereotype are typically locked in the same category as flat-earthers, astrologers and phrenologists. The framework for argument excludes criticism of the received model, because contemporary science is defined as excluding in principle any intelligent, supernatural causation or explanation.[36] Vocal proponents of intelligent design fail to receive very much grant money, won't be hired as professors (or, if hired, will not get tenure), and will be unlikely to get published in any official academic organs.

The intelligent design movement, spearheaded by law professor Phillip Johnson and thinkers in several disciplines, is mounting a wise attack on this citadel, but given the plausibility/power structure of Western science, their task is a daunting one.[37] However, with its powerful evidential argument against Darwinism and a savvy understanding of the sociology of knowledge, the movement shows great promise to uncover the truth of the matter. Power need not trump truth, but even if it does, truth remains truth.[38]

Furthermore, social conditions may favor the acquisition of knowl-

---

[36]This naturalistic assumption has not always been a presupposition of science. In fact, the leaders of the scientific revolution were theists and often Christians. On this, see Stanley Jaki, *The Road of Science and the Ways to God* (Chicago: The University of Chicago Press, 1978); and J. P. Moreland, *Christianity and the Nature of Science* (Grand Rapids, Mich.: Baker, 1989).

[37]For an explanation of this phenomenon, see Phillip E. Johnson, "What Is Darwinism?" in *Objections Sustained: Subversive Essays on Evolution, Law and Culture* (Downers Grove, Ill.: InterVarsity Press, 1998), pp. 23-33.

[38]Phillip Johnson's strategy is outlined in his *Defeating Darwinism by Opening Minds* (Downers Grove, Ill.: InterVarsity Press, 1997).

edge. Alvin Goldman notes that "the social dimensions or determinants of knowledge, or the ways in which social factors promote or perturb the quest for knowledge," need not necessarily "undermine objectivity."

> Even if knowledge is construed as true or rational belief, social practices might enhance knowledge acquisition. One social practice is trusting in the opinions of authorities, a practice that can produce truth if the trusted authorities are genuinely authoritative. . . . Even a scientist's pursuit of extra-epistemic interests such as professional rewards may not be antithetical to truth in favorable circumstances.[39]

The power of the correspondence concept of truth under oppression—truth as insistently representing reality, come what may—was spotlighted in two conferences for Russian and American literary critics. The first convened in California in 1988 and the second in Russia in 1990. American postmodernists were baffled by their Russian counterparts' insistence on absolute values, truth and humanism, based on the spiritual worldview rooted in the Russian Christian tradition. J. Hillis Miller, a deconstructionist, was amazed that these Russians clung to the outmoded notion of truth: "Nothing at all like the Soviets' views about literature exists today among literary scholars in the United States, except among certain extremely conservative critics."[40]

The Russians, recently freed from communism at the time of the second conference, were equally amazed at the Americans' rejection of objective truth. Their Russian literature served as a bulwark of spiritual truths during a time of atheistic oppression.[41] The old Soviet regime also persecuted dissenting artists because of their insistence that art could communicate truths that threatened the unjust political system.[42] Yet if truth is a mere social construction, with no outside reference to an independent reality, it has no ability to anchor protest, to inspire dissent, to orient the soul toward what is objectively good and to liberate

[39]Goldman, "Social Epistemology," p. 746.
[40]J. Hillis Miller, "Literature and Value: American and Soviet Views," *Profession* 92 (1992): 22-26; quoted in Veith, *Postmodern Times*, p. 172.
[41]See Veith, *Postmodern Times*, p. 173.
[42]Ibid.

those ensnared in error—against all odds. As Solzhenitsyn said, "One word of truth outweighs the world." But for postmodernists this is hopeless modernism and objectivism. For them, the world outweighs any "truth," since "truth" is only a product of differing cultures where no one has the last word. Remember those quotation marks around truth; postmodernists cannot live without them. Christians cannot live with them.

Postmodern Pragmatism and Truth

While the postmodernist view of truth trades on the idea of social construction through linguistic practice, it also typically defaults to some kind of pragmatic conception of truth. If truth is not what designates reality, it becomes a tool for achieving certain ends. Richard Rorty, for example, considers himself a neo-pragmatist in the school of John Dewey. Postmodernist pragmatism lacks the optimism of earlier schools but shares with them an instrumental view of truth: truth is what gets things done. Accordingly, Rorty speaks not of refuting other views as objectively false—that would assume the correspondence view of truth that he rejects—but of "redescribing" situations with a new vocabulary in order to win people over to one's view. The redescription is no better or worse with respect to reality than any other description, but it may work—that is, it may convince people to adopt one's own preferred vocabulary. Rorty's "ironist" view replaces the "metaphysical" view that attempts to find and defend objective truth.

> The ironist's preferred form of arguments is dialectical in the sense that she takes the unit of persuasion to be a vocabulary rather than a proposition. Her method is redescription rather than inference. Ironists specialize in redescribing ranges of objects or events in particularly neologistic jargon, in the hope of inciting people to adopt and extend the jargon. An ironist hopes that by the time she has finished using old words in a new sense, not to mention introducing brand-new words, people will no longer ask questions phrased in the old words.[43]

---

[43]Richard Rorty, *Contingency, Irony, and Solidarity* (New York: Cambridge University Press, 1989), p. 78.

Notice that Rorty is not concerned with *propositions*, that which marks out reality through language. He is concerned with *vocabularies*, the kind of words we use. The relationship of those words to the reality outside of them is not an issue for him. What Rorty is trying to dignify, through his own jargon, is what historically has been called a "snow job" or a "con job." It is not an argument, because arguments seek to persuade on the basis of logic and evidence marshaled to the effect that something is true or false. Rorty speaks simply of manipulating language. This is propaganda, not argument. Nazis, communists, fascists and assorted racists have excelled in such redescriptions. Such a "dialectic" may well "work," but that does not make it a proper intellectual procedure. Moreover, it leaves one with no sufficient reason to believe that any persuasive effort by an "ironist" should be preferred to any other ironic maneuver.

Many ideas may "work" and yet be objectively false. For instance, after a dissolute life, a man may reform on the basis of believing he lost a large sum of money. He becomes successful and credits the turning point to be when he determined to straighten up after misplacing a large sum. However, he later learns that the money had been stolen. His belief that he lost the money is proven false; yet it worked well to incite his success.[44] This kind of example shows the difference between (1) the truth or falsity of a belief and (2) the effect or consequence of a belief. Yet postmodernist pragmatists tend to conflate these disparate notions.

In 1908 G. K. Chesterton quipped that the one thing that works best for the human soul is the truth itself, something pragmatism cannot provide.

> I agree with the pragmatist that apparent objective truth is not the whole matter; that there is an authoritative need to believe the things that are necessary to the human mind. But I say that one of those necessities precisely is a belief in objective truth. . . . Pragmatism is a matter of human needs; and one of the first of human needs is to be something more than a

---

[44]See Winfried Corduan, *No Doubt About It: Basic Christian Apologetics* (Nashville: Broadman & Holman, 1997), pp. 59-61.

pragmatist. . . .The pragmatist, who professes to be specifically human, makes nonsense of the human sense of actual fact.[45]

This, of course, echoes Jesus' declaration, "If you hold to my teaching, you are really my disciples. Then you will know the truth, and the truth will set you free" (Jn 8:31). Only truth will liberate, morally and spiritually and culturally.[46]

Self-Reference, Consistency and Perspectivism

The final problem for the postmodernist view of truth is that of self-reference and consistency. This criticism has been voiced many times against many thinkers, but it remains irrefutable. Consider the statement:

> All "truth" is a social construction of language and nothing more. It cannot orient us to any objective reality outside a system of discourse.

This statement refers to *all truth* and says that truth is *nothing but* a contingent construction that cannot connect us to objective reality *at all*. This claim includes the statement itself in its description or range of reference. Therefore, the postmodernist claim about truth is merely a social construction—and nothing more. But if it is only a social construction, then the statement itself cannot accurately depict the reality it purportedly describes. Therefore, it is false. Put another way, the statement sets up truth conditions or reality requirements that it cannot fulfill. It commits intellectual suicide. In Alvin Plantinga's terms, a statement is "self-referentially inconsistent" when it refers to or implicates itself and ends up refuting itself because it cannot account for itself.[47]

Some postmodernists appear to notice this nasty and inescapable

---

[45]G. K. Chesterton, *Orthodoxy* (1908; reprint, New York: Doubleday, 1959), pp. 36-37.

[46]For a critique of the inadequacy of pragmatism, see George Grant, *Philosophy in the Mass Age*, ed. William Christian (1959; reprint, Toronto: University of Toronto Press, 1995), pp. 75-89. See also Douglas Groothuis, "Some Problems with Pragmatism," on the Douglas Groothuis and Rebecca Merrill Groothuis Web page: <www.gospel com.net/ivpress/groothuis>.

[47]Alvin Plantinga, "Reason and Belief in God," in *Faith and Rationality: Reason and Belief in God*, ed. Alvin Plantinga and Nicholas Wolterstorff (Notre Dame, Ind.: University of Notre Dame Press, 1983), p. 60.

philosophical problem. While discussing the deconstructionist claim that all truth is socially contingent, Kenneth Gergen writes this in parentheses, "Reader beware, the same may be said of this book, and as well of the saying so."[48] Nothing more is made of this titanic admission of philosophical suicide. If Gergen's ideas are themselves nothing but contingent constructions with no referent residing in reality, they cannot be any more true or false than anything else that may be advanced. Gergen's sentence logically disqualifies his entire project. I once illustrated this point at a conference at which I was speaking by reading this sentence and then tossing the book across the room while declaring, "So much for Gergen . . ."

This point of philosophical failure can be illustrated also by Nietzsche's philosophy of perspectivism, which has significantly shaped many postmodernist approaches to truth. Nietzsche claimed that there are no facts but only interpretations (or constructions) created according to one's particular need to enhance one's life, what he called "the will to power." There is "no true world," only "a perspectival appearance whose origin lies in us."[49] Everything is a matter of relative and pragmatic perspective, with no method by which to adjudicate rationally between perspectives in order to discern an objective truth true for everyone. Nietzsche claims: "There are many kinds of eyes. Even the sphinx has eyes—and consequently there are many kinds of 'truths,' and consequently there is no truth."[50]

Nietzsche put this forward as an account of the human situation, as an explanation for human knowing, being and acting. Yet if Nietzsche's own view is nothing but a relative perspective whose origin lay in himself only and not a fact of the matter, his own view cannot successfully describe the lay of the land. It summarily executes itself, however poetically or passionately enunciated. Moreover, Nietzsche condemns many other views as flatly false, including all nonperspectivist views. Con-

---

[48]Kenneth J. Gergen, *The Saturated Self: Dilemmas of Identity in Contemporary Life* (New York: HarperCollins, 1991), p. 109.
[49]Friedrich Nietzsche, *The Will to Power* 15, ed. Walter Kaufmann (New York: Vintage, 1967), pp. 14-15.
[50]Ibid., p. 291.

sider this excoriation: "In Christianity neither morality nor religion has even a single point of contact with reality."[51] Nietzsche (implicitly) claims that this statement against Christianity corresponds to reality and that Christian truth claims fail to correspond to reality. Hence Nietzsche reverts to a view of truth he elsewhere earnestly denies. No amount of contrarian zeal can make contradictions true.

This highly problematic element of Nietzsche's philosophy was once pointed out in a graduate seminar in philosophy at a state university, which was attended by a friend of mine. The professor, a die-hard perspectivist, admitted that the kind of objection I just gave was a daunting logical problem for Nietzsche but hoped that someone would work it out at some time. On this note of optimism the discussion ended, without any chastening of Nietzsche for being self-contradictory and, therefore, false in his perspective. Professional optimism notwithstanding, there is no hope for this kind of perspectivism. Scruton's assessment of Nietzsche's untrue perspective on truth cuts to the core: "Don't come down this path, his writings tell us, for this way madness lies."[52]

To some degree, we all have differing perspectives (which can be biased, prejudiced, ignorant, arrogant, uninformed and so on), but our perspectives only affect our sense of what is true; they do not determine truth. A perspective may be partially true, largely true or mostly false, but its worth is gauged by its truth value. A perspective is not, in itself, truth; it is a perspective *on* or *about* something else—something outside of itself. A perspective *refers* to reality, either successfully (by being true) or unsuccessfully (by being false). Perspectvism reduces to a kind of collective autism: everyone has a perspective; no one has the truth; but perspectivism as an epistemology is supposedly true . . . and the philosophical immolation continues.

On a commonsensical level, postmodernist constructivism or per-

---

[51]Friedrich Nietzsche, *The Antichrist*, in *The Portable Nietzsche*, ed. Walter Kauffman (New York: Viking), p. 581.

[52]Scruton, *An Intelligent Person's Guide*, pp. 27-28. For a helpful overall assessment of Nietzsche's philosophy, see Irving M. Zeitlin, *Nietzsche: A Re-examination* (Cambridge, Mass.: Polity Press, 1994), and James Collins, *God in Modern Philosophy* (Chicago: Regnery, 1959), pp. 257-67.

spectivalism also rules out the concept of lying. One lies when affirming the opposite of what one takes to be objectively true: either affirming what should be denied or denying what should be affirmed, given the facts of the matter.[53] However, if everything is a matter of interpretation or redescription or perspective *all the way down*, then there are no bedrock facts at all—no facts to relay and no facts to obscure. One's words create all the reality we can ever "know." The clear consequence of such a view is that lies are nonexistent because they are impossible. This is so radically counterintuitive as to be absurd. Lies, lying and liars have existed, do exist and will exist—in abysmal abundance. Perjury is still a crime, as is defamation of character, libel, slander and the obstruction of justice. Some are rightly convicted of these prevarications. The ninth commandment not to bear false witness against one's neighbor (Ex 20:16) is still broken, even in postmodern times. Just as Judas denied Jesus with a *lying* kiss, people continue to exchange the truth for a lie (Rom 1:25).

Christianity and the Correspondence View of Truth

Let us bring all this philosophizing back to the meat and marrow of Christian truth. The theological statement "Jesus is Lord of the universe" is either true or false. Whether it is coolly uttered or it is proclaimed with great emotion, it has only one truth value: either true or false. It either honors reality or it does not. The Christian claims that this statement is true irrespective of anyone's opinion (see Rom 3:4). This is because truth is a quality of propositions and beliefs. It is not ratified by any subjective response or majority vote or cultural fashion. The statement "The world is spherical" was true even when the majority of earthlings believed their habitat to be flat. The ancients who believed the statement "The world is flat" assented to a false proposition. Both the statement and the belief were false, because they did not connect with extrinsic reality.

The correspondence view of truth entails that propositional or de-

---

[53]One's intentions are paramount in lying; one does not lie if one intends to affirm the truth and accidentally denies it because one was misinformed. Nevertheless, there are many cases where lies are intended and do, in fact, deny realities.

clarative statements are subject to verification and falsification. A statement can be proven false if it can be shown to disagree with objective
reality. The photographs from outer space depicting the earth as a blue
orb (along with other evidence) falsified any stubborn flat-earth claims.
Certainly, not all falsification is as straightforward as this, but if statements are true or false by virtue of their relationship to what they attempt to describe, this makes possible the marshaling of evidence for
their veracity or falsity.

Therefore, Christians—who historically have affirmed (whether implicitly or explicitly) the correspondence view of truth—believe that
there are good historical reasons to believe that Jesus Christ rose from
the dead in space-time history, thus vindicating his divine authority
(see Rom 1:4; 1 Cor 15:1-11). The apostle Paul was adamant about this:
"And if Christ has not been raised, our preaching is useless and so is
your faith. More than that, we are then found to be false witnesses
about God, for we have testified about God that he raised Christ from
the dead" (1 Cor 15:14-15). Without the correspondence view of truth,
these resounding affirmations can only ring hollow.[54] Therefore, the
correspondence view of truth is not simply one of many options for
Christians. It is the only biblically and logically grounded view of truth
available and allowable. We neglect or deny it to our peril and disgrace.
Truth decay will not be dispelled without it.

---

[54]This is taken up in chapters six and seven.

5

The Postmodernist Challenge to Theology

Postmodernism poses a plethora of challenges to Christian theology. Those who are receptive to postmodernist ideas believe that Christian theology must abandon its residual attachments to modernism and embrace a new model more in accord with postmodernist thinking. Others are less radical but still take postmodernism as a generally helpful development that can open theology to new avenues of thought and relevance. This chapter will argue that both approaches are deeply problematic.

Instead of attempting a comprehensive theological response to postmodernism, I will address a few areas of central concern. First, given the postmodernist critique of language, some are claiming that an emphasis on the Bible as propositional revelation is questionable or even errant. They argue that our view of Scripture must be reevaluated. Community should take precedence over doctrinal propositions. Second, along these lines, some claim that theology should be primarily narratival in nature and not systematic or abstract and conceptual. Telling the Christian story should replace stipulating Christian doctrine.

These contentions need a careful investigation if theology is to rise to the challenge of postmodernism.

Propositions, Truth and Theology

Roughly stated, the task of Christian theology is to identify and articulate the revealed truths of Scripture in a logical, coherent and compelling manner. As Carl Henry put it in the introduction to his magisterial six-volume *God, Revelation, and Authority* (1976-1983): "The fundamental issue remains the issue of truth, the truth of theological assertions. . . . Durable theology must revive and preserve the distinction between true and false religion."[1] Theology is not merely an endeavor of academic theologians but the concern of every Christian who desires to understand and apply God's truth for life and make it known to others. Consequently, our theology affects all that we do, whether or not we have thought it through systematically. It directs our sermons, our spirituality, our evangelism and apologetics (or lack thereof), and our personal and social ethics. In other words, theology is indispensable and inescapable. This underscores the urgency of developing a theology that is faithful to Scripture and that speaks forcefully and truthfully to our postmodern situation.

The defense of propositional revelation has always been a central tenet of evangelicalism and a primary plank in the debate over biblical inerrancy. Chapter three defended a propositional view of truth and demonstrated that Scripture presents God's truth as revealed, objective, absolute, universal, eternally engaging, antithetical, systematic and an end in itself. There is no reason for theology to alter or adjust this understanding of truth when it comes to Scripture as God's revelation or with respect to the formulations of theological systems. Theology should affirm that the entire content of the Bible is true. Since the Bible is God's word, every truth claim it makes is factually accurate.[2] Of

---

[1]Carl F. H. Henry, *God, Revelation, and Authority* (Waco, Tex.: Word, 1976), 1:14.

[2]I cannot here give a defense of the doctrine of inerrancy, although it goes hand in hand with a proposition view of biblical revelation. The most detailed defense of inerrancy is found in Henry's six volumes, *God, Revelation, and Authority.* An excellent article on the logic of inerrancy is J. P. Moreland, "The Rationality of Inerrancy," *Trinity Journal NS,* spring 1986, pp. 75-86.

course, Scripture gives us a wealth of literary forms—poetry, history, wisdom literature, prophecy and more—but every form has propositional content. In other words, Scripture is informative and correct on every matter it addresses. It discloses knowledge about the nature of God, humanity, salvation, ethics, history and events to come. This revelation came through a variety of cultures and individuals, but it is no less propositional for that.

The language of Scripture consists of more than declarative statements such as "Jesus wept." It also presents questions (Jesus' statement "My God, my God, why have you forsaken me?"), imperatives ("Thou shalt not bear false witness against your neighbor"), requests ("Lead us not into temptation") and exclamations ("Hallelujah!"), which are not, strictly speaking, propositional. Nevertheless, they are always presented in an intellectually rich environment of propositional truths, and their meaning can be transposed into propositions quite easily. For example, God says, "Thou shalt not commit adultery." A command is not propositional because it does not refer directly to an objective state of affairs, although it assumes several propositions. It is true that God gave this command, and it is true that adultery is immoral because it violates God's very character and cuts against the grain of the moral world that God has made. The statement can be easily transposed into the proposition "Adultery is morally wrong." The foremost contemporary defender of propositional revelation, Carl Henry, is right on target: "Regardless of the parables, allegories, emotive phrases and rhetorical questions used by these [biblical] writers, their literary devices have a logical point which can be propositionally formulated and is objectively true or false."[3]

Poetic utterances are also propositional, no matter how imaginative or emotional they may be. David cries out, "Cleanse me with hyssop, and I shall be clean; wash me, and I shall be whiter than snow" (Ps 51:7). This is the metaphorical language of contrition, confession and hope. It also makes claims concerning objective reality. Consider some

---

[3]Carl F. H. Henry, *God, Revelation, and Authority* (Waco, Tex.: 1979), 3:453; quoted in Alister McGrath, *A Passion for Truth* (Downers Grove, Ill.: InterVarsity Press, 1995), p. 172.

of the propositions it encompasses:

1. David prayed this prayer.
2. David needed to be forgiven by God, or more poetically, "cleansed" and "washed."
3. God heard David's prayers.
4. God forgave and restored David.
5. David believed statements 1-4.

Undoubtedly, God's revelation comes through historical events (supernatural or otherwise), personal experiences (Ex 3; Is 6), the witness of creation (Ps 19; Rom 1—2). But these modes of revelation are all communicative, intelligible and informative. They can be understood in terms of propositions. An event wrought by God—such as the parting of the Red Sea or the resurrection of Christ—is not itself a proposition, but it is a fact that can be accurately described in propositions.[4]

Divine revelation was given to people in various communities. However, the source of the revelation was not the community but God working through communities to make objective truth known. Henry's thesis is to the point, despite some postmodern detractors: "God's revelation is rational communication conveyed in intelligible and meaningful words, that is, in conceptual-verbal form."[5] Although Henry's concern was not postmodernism as much as neo-orthodoxy and theological liberalism, his affirmation still stands.

> Issuing from the mind and will of God, revelation is addressed to the mind and will of human beings. As such it involves primarily an activity of consciousness that enlists the thoughts and bears on the beliefs and actions of its recipients.[6]

Those who regard a high view of propositional revelation as reflecting an outmoded modernist approach to theology, confuse the *effects* of God's revelation with its *nature* when they claim that revelation comes

---

[4]See Ronald Nash, *The Word of God and the Mind of Man* (Grand Rapids, Mich.: Zondervan, 1982), pp. 43-46.
[5]Henry, *God, Revelation, and Authority*, 3:248. Henry's entire treatment of propositional revelation is excellent, and remains the best philosophical and theological treatment of the matter.
[6]Ibid.

through the community of faith and the experience of Christians, as we will see below. God's revelation, rightly received, creates community, whether the community of ancient Israel, the early church or the body of Christ today in various locations around the world. God's revelation also produces relationships between believers and between believers and unbelievers. Revelation, when it is truly understood through the illumination of the Holy Spirit, likewise induces certain emotions such as reverence for God, joy over salvation, sorrow over sin, outrage over evil and hope for the future restoration of the universe. But these communities, relationships and emotions are the results of God's objective revelation. They do not constitute or comprise that revelation itself. Moreover, these responses would not be possible without God's prior disclosure of objective truth. David's prayer of contrition and hope was uttered because God's disclosure (through the prophet Nathan) convicted him of his sin (2 Sam 12) and assured him that God would hear his prayer and would forgive and restore him. Prayer or community without revealed truth is pointless and pathetic. "Where there is no revelation, the people cast off restraint; but blessed are those who keep the law" (Prov 29:18).

When postmodernists seek to disparage metanarratives, deconstruct truth into language games and render spirituality a mixture of subjectively compelling elements, evangelicals must bring objective truth back to the table as the centerpiece of concern. The issue is whether God speaks in ways we can understand. As Schaeffer said a generation ago, "The whole question [for modern people] . . . is whether there is anyone adequately there in the universe to *speak*."[7] Several evangelical thinkers have made, I believe, key mistakes with regard to the nature of truth and biblical revelation that inadvertently let loose the contagion of truth decay, thus threatening our ability to hear God speak in Scripture. I cannot treat their ideas exhaustively, but will attempt to highlight what I take to be their essential confusions and errors.

---

[7]Francis A. Schaeffer, *He Is There, He Is Not Silent* (Wheaton, Ill.: Tyndale, 1972), p. 54. Schaeffer was concerned with existentialism and language philosophy, but his point still stands for postmodernism.

McGrath and Grenz on Propositional Revelation

Making propositional revelation central is not an error of rationalism or modernism, as some evangelical theologians now allege. Alister McGrath claims that Carl Henry and others have "laid too much emphasis upon the notion of a purely propositional biblical revelation."[8] He then caricatures this view: "Any view of revelation which regards God's self-disclosure as the mere transmission of facts concerning God is seriously deficient, and risks making God an analogue of a corporate executive who disperses memoranda to underlings."[9]

Henry, however, does recognize that God makes himself known (self-disclosure) through a variety of media. His insistent argument, which Christians must appropriate if we wish to reverse postmodernist truth decay, is that God's revelation is irreducibly propositional, although this propositional truth comes to us in many forms and has many effects on us. Henry would agree with McGrath's statement that "Revelation concerns the *oracles* of God, the *acts* of God, and the *person and presence* of God."[10] However, it must be the case that the oracles are true oracles of God (as opposed to the counterfeits of the false prophets), that the acts of God are rightly interpreted propositionally, and that the person and presence of God is cognitively apprehended as well as affectively felt.

Stanley Grenz agrees with McGrath's critique when he says that a "postmodern articulation of the gospel is postrationalistic. It no longer focuses on propositions as the central content of Christian faith."[11] Grenz thinks that a personal encounter or experience of God articulated within the community of faith should characterize our witness, not a focus on propositional truth. At points, Grenz seems to give up or at least dilute the notion of propositional truth. At other points, he simply minimizes its relevance for postmodern situations. Like Lesslie Newbigin, Grenz appeals to Michael Polanyi's notion of "universal intent" as ex-

---

[8]McGrath, *Passion for Truth*, p. 106.
[9]Ibid., p. 107.
[10]Ibid.
[11]Stanley Grenz, *A Primer on Postmodernism* (Grand Rapids, Mich.: Eerdmans, 1996), p. 171.

emplary for theology. This means that our theological statements intend on being universal in scope, but we should distinguish a *"concern for universality"* with any *claim about* universality," since for "Polanyi, truth always transcends our apprehension of it."[12] Grenz appears to endorse Polanyi's idea that if "propositions themselves [express] final truth" this "represents a truncated view of belief."[13] On the other hand, Grenz says that a "faith community claims to represent in some form the truth about the world and the divine reality."[14] He also writes of the "propositions we accept as reflecting the nature of reality."[15]

This seems confused. "Propositions themselves" either express truth or they do not, as long as the propositions are unambiguous. There is no middle option. For that matter, nothing but a proposition can express truth in a conceptual sense.[16] (Truths can be *manifested* through divine actions, as we have pointed out, but these factual actions still bear witness to the propositions they embody.) No one proposition can express all the truth, but this hardly disqualifies a theological proposition from expressing specific and fundamental "final truths." No human theology can lay claim to perfection, but particular statements are true in a definitive and final sense, such as "Jesus is Lord," "God is triune," "Humans are sinful," "Jesus' death atoned for human sin," "There is a hell" and so on. Christians are concerned both to "express universality" and, therefore, to make a "claim about universality." Jesus' lordship covers every square inch of the universe (Acts 4:12; Col 1:15-19). No human (or angel, for that matter) has a perfect or comprehensive grasp of what Jesus' lordship entails, but this does not mean that we cannot utter "final" or "universal" truths about Jesus, his gospel and his kingdom. Divine mysteries remain, but they are placed within a framework of intelligible claims that make possible knowledge of God and his ways.

---

[12]Stanley Grenz, *Revisioning Evangelical Theology* (Downers Grove, Ill.: InterVarsity Press, 1993), p. 78.
[13]Ibid., p. 79.
[14]Ibid.
[15]Ibid., p. 81.
[16]Beliefs also express truths, but beliefs affirm propositions, so the proposition is still necessary and primary.

The Truth of God Incarnate

Consider Jesus' identity as God incarnate. One can formulate this truth in various propositions, each with a greater level of conceptual sophistication.

1. Jesus is truly divine and truly human.
2. Jesus is one person with two natures: divine and human.
3. Jesus' two natures express a hypostatic union of divinity and humanity in one person.

All three statements are objectively true because they correspond with the reality of Jesus Christ as God incarnate. These propositions "themselves express final truth," but they each do so with a different level of conceptual content and specification. None of these statements supplies the comprehensive truth of the incarnation (nor does the Council of Chalcedon's highly nuanced articulation), but they are all equally true and biblically congruent. These truths may serve as a foundation for further knowledge and clarification, but they *succeed* in their intent to be universally true. "Universal intent"—trying to get reality right—Grenz to the contrary, is not sufficient for theologizing, although it is necessary.

Theology: First-Order Propositions

Grenz, following postliberal theologian George Lindbeck, claims that theology and "its propositions are second-order propositions," which derive from religious experience and communal life.[17] Grenz's appropriation of Lindbeck is troubling because Lindbeck stresses that doctrine has a regulative function in various communities that is not directly (if at all) propositional. If so, doctrinal "truths" only apply within the community; they cannot successfully or normatively refer to a reality outside of the community. As Paul Griffiths points out, this view of doctrine (sometimes called "rule theory") rejects the idea that "doctrine-expressing sentences primarily [are] expressive of propositions, and so bearers of truth-value and conveyers of information about extramental and extralinguistic realities."[18]

---

[17]Ibid., pp. 77-78.
[18]Paul Griffiths, *An Apology for Apologetics* (Maryknoll, N.Y.: Orbis, 1991), p. 39.

If rule theory is correct, the doctrine of a Buddhist community and the doctrine of a Christian community cannot contradict each other, since they refer only to internal practices or rules of those respective communities and not to objective truths expressed in propositions. But since the beliefs held in both communities do lay claim to final realities outside of themselves, this cannot be the case.[19] Consider, as an example, two key doctrines. The Buddhist nirvana (an impersonal state beyond desire) and the Christian Trinity (a tripersonal being with desires) cannot both be the ultimate reality. One cannot find final refuge both in the Buddha and in the Christ. They are contradictory, antithetical. Such is the nature of all truth claims, in religion and elsewhere. truth claims exclude whatever contradicts them.

Therefore Grenz's use of Lindbeck's concepts tends to undercut his own positive remarks about propositions. Theological propositions should have a first-order status in theology and all of life. Theology ought to be derived first from Scripture, not community or experience, although these will always shape our theologies in various ways. Revealed truths, articulated theologically, ought to guide our lives, give us hope and make us discerning because the Revealer of these truths is trustworthy and good. Theology, rightly received, *results* in rules for godly living, but these rules are cognitively meaningful only in relation to objective realities that are true for everyone, both inside and outside the community of faith.

The apostle John enjoins us to "test the spirits to see whether they are from God." This is done by checking their doctrine—their propositional affirmations—concerning Christ's identity (1 Jn 4:1-4). Paul speaks of "the knowledge of the truth that leads to godliness" (Tit 1:1). A deep knowledge of objective truth leads to subjective godliness demonstrated by Christians both within and without the Christian community, before the watching world. Schaeffer is correct:

> Our calling is not primarily to an alternate lifestyle. Considering what the Bible teaches, what is crucial is not the word *community*, nor the form the practice of community takes.

---

[19]Ibid., pp. 39-44.

Our primary calling is to truth as it is rooted in God, his acts and revelation; and if it is indeed truth, it touches all of reality and all of life, including an adequate basis for, and some practice of, the reality of community.[20]

Henry has eloquently argued that God's revelation is inherently, intrinsically and incorrigibly cognitive; its intellectual content fuels our existential transformation as we submit to and internalize these truths, graciously made known to us by the Spirit of truth (Jn 16:13). He highlights the first-order nature of divine revelation:

> Revelation is actual only as God gives himself to our knowing. All a priori conceptions, all conjectural postulations, all subjective expectations are answerable to and subject to what is given through divine self-revelation. The objective given reality with which theology must begin is God manifesting himself in his Word.[21]

The purpose of divine revelation is not merely the enunciation of a set of true propositions. Nevertheless, without these true propositions, revelation vanishes as a conceptual category, for there remains no cognitive content to be revealed. Revelation is God's effort to make himself known in ways that bear on every dimension of the human being—the mind, the emotions, the imagination and the will. The entire person must bow before the Creator and Redeemer in submission to the Holy Spirit. We are to love God with all our heart, soul, mind and strength as our first priority; within that first-order theological affirmation, we then love our neighbor as ourselves (see Mt 22:37-39).

Logical Consistency and Theology

This whole-personed submission to God ought to stem from a logical understanding of what Scripture teaches and how it applies to us today. As God said through Isaiah, "Come now, let us reason together" (Is 1:18). Yet some have rejected logical consistency as a criterion for theology, taking it to be a holdover from the rationalism of Enlightenment modernism. McGrath accuses evangelical leaders such as Carl Henry,

---

[20]Francis A. Schaeffer, *The God Who Is There*, 30th anniv. ed. (Downers Grove, Ill.: InterVarsity Press, 1998), p. 207.
[21]Henry, *God, Revelation, and Authority* 3:275.

John Warwick Montgomery, Francis Schaeffer and Norman Geisler of succumbing to "a strongly rationalist spirit" that is ill-advised. He maintains that "even Carl Henry can offer such hostages to fortune in his affirmation of belief in a 'logically consistent divine revelation.' "[22] McGrath proposes that Henry puts revelation at risk by subjecting it to logical consistency. Henry's appeal to logic makes it "a more fundamental authority" than Scripture itself. McGrath asks, "What logic is to be allowed this central role? Whose rationality provides the basis of scriptural authority?"[23]

Henry and his followers supposedly do not recognize the effect of sin on human rationality.[24] McGrath scolds them: "Evangelicals, of all people, cannot allow revelation to be imprisoned within the flawed limits of sinful human reason."[25] He illustrates his worries by discussing how theologians have handled christological questions. Tertullian, an early church fideist, is cited as instructive, for he "pointed out the danger of grounding or judging the gospel in what passed for human wisdom."[26] Henry has "rendered evangelicalism intensely—and needlessly —vulnerable at this point," because of his insistence on logical consistency for the possibility of knowledge.[27]

McGrath fails to make crucial distinctions. First, in saying that logical consistency is a criterion for understanding Scripture, one is simply appealing to a basic fact of all intelligible discourse, as I pointed out in chapter three. Humans are made such that we cannot believe explicitly contradictory things (although we may, because of ignorance or confusion, accidentally believe contradictory things). But even if we could knowingly believe contradictory things, they could not both be true! Jesus did not both (1) rise from the dead and (2) fail to rise from the dead—in the same way, at the same time. As Henry tellingly says, "If the law of contradiction is irrelevant in the sphere of

---

[22]McGrath, *Passion for Truth*, p. 170. He is quoting Henry, *God, Revelation, and Authority* 3:476.
[23]McGrath, *Passion for Truth*, p. 170.
[24]Ibid.
[25]Ibid.
[26]Ibid., p. 171.
[27]Ibid.

transcendent ontology [God's being and nature], then God and the non-God, the divine and the demonic, cannot be assuredly differentiated."[28]

Moreover, as Henry and others have developed at length, John's Gospel (1:1-3) refers to the preincarnate Christ as the Logos (or Word). This means, among other things, that the personal Word is intelligible and rational, that he created a knowable world peopled by creatures who can know truth through rationality. The Word is God communicating, God speaking. Early Christian apologists employed this notion to argue that any truth discovered by non-Christian philosophers was only possible because of God, the Logos.[29]

Dividing revelation from logic generates a dangerous and false dichotomy. When McGrath asks, "Which logic, whose rationality?" he befuddles matters, since no human owns or controls logic and logic does not change with the individuals who employ it. Humans use logic either poorly or wisely; humans do not create logic—although they may manipulate opinion, employ propaganda and offer fallacious arguments. The basic laws of logic (such as noncontradition and excluded middle) and argument forms (such as *modus ponens* and *modus tolens*) constitute proper thinking. These are not contingent social constructions, as I argue in chapter seven.

Moreover, McGrath himself appeals to logic in his own denigration of logic. This is inescapable, even if self-contradictory. He argues:

1. Human reason is fallen.

2. Logical tests for revelation unnecessarily play into the hands of secular critics.

3. Therefore: Human reason should not be used to test revelation.

4. Therefore: Those who use reason to test revelation are mistaken.

The problem is that premise (1) is ambiguous and premise (2) is false. Therefore, conclusions (3) and (4) do not follow logically from premises (1) and (2). Let us see why.

Human *reason-ing* is affected by sin in that we often do not attend to

---

[28]Henry, *God, Revelation, and Authority* 2:60.
[29]Ibid., 3:164-247; and Nash, *Word of God*, pp. 59-70.

matters logically or we reason in only a half-hearted or slothful way. We employ logical fallacies without knowing it, and our stock of facts from which we argue is sometimes limited in ways that hinder our thinking. As Pascal mused:

> The mind of this supreme judge of the world [i.e., the rational human] is not so independent as to be impervious to whatever din may be going on near by. It does not take a cannon's roar to arrest his thought; the noise of a weathercock will do. Do not be surprised if his reasoning is not too sound at the moment, there is a fly buzzing in his ears; that is enough to render him incapable of giving good advice.[30]

The greatest problem with human reasoning occurs when it vainly attempts to become autonomous of God and divine revelation.[31] This is the fault of human hubris, not of reason itself. Paul indicts such people: "Although they claimed to be wise, they became fools" (Rom 1:22). Being finite entities in the created cosmos calls for an openness to a disclosure of truth from a source beyond ourselves. It is reasonable to expect to receive information beyond what human reason *left to itself* can provide.[32] I cannot simply observe my environment, use the laws of logic and—without scriptural revelation—deduce the existence and nature of the holy Trinity. However, I can discover the truth of the Trinity through divine revelation and rationally comprehend the basic framework of this doctrine as central to all of Scripture.[33]

Nonetheless, the hazards of human reasoning count nothing against the validity of logic itself, which flows from the being of God and is in-

---

[30]Blaise Pascal, *Pensees*, ed. Alban Krailsheimer (New York: Penguin, 1966), 48/366, p. 43.

[31]See Schaeffer, *God Who Is There*, esp. sect. 1 and 2.

[32]For a concise but strong case for a reasonable openness to revelation beyond what reason alone can provide, see R. Douglas Geivett and W. Gary Phillips, "A Particularist View: An Evidentialist Approach," in *Four Views on Salvation in a Pluralistic World*, ed. Dennis L. Okholm and Timothy R. Phillips (Grand Rapids, Mich.: Zondervan, 1996), pp. 216-29. On the relationship of human reason and divine revelation, in aphoristic form, see Pascal, "Submission and Use of Reason," in *Pensees* 13/167-88, pp. 83-85.

[33]For an excellent treatment of the Trinity, see Millard Erickson, *God in Three Persons* (Grand Rapids, Mich.: Baker, 1995).

trinsic to our created natures and cognitive structure.[34] There is more to being in the image and likeness of God (Gen 1:26) than being rational, but we are not less rational for that. Reason itself is not fallen. Reason is a fact of God's reality—of his character, of the order of his creation, and of the minds of his rational creatures. Human reasoning, however, is subject to all manner of ills because we are sinners who abuse God's good gifts.

D. Elton Trueblood argued that revelation must be tested by reason "for the simple reason that there are false claims to revelation. We know, in advance, that many alleged revelations are false, because there are absolutely contradictory claims." More pointedly: "Unless the law of contradiction is recognized as the necessary condition of all rational discussion, we give up everything."[35] If McGrath asks us to suspend basic logic for core Christian claims (because reason is fallen), why not suspend it for non-Christian claims as well? For instance, Christian apologists have deemed pantheism illogical. It claims that (1) everything is one and divine, but that (2) individuals exist who typically don't recognize this oneness and divinity. Rationality sees these pantheistic truth claims as contradictory because a comprehensive divine oneness rules out real individuality and also the possibility of ignorance or a lack of divine realization.[36] If Christians defensively cloak themselves in mystery without invoking logic, they lose their ability to criticize other worldviews. Ironically, McGrath has written a book on Christian apologetics, which discredits other worldviews as illogical and, therefore, unworthy of belief.[37] Yet in *A Passion for Truth* he seems to disparage or at least minimize the role of reason with respect to propositional revelation.

---

[34]Arthur Holmes has given an excellent account of how and why humans commit intellectual errors in *All Truth Is God's Truth* (Grand Rapids, Mich.: Eerdmans, 1977), pp. 49-69. However, Holmes does not concur with McGrath's ideas on "fallen human reason."

[35]D. Elton Trueblood, *Philosophy of Religion* (Grand Rapids, Mich.: Baker, 1957), p. 32.

[36]See Winfried Corduan, *No Doubt About It* (Nashville: Broadman & Holman, 1997), pp. 92-95.

[37]Alister E. McGrath, *Intellectuals Don't Need God, and Other Myths* (Grand Rapids, Mich.: Zondervan, 1993).

It must be granted that although right reasoning will not lead us astray when prayerfully applied to the deposit of revelation in Scripture, human reasoning is, nonetheless, faulty and fragile. Therefore, conclusions about theological matters should be open to correction, clarification, revision and amplification—given more evidence, better arguments, and a more open and humble spirit before God. Yet these realities of our fallen estate do not forbid a strong measure of certainty in many theological matters (if we have exercised proper diligence in study). However, they do guard against any arrogance and triumphalism that forgets that the divine image in us is marred in every dimension, rationality included.

McGrath's attack on the supposed rationalism of Carl Henry and many other evangelicals rings hollow for another reason. McGrath claims that insisting on logical consistency plays into the hands of critics such as Spinoza who view the incarnation as a contradiction as illogical as a square circle.

> Yet why should evangelicals feel under any such pressure to conform to the highly questionable dictates of the limits of fallen human reason? And how often has it been pointed out, even by secular philosophers, that "logic is the enemy of truth"?[38]

This poisons the well by accusing Henry of conforming to "fallen human reason," which we have already addressed. Moreover, no secular philosopher—premodern, modern or postmodern—would be persuaded by the Christian who says, "We don't conform our theology to fallen human reason, so we need not make the concept of the Incarnation intelligible to outsiders (or even ourselves). Now that this is settled, please accept our theology and follow our God." This would only give more fuel to the charge that Christianity is illogical and anti-intellectual if not unintelligible.

As for the statement "logic is the enemy of truth," I know of no philosopher who ever held this. In fact, it would be difficult even to *be* a philosopher and hold this. McGrath gives no reference. If anyone holds this, it reveals their illogic and their inability to discover truth ratio-

---

[38]McGrath, *Passion for Truth*, p. 171.

nally. This slogan provides absolutely no help for Christian theology.

The invocation of the category of "mystery" in describing Christian doctrine (whether concerning the incarnation or other concepts), as some theologians are too prone to do, must be done with great care, and only after intense intellectual scrutiny. A logical contradiction is not a mystery; it is a falsehood. Regarding the incarnation, the appeal to logical consistency is not a modernist mistake, which, when corrected, exonerates Christian theology from secular appraisal. Beyond the basic framework spelled out by the Council of Chalcedon (which is faithful to Scripture), philosophers and theologians have tried in various ways to make the notion of one person with two natures intelligible and consistent. McGrath himself gives some helpful ways of explaining Christ's deity and humanity in another book. Consider an analogy of a friend who holds dual citizenship. Although we typically think that one can be a citizen of only one country, this man is a citizen of both England and Switzerland. McGrath says:

> A logical contradiction exists if, and only if, being British excludes being Swiss. But it does not. And why, at the theological level, should being human exclude Jesus from being divine? Might he not be a citizen of heaven as well as earth? [39]

This is not a complete apologetic but is intellectually suggestive and appeals to the need for logical consistency for a statement to be true.

More philosophically, Gordon Lewis and Bruce Demerest argue that the divinity and humanity of Christ do not contradict each other. To make the argument they explain the difference between contraries and subcontraries. If two statements are contraries, they cannot both be true, but both can be false, such as "All dogs are brown; no dogs are brown." If two statements are subcontraries, they can both be simultaneously true but cannot both be simultaneously false, such as "Some dogs are brown; some dogs are not brown."

Within his one person, some of Jesus Christ's attributes are divine and some are not divine (human). The truths about Jesus' humanity are in a subcontrary relationship with the truths about his divinity. The di-

---

[39]Ibid., p. 126.

vine attributes do not conflict with the human attributes, as would be the case if we said, "All of Christ's attributes are divine and some of Christ's attributes are not divine." That would be a flat contradiction and, therefore, false, because "the affirmation and the denial of the universal truth claim could not be true."

> In contrast, in a subcontrary relationship neither the affirmation nor the denial is universal, hence both may be true. For example . . . "Some of the attributes of a person are physical" and "Some of the attributes of a person are nonphysical." Similarly, "Some attributes of the person of Jesus Christ are divine and some are human." Neither the divine set of attributes nor the human set of attributes is said to be all that he has, and so neither affirmation is necessarily false.[40]

The logical category of a subcontrary relationship comes from Aristotle (a premodern!) but serves theology well here. This is not modernistic rationalism but rather faith seeking understanding through God-given logic. Lewis and Demarest admit their "lack of full comprehension" of "how the divine and human attributes exist together, but that is not sufficient ground for attributing logical nonsense to the focal point of God's century-spanning redemptive program!" In understanding the incarnation they "acknowledge complexity . . . but not contradiction."[41]

Invoking Postmodernism Illicitly
Sounding very postmodernist, McGrath asserts that "the notion of 'universal rationality' is a fiction, a dream, and a delusion." He is so concerned about the purported errors of the modernist attempt to establish a "universal rationality" that he enlists an epistemological nihilist, Paul Feyerabend, for his cause. Feyerabend says:

> There is hardly any difference between the members of a primitive tribe who defend their laws because they are the laws of the gods . . . and a

---

[40]Gordon Lewis and Bruce Demarest, *Integrative Theology* (Grand Rapids, Mich.: Zondervan, 1992), 2:350.
[41]Ibid. For more on the logic of the incarnation see Millard Erickson, *The Word Became Flesh: An Incarnational Theology* (Grand Rapids, Mich.: Baker, 1993).

rationalist who appeals to objective standards, except that the former know what they are doing while the latter does not.[42]

Instead of attacking this radical constructivism, McGrath calmly adds that "this comparison has alarmed many; it has, however, yet to be refuted by a philosopher of science."[43] It is not true that Feyerabend's philosophy of science has won the day academically.[44] (His motto for describing the philosophy of science was "anything goes." Would we want to apply that to theology?)[45]

Moreover, inasmuch as the tribespeople mistakenly attribute events to the gods instead of natural laws, they are flat-out mistaken. If they take the earth to be flat and the sun to move, they are mistaken as well. Many of their false beliefs keep them in the thrall of superstition. Primitive tribes have not found vaccines for polio or smallpox, nor can they repair a detached retina, remove brain tumors, perform heart transplants or send in paramedics by helicopter. These benefits are attributable to the advances of modern science, which originated within a Western, theistic worldview,[46] and which has used rationality to discern many truths and cure many ills. One need not be a secular rationalist— who rejects divine revelation—to see the matter in this light. McGrath throws out the rational baby with the rationalistic bath water.

In a critique of John Hick's theory of religious pluralism, McGrath claims that "in these postmodern times . . . the idea of a universal morality has been abandoned."[47] This is true for some contemporary thinkers but not all, as I argued in chapter two. But he also claims that "no

---

[42]Paul Feyerabend, *Science in a Free Society* (London: Verso, 1983); quoted in McGrath, *Passion for Truth*, p. 90.

[43]McGrath, *Passion for Truth*, p. 90.

[44]On the philosophy of science, see J. P. Moreland, *Christianity and the Nature of Science* (Grand Rapids, Mich.: Baker, 1989).

[45]See Paul Feyerabend, "Anything Goes," in *The Truth About the Truth*, ed. Walter Truett Anderson (New York: G. P. Putnam's Sons, 1995), pp. 199-203. For a biographical and critical interaction with Feyerabend's ideas, see John Horgan, *The End of Science: Facing the Limits of Knowledge in the Twilight of the Scientific Age* (New York: Broadway Books, 1996), pp. 47-56.

[46]On this, see Diogenes Allen, *Christian Belief in a Postmodern World: The Full Wealth of Conviction* (Louisville: Westminster John Knox, 1989), pp. 23-34.

[47]Alister McGrath, in *Four Views*, p. 67.

universal moral framework exists by which such a public and universal judgment can be made" about what religion is morally superior.[48] McGrath is not being merely descriptive. He thinks that the move away from metanarratives and attempts to explain the big picture is healthy. Because "the old certainties of the Enlightenment" are dying, the "belief in cultural or experiential metanarratives . . . is acknowledged to be at best flawed and at worst an invitation to oppression."[49] He is also happy to report that "claiming privileged access to a total and comprehensive knowledge of reality is generally treated with intense skepticism" because such knowledge cannot be verified or falsified.[50] McGrath quotes Terry Eagleton's observations with approval:

> Post-modernism signals the end of such "metanarratives" whose secretly terrorist function was to ground and legitimate the illusion of a "universal" human history. We are now in the process of awakening from the nightmare of modernity, with its manipulative reason and fetish of the totality, into the laid-back pluralism of the post-modern, that heterogeneous range of life-styles and language games which has renounced the nostalgic urge to totalize and legitimate itself.[51]

Although McGrath does not mention this, Eagleton's review is *critical* of postmodernism;[52] nonetheless, Eagleton's description of postmodernism is apt, and it is not good news for Christian theology. The error of modernism was the construction of a false totality based on autonomous reasoning and humanistic utopianism that excluded divine revelation. The new error of postmodernism is the abandonment of metanarrative, and the acceptance of relativism and cultural constructivism. In the review McGrath cites, Eagleton expresses concern that Jean Francois Lyotard's postmodernist rejection of metanarrative al-

---

[48]Ibid., p. 69.

[49]Ibid., p. 200.

[50]Ibid., p. 158.

[51]Terry Eagleton, "Awakening from Modernity," *Times Literary Supplement*, February 20, 1987, p. 195; quoted in McGrath, *Passion for Truth*, p. 187. Eagleton's article is a review of two books by Jean-François Lyotard which defend postmodernism. Eagleton pans both books and the postmodernist project as a whole.

[52]See Terry Eagleton, *The Illusions of Postmodernism* (Cambridge, Mass.: Blackwell, 1996). This is a neo-Marxist critique written after the review McGrath cites.

lows no standpoint from which to condemn social injustice, such as Na-
zism, as objectively evil. This is because, according to Lyotard, each
narrative "certifies itself in the pragmatics of its own transmission without having recourse to argumentation or proof."[53] Such is the result of
abandoning "universal rationality."

McGrath seems sanguine about the prospects of postmodernity, but
he fails to note that Christian theology is a metanarrative based on God's
self-disclosure. The postmodernists on which McGrath relies see the collapse of Enlightenment rationalism as the end of *all* metanarratives. If
Christians cannot appeal to universal standards of rationality and morality in their apologetic and their theological articulations, the postmodernist criticism of metanarratives ends up eroding the Christianity that
believers seek to present to the postmodern world. The very concept of
divine revelation presupposes that those who receive that revelation do
have some access to objective reality. God has made himself known in
creation, conscience, Christ and the Scriptures. Followers of Christ have
the privilege of knowing that Jesus is Lord; others do not (1 Cor 8:6).
Jesus' lordship covers all of reality, and all wisdom and knowledge is
found in Christ (Col 1:15-17; 2:3). We know only in part in this life (1 Cor
13:12), but we can know truly because we have been privileged with
knowledge from God, the omniscient and omnipotent Revealer.

This privileged knowledge leaves no room for pride and offers
plenty of room for growth and correction. We do not equate the supreme truth of God with our limited grasp of it, but we do have something to grasp, because God has grasped us in Christ by his matchless
grace.

McGrath likewise joins postmodernists in dismissing the correspondence view of truth through a kind of caricature.

> It is a travesty of the biblical idea of "truth" to equate it with the Enlight-
> enment notion of conceptual or propositional correspondence, or the
> derived view of evangelism as proclamation of the propositional correct-
> ness of Christian doctrine.[54]

[53]Eagleton, "Awakening from Modernity," p. 194.
[54]McGrath, *Passion for Truth*, p. 177.

Strangely enough, McGrath also writes of evangelism as proclaiming "an objective truth with the expectation that this will give rise to a subjective response—that is to say, a response which involves the heart, mind, and total being of those who hear it."[55] Truth cannot be objective unless it corresponds to objective reality. In another book McGrath stipulates that faith must involve assent "to belief in the existence of God and his promises."[56] He is rightly concerned about propositional proclamation apart from a call to commitment, but to say that the belief in the "notion of conceptual or propositional correspondence" is a "travesty" and a capitulation to Enlightenment notions is acutely befuddled. The truth necessarily makes demands on the totality of our being. It is truth *disclosed by God*, it is not some abstract and impersonal Platonic notion of truth. God's truth must be objective truth in order to make these all-encompassing subjective demands on us, his creatures. To limit theology or evangelism to formulating and reciting a clinical list of propositional truths would be to truncate both disciplines, but to remove truth as correspondence would be to abolish theology and evangelism entirely.

The Enlightenment notion of the nature of truth was not new to the Enlightenment. The correspondence view of truth is ancient, going back to Plato, Aristotle and to the Bible itself. Christianity and Enlightenment thought are in basic agreement on the *nature of truth*; the disagreement concerns *what is true, how truth is known* and *what effect truth should have on us*. McGrath, like many evangelicals flirting with postmodernism, fails to make these substantial philosophical distinctions.

Middleton and Walsh on "Strange Truth"

Some thinkers argue that any claim to objective truth is an arrogant and futile attempt at realism (the belief that reality can be truly described in language that corresponds to facts). J. Richard Middleton and Brian J. Walsh in *Truth Is Stranger Than It Used to Be* (1995) agree with postmodernists in claiming that critical realism is wrongheaded. Critical realism,

---

[55]Ibid., 178.
[56]McGrath, *Intellectuals Don't Need God*, p. 49.

roughly put, acknowledges that our grasp of reality is partial and mediated by our cultures and experiences; but it rejects constructivist and coherentist views of truth. Yet for Middleton and Walsh critical realism

> still seems to hide a pretentious aspiration to "get reality right." . . . Such an aspiration, however, is epistemologically impossible to realize. Indeed, it rests upon the conviction that a final, universally true perspective can be achieved."[57]

However, this "has proven to be bankrupt and has legitimately been deconstructed by postmodern thought."[58] These writers create a straw man, draw a false dichotomy, refute themselves and claim far too much for postmodern thought.

The straw man is in their assertion that critical realism assumes that a "final, universally true perspective can be achieved." Critical realists, like myself, do not claim that they can achieve a perfect or exhaustive system of truth. However, the perfect system does exist in the mind of God, who knows all things truly and makes many truths known through revelation. Nevertheless, *some* truths—truths that are universal and final concerning God's character, salvation and ethics—can be known even by erring mortals. In this sense, Middleton and Walsh's accusation sticks, but it fails as an argument against critical realism. Some perspectives or worldviews are better than others because they are truer than others. But this idea must be abandoned if one abandons some form of realism, as do these authors.

It is a false dichotomy to force a choice between claiming to achieve a "final universally true perspective" and giving up on realism (and, therefore, objective truth) entirely. Critical realism realizes that we are always in process in the attempt to achieve a truer overall perspective or worldview. However, the alternative (some form of nonrealism or antirealism) necessitates the loss of truth completely.[59] Theological perspec-

---

[57]J. Richard Middleton and Brian J. Walsh, *Truth Is Stranger Than It Used to Be* (Downers Grove, Ill.: InterVarsity Press, 1995), p. 168.
[58]Ibid.
[59]For a discussion of realism and its alternative, see Panayot Butchvarow, "Metaphysical Realism," in *Cambridge Dictionary of Philosophy*, ed. Robert Audi (New York: Cambridge University Press, 1995), pp. 488-89.

tives ought to "get it right" as often as possible; correct theology is not impossible if the Scriptures teach the truth and if the Holy Spirit is still leading believers into the truth as we submit to Christ and apply ourselves earnestly and honestly to the task of knowing (Jn 16:13; Heb 5:14).

Middleton and Walsh's statement about critical realism is self-refuting because they claim that critical realism is not the fact of the matter. This criticism itself is a factual claim about reality: a claim that purports to "get it right" by saying that realism is wrong. If so, Middleton and Walsh are implicitly endorsing a kind of realism by asserting the objective falsity of critical realism. Therefore, their claim is false because it is self-contradictory. One cannot logically assume what one denies.

Finally, as I have argued repeatedly, postmodernist thought has *not* deconstructed the basic truths of logic, the credibility of objective truth or the power of rationality to discern truth. It has not triumphed philosophically! This is the case for Nietzsche's perspectivism, Rorty's ironism, Foucault's reduction of truth to power, Derrida's deconstruction, Lyotard's claim that metanarratives lead to oppression and more. To enlist these writers for Christian purposes is unwise and ill-fated.[60]

Murphy on Unsurpassability

Another thinker attempts to recast the theological notion of truth to fit what she calls "Anglo-American Postmodernity."[61] This phrase refers not to French deconstructionists or other continental thinkers but to thinkers such as Richard Rorty and W. V. Quine. Nancey Murphy rejects foundationalist epistemology and the correspondence view of truth in favor of a contextualist and coherence view of truth.[62] Truth is not established by language's ability to refer successfully to a knowable objective reality. Rather, Murphy understands truth to mean a claim that is "unsurpassable" within one's best theories. In other

---

[60]For a thorough critique of Middleton and Walsh, see Peter Payne's review essay of *Truth Is Stranger Than It Used to Be*, in *Religious and Theological Studies Fellowship Bulletin*, November-December 1996, pp. 16-25.

[61]Nancey Murphy, "Philosophical Resources for Postmodern Evangelical Theology," *Christian Scholar's Review* 26, no. 2 (winter 1996): 184-205.

[62]I will discuss foundationalism in chapter seven.

words, certain statements made within the context of particular theories have an unrivaled intellectual power to serve as the unifying focus of the theory.

Murphy, however, has confused metaphysical concepts with epistemological concepts. Truth, for Murphy, means that an idea is unsurpassable within a system of thought or an epistemological context. This understanding of truth does not refer to objective realities distinct from thought and language but to an *epistemological* notion of certainty within a particular philosophical system. The concept of truth, however, is a *metaphysical* notion with respect to objective reality. Whether or not anyone knows something to be true does not affect its truth-value.[63] For instance, it is true that there is a certain number of Christians on the planet at any given time. But no one, save God, knows what that exact number is.

Murphy thinks that the statement "God exists" is true only in relation to our theories. It is true because it coheres with all our other statements; it has the place of being "unsurpassable" within those theories. The real question, though, is whether the statement "God exists" is true with respect to reality itself (metaphysics), not whether it is true with respect to the coherence of our theories (epistemology). A worldview must be internally coherent to be true, but coherence is only a *necessary* condition for truth; it is not a *sufficient* condition (as discussed in chapter four).

The statement "Brahman is the ultimate and only divine reality" is unsurpassably "true" within an Advaita Vedanta (or nondualist) Hindu theology/system and may cohere with other theological statements within that system. The statement "The Trinity is the ultimate reality" is unsurpassably "true" within the Christian theology/system. Nevertheless, Brahman and the Christian God cannot both exist as the superlative reality, since God is a personal being and Brahman is an impersonal essence. Keith Yandell points out that Murphy's confusion has rather drastic philosophical consequences:

---

[63]On this, see Michael Jubien, *Contemporary Metaphysics* (Malden, Mass.: Blackwell, 1997), pp. 77-82, and chapter four of this book.

Monotheists hold that God existed before the earth was formed; that considerably predates our theories. Professor Murphy identifies *God exists* with . . . [the notion] that we have theories [about God]. Hence if we didn't exist or existed theoryless, *God exists* would be false. All of this makes God's existence too fragile as well as too late. It is hard to distinguish it from the claim that all there is to God is a bunch of ideas in us.[64]

For Murphy and those who follow her Anglo-American postmodernism, truth becomes relativized to theories, none of which can be checked against an independent reality. Unless the statement "God exists"—or any other theological assertion—can have a mind-independent and theory-independent reality, it cannot do justice to the biblical view of truth or serve as a basis for rational engagement with non-Christian worldviews.

There is a better way for Christian theology than making accommodations to postmodernist errors—the way of God's gripping and knowable truth. We have, by God's grace, a True Story to tell.

Back to God's Metanarrative
The grasp of God's grace encompasses all of cosmic and human history in one grand narrative or story—a story we can apprehend truly, if only partially. Despite my disagreements with Grenz at some points, he puts it well:

> Our world is more than a collection of incompatible and competing local narratives. Contrary to the implications of Lyotard's thesis, we firmly believe that the local narratives of the many human communities do fit together into a single grand narrative, the story of humankind. There is a single metanarrative encompassing all people and all times.[65]

Postmodernists are correct in emphasizing the centrality of stories in culture, from bedtime stories told to children, to the historical narratives of nations and peoples. Their downfall comes in shrinking the metanarrative to a micronarrative and then severing these stories from

---

[64]Keith E. Yandell, "Modernism, Post-Modernism, and the Minimalist Canons of Common Grace," *Christian Scholar's Review* 27, no. 1 (fall 1997): 23.
[65]Grenz, *Primer on Postmodernism*, p. 164.

objective truth. These isolated and insulated ministories have been
freeze-dried and shrink-wrapped for postmodern consumption, but
they fail to nourish, satisfy or inspire—however much they may distract us from broader concerns.

We tell and hear stories to find meaning, not just for entertainment.
Stories involve a place for human significance, plot and character development, moral value and resolution. More significantly, they require a
storyteller, a narrator. Howard Synder explains:

> You simply can't have a story without a story-teller. A tale demands a
> teller as surely as tale and tell come from the same root. No teller, no tale.
> Without a novelist, no novel; without dramatist, no drama. This is obvi-
> ous, yet its major meaning is often missed: A story requires a person as
> surely as lungs need air. The existence of a story is proof positive of the
> existence of a person. This means that story requires a consciousness, that
> strange fact of self-awareness, including will, intention, imagination, and
> purpose, the constituents of personality.[66]

Christian theology—whether articulated in books, articles, seminary
classes, Christian colleges or preaching and teaching in the local church
—ought to capitalize on the postmodernist fascination with narrative
by speaking of God's own story in all its richness, complexity and
drama. It is a drama in four principle acts: creation, fall, redemption
and consummation. But we must set forth this narrative, not as just one
among many micronarratives that give meaning to disparate communities but as the cosmic Story of the Creator himself, who not only has
given us the key to history in Scripture but has entered history in the incarnation for the sake of our liberation from sin and death. Hopelessly
conflicting micronarratives ("You have your truth; I have mine") give
no final meaning to life; they set up ghettos instead of charting the
terms, rights, gifts and responsibilities of being citizens in God's world,
of being actors in God's divine drama. God is the personal being who
tells us the true Story and orchestrates the whole Story.

Charles Jencks, a leading analyst of postmodernist architecture and

---

[66]Howard Synder, *EarthCurrents: The Struggle for the World's Soul* (Nashville: Abing-
don, 1995), p. 263.

art, discerns that postmodernism's rejection of metanarratives places it at a cultural impasse. Thinking that traditional religions have nothing left to offer, he presents the outline of a "new metanarrative" that strives rather desperately to anchor meaning in an aboriginal nothing-ness from which came chaos, from which evolved order and increasing complexity.

> In the beginning (one cannot expunge the biblical overtones) was the quantum vacuum, or plenum, the seething nothing that, because of the Uncertainty Principle, allows particles to come into and go out of exist-ence for short moments. . . . Whatever happened (according to the Stan-dard Model), there was a hot explosion and expansion.[67]

From this Jencks pronounces about life coming from nonlife, purpose emerging from nonpurpose and, eventually, culture springing forth from nature. This is the new "universe story"—a tale told by no one, full of speculation and folly, signifying insignificance.[68] All biblical con-cepts have been theologically expunged, but the psychological quest for a unifying and inspiring Story remains.

Jencks's authorless and meaningless story reveals the prodigious and prodigal quest of postmodernism for some larger meaning beyond contingently constructed cultures. Nevertheless, capitalizing on the "Uncertainty Principle" and speaking of a "seething nothing" is philo-sophically bankrupt in at least two ways.[69] First, if all began with noth-ing, there would still be nothing because "from nothing, nothing comes" (*ex nihilo nihil fit*, as the ancients said). "Nothing" (or the ab-sence of everything), which has no properties whatsoever, by definition and necessarily has no causal properties or causal powers. We know, as John Locke said, "by intuitive certainty, that bare nothing can no more produce any reality, than it can be equal to two right angles."[70] "Noth-ing" is ontologically paralyzed, inert and incapacitated. Invoking exotic

---

[67]Charles Jencks, *What Is Postmodernism?* 4th ed. (Lanham, Md.: National Book Net-work, 1996), p. 72.

[68]I am here playing on Shakespeare's famous phrase "A tale told by an idiot, full of sound and fury, signifying nothing."

[69]Jencks, *What Is Postmodernism?* p. 72.

[70]John Locke, *An Essay Concerning Human Understanding*, 4.10.

terms from physics does not solve the problem of the nullity, vacuity and uselessness of nothingness.[71]

Second, even if we grant that nothing produced everything without a cause or reason, then there would be no reason for anything's existence. History—whether cosmic or human or subhuman—would utterly lack any meaning, purpose, value or significance because its foundation would literally be in nothing; its origin would be in emptiness. This is hardly a metanarrative to inspire beleaguered and confused postmoderns. We are simply thrown back to social constructions, contingencies and chaos—the very things Jencks wants to transcend. His impersonal and arbitrary universe leaves persons adrift and rudderless.

If Christian theology is to hold its ground and advance in confronting the challenges of postmodernism, it must clearly and powerfully affirm the propositional truth of God-inspired Scripture and its rational knowability. Along with this, it must recognize and heed the demands and privileges of God's great cosmic Story of creation, fall, redemption and consummation. This Story, if not objectively true, becomes merely one of many tales told by the errant narrators of postmodernity. Nothing less than the wedding of propositional truth and God's Story will meet the need of our postmodern hour. Nothing less will honor the great and true Storyteller of the universe.

---

[71]See Dallas Willard, "The Three-Stage Argument for the Existence of God," in *Contemporary Perspectives on Religious Epistemology*, ed. R. Douglas Geivett and Brendan Sweetman (New York: Oxford University Press, 1992), pp. 215-16; and G. E. M. Anscombe, "'Whatever Has a Beginning of Existence Must Have a Cause': Hume's Argument Exposed," *Analysis* 34 (1974): 145.

6

POSTMODERNISM
& APOLOGETICS
Dangers to Avoid

Considering what we have argued about the effects of postmodernist truth decay, how ought Christians defend the biblical worldview in the post- modern world? Edward John Carnell was right in affirming that "since apologetics is an art and not a science, there is no 'official' way to go about defending the Christian faith. The defense must answer to the spirit of the times."[1] However, not all apologetics strategies are equally judicious. Some today have claimed that the church is sadly stuck in a modernist apologetic methodology, unable to meet the challenges of a postmodern world. Prolific author and theologian Alister McGrath rec- ommends a "person-centered apologetics" that "aims to remain faithful to the gospel while ensuring that it fully address the contemporary situ- ation." Few could argue with this as a general principle, but McGrath's following advice is more controversial. Although "we do not need to throw away Christianity's claim to truth,"

---

[1]Edward John Carnell, *Christian Commitment: An Apologetic* (New York: Macmillan, 1957), p. vii.

We . . . need to realize that it is now bad tactics to major on the truth question. If we are going to get a hearing in today's culture, we need to be able
to show that Christianity has something relevant and attractive to offer.
The bonus is that this attraction is securely grounded in God's self-revela-
tion, not invented yesterday in an effort to get a hearing in the marketplace.[2]

Some have even advised abandoning the notions of rational cogency,
objective truth and an emphasis on propositions in favor of a more
communal and experiential kind of apologetic. Before outlining a contemporary apologetic strategy in the next chapter, I will assess three re-
visionist proposals that bring into question standard assumptions in
apologetics. I will argue that we must continue to "major on the truth
question," not as a "bonus" but as the essence of apologetics. Yet we
must do so in a way that is savvy to postmodern *realities*, without capitulating to postmodernist *philosophies*.

Willimon on "Jesus' Peculiar Truth"

William Willimon is a well-known writer who is probably more happy
with the designation of "postliberal" than "postmodern." The purpose
of this book is not to analyze postliberalism, although the topic came up
in chapter five. However, Willimon's apologetic proposal in a *Christianity Today* article called "Jesus' Peculiar Truth" shares several themes
with postmodernism and deserves a critique.

He recounts an exchange in which he supposedly trumped someone
who was worrying about the exclusivity of objective Christian truth.
Willimon responded, "Isn't it curious that Jesus did not say to his disciples, 'I am here to tell you *about* the truth?' He says, "I *am* the truth."[3]
He thinks that John 14:6 downplays objective truth by affirming Jesus
personally as the truth. This is a false inference. Scripture teaches that
God's truth is equally objective and personal. Jesus personifies truth
precisely because all that he says is true and his life reflects and embod-
ies perfect holiness by being true to the truth. No one is truer than Jesus,

[2]Alister McGrath, *Evangelicalism & the Future of Christianity* (Downers Grove, Ill.:
InterVarsity Press, 1995), p. 103.
[3]William H. Willimon, "Jesus' Peculiar Truth," *Christianity Today*, March 4, 1996, p. 21.

so he can say, "I am the truth." If this statement is not itself objectively true, it has no meaning whatsoever. Gordon Clark's comments are on target:

> Like other words, truth too can be used figuratively, by metonymy, in which the effect is substituted for the cause. Thus when Christ says, "I am the Way, the Truth, and the Life," the word "truth" is just as figurative as the word "life." As Christ is the cause of life, so is he the cause of truth. That water freezes and that a sinner may be justified by faith are true because Christ creatively said, Let it be so.[4]

There is more to Jesus' statement "I am the truth" than metonymy, but nothing in his declaration implies that some nebulous idea of personal truth trumps propositional truth. "I am the truth" is true; it is a truth about a person, Jesus Christ.

Willimon laments the intellectual and moral state of our culture but wonders if relativism is really the problem. This is a strange comment given the very high percentage of Americans who are relativistic. Nevertheless, he concedes that "the concept of absolute truth is a necessary corrective for a society wallowing in pop-psychotherapeutic, feel-good strategies" with people more concerned about feelings than truth.[5] He goes on to say that "Christians who argue for the 'objective' truth of Jesus are making a tactical mistake," because Jesus did not "arrive enunciating a set of propositions that we are to affirm. . . . Jesus never asks us to agree; he asks us to join up, to follow."[6] Instead of "cognitive assent, he asked for a life of discipleship involving the whole self, not just the mind."[7] Willimon continues, "Truth is a person, personal," although it is not "sheer subjectivity" since truth is inseparable from Jesus himself.[8]

Willimon to the contrary, Jesus *did* present "a set of propositions we are to affirm." He taught by declaring true propositions that ought to be

---

[4]Gordon Clark, "Truth," in *Evangelical Dictionary of Theology*, ed. Walter Elwell (Grand Rapids, Mich.: Baker, 1984), p. 1114.
[5]Willimon, "Jesus' Peculiar," p. 21.
[6]Ibid.
[7]Ibid.
[8]Ibid., p. 22.

believed as true, given his character and the arguments and evidence to which he appealed. When he said, "My yoke is easy and my burden is light" (Mt 11:30), he was calling people to affirm this as true. Otherwise, there would be no reason to take on that yoke, to trust him. Jesus also affirmed, "I told you that you would die in your sins; if you do not believe that I am the one I claim to be, you will indeed die in your sins" (Jn 8:24). Believing the truths that Jesus taught about himself is essential to salvation and discipleship. We must affirm the propositions he professed if we are to believe and obey him. If I believe someone who says to me, "The theater is on fire," I must assent to this proposition. Having assented, I will flee the scene. These truths imply action. Jesus' objective truths imply existential obedience. The two are inseparable.

Jesus called his disciples to believe truths as a necessary condition of salvation and discipleship. In addition, one must entrust oneself to Christ as Lord. This involves a whole-hearted commitment beyond bare assent. However, without the assent, the devotion makes no sense. Christian faith involves both intellectual assent (*fides*) and personal trust (*fiducia*); in fact, the latter is logically dependent on the former for its rationale.[9]

Willimon is also afraid that an apologist who appeals to objective truth gives his audience the false assumption that they thereby know the truth, when, in fact, we lack "the resources, on our own, to think about matters like God, truth, peace, justice, before knowing Jesus, who is for us the way, the truth, and the life."

> Arguing that Christ and his way are "objectively true," we run the risk of deceiving people into thinking that they are already capable, just as they are, of thinking about these matters without first knowing Jesus, without conversion. That is why the gospel consistently avoids asking for mere intellectual agreement.[10]

Willimon assumes that an appeal to objective truth makes truth too

---

[9]On the relationship of truth, faith and trust, see Alister McGrath, *Intellectuals Don't Need God and Other Modern Myths* (Grand Rapids, Mich.: Zondervan, 1993), pp. 48-60; and Harold Netland, *Dissonant Voice: Religious Pluralism and the Question of Truth* (Grand Rapids, Mich.: Eerdmans, 1991), p. 128.

[10]Willimon, "Jesus' Peculiar," p. 22.

cheap, something "any fool can walk in off the street and get without cost or pain." In good postmodernist fashion, he takes this to be a "bad legacy of the enlightenment" which tried to devise truth systems that would be approachable to any rational person.[11]

Willimon fails to make rudimentary distinctions crucial for apologetics. As I argued in earlier chapters, unless we have a sense of what objective truth is (correspondence to reality), the claims of Christ will be absorbed into postmodernist constructivism and relativism. Pre-evangelistic work is needed to spell out what the nature of truth is. Furthermore, in order for one to commit oneself to Jesus, one must take his message to be objectively true. Jesus gave evidence and arguments for his identity as God Incarnate. He cited his miracles, his character and his fulfillment of Scripture as proof of the truth he taught and lived. People assessed the truth-value of these claims prior to their conversion (even if they still had some unresolved questions about his identity). Otherwise, there would be no reason for their conversion. Carl Henry puts it well:

> If the truth of revelation cannot be known prior to commitment to Christ, then men cannot be culpable for its rejection; moreover, it would be a waste of time and energy to try to persuade them of its validity.[12]

We come to know God's truth much more fully and internally through the Holy Spirit after conversion, but unless we apprehend something of God's truth before conversion (through God's general revelation and common grace), the very logic of conversion fades away.

Willimon's viewpoint implies a radical fideism, which means the death of apologetics. Without arguments for the gospel's objective truth, we can only call people to commit; we are in no better intellectual condition than any other contender in the postmodern marketplace. In fact, we are in worse shape, since other worldviews—such as Islam and secular humanism—resist postmodernist constructivism and engage in their own objective apologetic efforts.[13]

---

[11]Ibid.

[12]Carl F. H. Henry, *God, Revelation, and Authority* (Waco, Tex.: Word, 1976), 1:229.

[13]I do not deny the fact that God may call people to himself despite the lack of a wise apologetic. But this does not justify fideism.

Willimon confuses a metaphysical claim—that objective truth exists —with an epistemological claim about how knowledge of objective truth is acquired. Enlightenment thinkers were utopian about the possibility of establishing all truth through unaided reason, but this does not disqualify the apologetic project of presenting Christianity as objectively true and rational. The apologist should realize that any number of subjective factors can serve as obstacles to belief, that apologetics needs to be person-specific and relational, that the truth of Christianity cannot be deductively proved beyond all shadow of doubt, and that good arguments can be rejected out of hand.[14] Nevertheless, we still must labor to "give the reason for hope that [we] have" (1 Pet 3:15) and to "contend for the faith" (Jude 3).

Natural theology also troubles Willimon. He thinks that appealing to nature as a premise from which to infer the existence of God will cause people to focus on the orderliness of nature as a basis for a God of order rather than asking the more *biblical* question, 'What *kind* of God exists?' "[15] Arguments from nature to God take many forms—some are compelling, others are not.[16] But to dismiss all of natural theology with the sentence "The Bible does not stress the orderliness of God, just that the God of Israel is true"[17] is unconvincing. God's signature is all over creation (Ps 19; Acts 14:17; Rom 1—2). Those who struggle to believe in God need solid arguments for his objective existence. This is especially urgent in areas, unlike the United States, where atheism runs high, such as Eastern Europe, Australia and Russia. It is ironic that Willimon rejects natural theology at just the time when it is experiencing a renaissance through the work of highly trained and well-respected Christian philosophers such as J. P. Moreland and William Lane Craig.[18]

Willimon muddles matters further by claiming that "what the God of Israel and the church promises us is not absolute truth reduced to

---

[14]On this, see chapter seven.
[15]Willimon, "Jesus' Peculiar," p. 22.
[16]I will outline these arguments in chapter seven.
[17]Willimon, "Jesus' Peculiar," p. 22.
[18]See J. P. Moreland, *Scaling the Secular City* (Grand Rapids, Mich.: Baker, 1987); William Lane Craig, *Reasonable Faith* (Wheaton, Ill.: Crossway, 1994).

propositions but the reality of the kingdom of God and eternal communion with the One who is the way, the truth, and the life."[19] But truth is propositional by definition. To say it should not be "reduced to propositions" evidences a deep befuddlement that masks as profundity. There could be no knowledge of the "reality of the kingdom of God" without propositional truth as a necessary condition for that knowledge and experience.

Willimon also appeals to the guidance of the Holy Spirit (Jn 16:13) as evidence that "Christian truth is not an achievement of clear thinking. It is a gift."[20] This is a false dichotomy. The Spirit can lead us to truth through clear thinking; apologetics calls unbelievers to think clearly about Christian truth claims. If they end up believing the gospel, all the glory goes to God for this gift (Eph 2:8; Tit 3:5). God himself says through Isaiah to his covenanted people, "Come now, let us reason together" (Is 1:18). Although Jesus spoke with divine authority, he employed cogent and careful arguments in his disputes with the religious leaders who sought to refute him.[21]

Kenneson Against Objective Truth

Philip Kenneson presents an even more radical alternative in his chapter "There Is No Such Thing as Objective Truth, and It's a Good Thing Too" from a collection of essays called *Christian Apologetics in the Postmodern World* (1995). Kenneson's effort is important because of its attempts to Christianize postmodernist themes from Richard Rorty and others.

Following Rorty, Kenneson identifies belief in objective truth as an impossible "view from nowhere approach" (all the while claiming he is not a relativist). The Enlightenment notion of objective truth as that which corresponds to reality was a wrong turn philosophically. This view generated anxiety about verifying which beliefs corresponded to reality. We have better options. We should not fret about rejecting the correspondence view since "most Christians throughout most of his-

---

[19]Willimon, "Jesus' Peculiar," p. 22.
[20]Ibid.
[21]See J. P. Moreland, *Love Your God with All Your Mind* (Colorado Springs, Colo.: NavPress, 1997), pp. 50-51.

tory have done well without the concept" of objective truth.[22]

On the contrary, the Bible itself presents its truth as objective, as I argued in chapter three. Christians throughout history have believed that the Bible's claims correspond to reality, and Kenneson gives no evidence to the contrary. This is not a "view from nowhere" (which would be impossible) but a true view from somewhere. For us, to view a thing means to view from somewhere. God views everything, so his omniscient view is a "view from everywhere." Our finite, human views are situated in space and time, but they are not necessarily at odds with reality thereby. Some things are viewed truly from somewhere.[23] A ten-year-old American child, a forty-year-old Japanese politician, a sixty-year-old Liberian farmer all know that torturing the innocent for pleasure is morally wrong. They also know that a triangle has three sides. All three persons properly identify objective truths.

Kenneson understands the correspondence view of what truth is,[24] but like Willimon, he confuses this view of truth with particular Enlightenment epistemologies. For instance, Descartes held to a correspondence view of the nature of truth, but his methodology of subjecting everything to doubt until he found what could not possibly be doubted—"I think; therefore, I am"—is arguably not the best way to do philosophy.[25] However, critiquing Descartes's methodology of finding *what is true* is a different enterprise than rejecting his basic view of *what truth is*.

Kenneson anticipates the objection that if we drop the concept of objective truth from apologetics we are left with only subjective "truth," such that we make things true merely by believing them. Against this, he enlists Rorty's idea that truth is merely a property of sentences, or ways we speak. Kenneson says:

---

[22]Philip Kenneson, "There Is No Such Thing as Objective Truth, and It's a Good Thing Too," in *Christian Apologetics in the Postmodern World*, ed. Timothy R. Phillips and Dennis L. Okholm (Downers Grove, Ill.: InterVarsity Press, 1995), p. 158.

[23]Against the "view from nowhere" objection, see John Searle, *Mind, Language, and Society* (New York: Basic Books, 1998), p. 21.

[24]Kenneson, "There Is No Such Thing," p. 157.

[25]It is worth noting that this basic approach to skepticism goes all the way back to the *premodern* Augustine in his *City of God*.

Truth cannot be out there—cannot exist independently of the human mind—because sentences cannot so exist or be out there. The world and God are out there, but descriptions of the world and God are not. Only descriptions of the world and God can be true or false.[26]

Therefore, we should stop worrying about "the way language does or does not hook up with reality," as do apologists such as James Sire and others.[27] If we shift to Rorty's view of truth, we can breath easier; no one needs to ask about objective truth.[28] Given the defects in Rorty's perspective, which I address in chapter eight, it is unlikely that he will provide a philosophical assist for Christians. This is especially true, since Rorty, an atheist, does not think that God is "out there" at all.

When Kenneson says that "truth cannot be out there" because sentences are not out there, he neglects the fact that God has a mind that knows every true proposition to be true and every false proposition to be false. This is crucial to what "all-*knowing*" means. Therefore, truth *does* exist outside of human sentences; it exists in the mind of God.

Kenneson drives a sharp wedge between objective states of affairs and sentences about these states of affairs (or realities); he also omits entirely the important concept of a proposition (discussed in chapter four). A sentence about Jesus Christ is not Jesus Christ, but the proposition that the sentence affirms or refers to—that is, the meaning of the sentence—is either true or false. If a Muslim says, "Jesus is not God," this sentence is *false* because of its relationship to that to which it refers, namely, Jesus. The sentence "Jesus is God" is *true* for the same reason; it "hooks up with reality." In divorcing sentences from objective realities, Kenneson's position defaults to linguistic relativism, whereby language cannot be connected to or verified by anything outside of language itself.

But Kenneson contradicts his principle that sentences and reality are not on speaking terms. By using a sentence, he writes that "the world and God are out there." That is, the world and God exist outside of language itself; they are extralinguistic realities. Yet if truth is *not* corre-

---

[26]Kenneson, "There Is No Such Thing," p. 159.
[27]Ibid., p. 160.
[28]Ibid., p. 161.

spondence with external states of affairs, how can Kenneson affirm that
these states of affairs—the world and God—actually exist "out there"?
His statement cannot play by its own rules; it contradicts itself and is
therefore false—another case of "self-referential inconsistency."[29] Kenneson is correct that truth and falsity apply to sentences (and, I add, ultimately to propositions and beliefs), but sentences *are made true or false*
by virtue of their relation to reality.[30]

Kenneson defers to Rorty to defend himself against relativism. Since
I argued that Rorty cannot so defend himself, he cannot defend Kenneson either.[31] However, Kenneson adds a new twist, saying that "because
I have neither a theory of truth nor an epistemology, I cannot have a relativistic one of either."[32] This posturing is impertinent. Kenneson *has*
given us a theory of truth. Inasmuch as he rejects correspondence and
embraces Rorty's nonrealism, his epistemology is "the web of belief"
view.

In viewing truth as a "web of beliefs" Kenneson embraces the coherence theory of truth (critiqued in chapter four), whereby truth is seen as
internal to the web, because "there is no standard of truth independent
of a set of beliefs and practices."[33] Instead of "asking whether one's language hooks up to reality," we should ask what "web of convictions, beliefs and practices must be in place before we can make the judgment
that a certain statement is true or false."[34] But to judge the truth or falsity of statements according to our beliefs begs the question of whether
our beliefs are true or false in the first place. We can make judgments on
the basis of our background beliefs, but our background beliefs are also
judgments on matters of truth and falsity.

Kenneson's perspective is fatal to apologetics. He says that his "new
paradigm" delivers us from uncertainty because "we *always* know for

---

[29]See Alvin Plantinga, "Reason and Belief in God," in *Faith and Rationality: Reason and
Belief in God,* ed. Alvin Plantinga and Nicholas Wolterstorff (Notre Dame, Ind.: University of Notre Dame Press, 1983), p. 60.
[30]For more on this, see chapter four.
[31]See the discussions of Rorty in chapters four and eight.
[32]Kenneson, "There Is No Such Thing," p. 161.
[33]Ibid., p. 163.
[34]Ibid.

certain what is true, because we are always in the grip of some belief."[35] Given that he has dropped correspondence as the nature of truth, Kenneson must conflate belief with truth, just as postmodernists do. Therefore, Muslims always know that Jesus is not God, and Christians always know that Jesus is God. This violates the law of noncontradiction: A cannot be non-A. Both states of affairs cannot exist in the same way at the same time.

When belief is conflated with truth, and there is no standard of truth independent of belief, there can be no rational reason to change one's set of beliefs, because all beliefs are merely self-referring. The beliefs are not really about any reality outside of themselves. Thus, Kenneson affirms the contradictory statement: "What we certainly know may change if and when our beliefs change."[36] In other words, I can know with certainty that a statement is true; then, when my beliefs change, I can know with certainty that the same statement is not true. This is impossible. We can only reestablish sanity by distinguishing belief from truth and falsity. I may be psychologically certain of an objective falsehood (I *believe* that Texas is larger than Alaska), but I cannot have certain *knowledge* of what is objectively false (because Alaska is larger than Texas).

All web theories of truth, Kenneson's or others, break down on the matter of why anyone would or should switch webs (worldviews) if they take their own web to be at least internally coherent. If there is no standard to judge one's beliefs against reality, why change a set of beliefs, except for some self-serving purpose? We have many examples of people, such as C. S. Lewis, who changed worldviews on the basis of good arguments that refuted their previous beliefs.[37] Despite this, Kenneson says the web paradigm makes us "passionately evangelic." It encourages us to

persuade others to accept our beliefs because if they believe what we

---

[35]Ibid.
[36]Ibid.
[37]See C. S. Lewis, *Surprised by Joy* (New York: Harcourt, Brace & World, 1955). Against the web theory (or conventionalism), see Winfried Corduan, *No Doubt About It: Basic Christian Apologetics* (Nashville: Broadman & Holman, 1997), pp. 66-70.

believe, they will see what we see; and the facts to which we point in
order to support our interpretations will be as obvious to them as they are
to us.[38]

This further undermines apologetics because there could be no rational argument by which to persuade one to change beliefs. It is a truism
that *if* someone believes what we believe, they will accept our interpretations. This simply means that if you believe what we believe, you
will, in fact, believe what we believe. This is not an apologetic; it is a
tautology. The issue is why anyone should accept Christian beliefs at
all.[39]

Kenneson also betrays his whole project by asserting that facts support interpretations. On his view, facts cannot support interpretations,
since there are no facts independent of interpretations. Kenneson thinks
it makes no "sense to think of reality as it is itself, apart from human
judgment."[40] So, like Nietzsche he has disqualified facts from meaning
anything independent of our interpretations of them. Everything becomes interpretation.[41] To appeal to facts to support interpretations is to
lapse into the supposedly discredited correspondence view of truth.

Kenneson claims his model of truth has several advantages over the
correspondence view. It makes the church the touchstone, for when objective truth is abandoned, we must demonstrate a way of life that is attractive to outsiders. The Christian must now disregard "the view from
nowhere" and emphasize the "convictions and practices [that] are
themselves an embodiment of what they take to be good and true."[42]

Kenneson, despite himself, seems to presuppose a correspondence
view of truth to make this claim about the church. To embody a practice
that one takes to be good and true is to put into effect a truth about reality. Kenneson has left out half of the equation. If Kenneson simply says
that his claim is true only in reference to his particular ecclesiastical lan-

[38]Kenneson, "There Is No Such Thing," p. 164.
[39]See James W. Sire, *Why Should Anyone Believe Anything At All?* (Downers Grove, Ill.:
InterVarsity Press, 1994).
[40]Kenneson, "There Is No Such Thing," p. 164.
[41]See chapter four for a discussion of perspectivism.
[42]Kenneson, "There Is No Such Thing," p. 162.

guage game, he has relativized the notion of truth such that he cannot present any reason for anyone outside of that ecclesiastical language game to accept it as their own.

Kenneson's main complaint seems to be that the concept of objective truth vitiates the incarnational witness of the church because it allows us to appeal to the truth apart from the character of our lives: "Believing that a certain proposition hooks up with the way the world really is does not require one to act in any certain way."[43] But this does not follow. The church is called to be a community constituted by the truth in the power of the spirit of Truth. We should be "speaking the truth in love" (Eph 4:15), which involves far more than simply uttering true statements. John Stott elaborates:

> "Speaking the truth in love" is not the best rendering of this expression,
> for the Greek verb makes no reference to our speech. Literally, it means,
> "truthing (*aletheuontes*) in love," and includes the notions of "maintain-
> ing," "living," and "doing" the truth.[44]

Followers of Christ must be true to (or consistent with) God's truth. This means that we are to conform our thoughts and our lives, through the power of the Holy Spirit, to the realities of God. Our impetus is gratitude for our salvation and love for other believers, the lost and God himself. Schaeffer, a hands-on apologist who died in 1984 before the ascendancy of postmodernism in Christian circles, saw clearly the need to declare, defend and demonstrate the truth of Scripture. He wrote in 1968:

> Both a clear comprehension of the importance of truth and a clear practice
> of it, even when it is costly to do so, is imperative if our witness and our
> evangelism are to be significant in our own generation and in the flow of
> history.[45]

---

[43]Ibid., p. 163.
[44]John Stott, *The Message of Ephesians* (Downers Grove, Ill.: InterVarsity Press, 1979), pp. 171-72.
[45]Francis Schaeffer, *The God Who Is There*, 30th anniv. ed. (Downers Grove, Ill.: InterVarsity Press, 1998), p. 214. See also Francis Schaeffer, *The Church at the End of the 20th Century* (Downers Grove, Ill.: InterVarsity Press, 1970), pp. 71-77.

When objective truth is removed, the community becomes merely self-referential and ultimately autistic. It has its web of beliefs; it engages in various practices. But it cannot be said that the community reflects objective realities. This leaves members of the community with no compelling reason to adhere to these beliefs. What are these beliefs *about*, if not something outside of the community that gives it its compelling relationship to reality?[46]

Kenneson's paradigm for truth and epistemology is contradictory and cuts out the ground from under any rational apologetic for the truth of the Christian faith. If there is no objective Christian truth, there is no Christian witness to that truth, no embodiment of that truth and no apologetic endeavor at all. We are left with only relativistic redescriptions, a la Rorty—and a few inspirational epigrams from Wittgenstein. In the end Kenneson's program is a kind of religious constructivism with a postmodernist atheist, Richard Rorty, overseeing the philosophical building program. Here, as elsewhere, we should remember Paul's sobering words, "See to it that no one takes you captive through hollow and deceptive philosophy, which depends on human tradition and the basic principles of this world rather than on Christ" (Col 2:8).

There *is* such a thing as objective truth, and it's a good thing too!

Newbigin's Uncertain Truth

Lesslie Newbigin (d. 1998) was a long-time missionary and Christian statesman who, later in life, wrote several books addressing the question of how Christians should face postmodern times. He has much to say of value concerning the nature of the Christian life and commitment in our day. Although his critique of non-Christian worldviews and attitudes was often insightful, his concept of truth and its defense were unsteady at times. The consistent application of his ideas leads to a diminishing of apologetic effort, and this is ill advised for the challenges we face. In some ways this thinking was postmodernist.

First, Newbigin's view of truth appears to be inconsistent. At times

---

[46]On the nature of Christian community, see Richard Keyes, *Chameleon Christianity* (Grand Rapids, Mich.: Baker, 1999), pp. 87-102.

he sounds as if he endorses the correspondence view, while at others he seems to deny it. Newbigin emphasizes that the gospel is a "public truth," a reality to proclaim and live out before the world. He says that we have to proclaim the gospel "not as a package of estimable values, but as the truth about what is the case, about what every human being and every society will have to reckon with."[47] He also makes this admirable statement:

> I am responsible for seeking as far as possible to insure that my beliefs are true, that I am—however fumblingly—grasping reality and therefore grasping that which is real and true for all human beings and which will reveal its truth through further discoveries as I continue to seek.[48]

This agrees with the view of truth I have presented. I also applaud this statement: "When I say 'I believe' [in Christianity] I am not merely describing an inward feeling or experience; I am affirming what I believe to be true, and therefore what is true for everyone."[49] Statements such as these were enough to make Philip Kenneson claim that "the proposals of Lesslie Newbigin [are] never quite satisfying."[50] Yet Newbigin also makes statements that may be taken to deny—and to misrepresent—the correspondence view of truth. When discussing the notion that "belief-statements are merely subjective," he says that this

> presupposes the possibility of an "objective" knowledge which is not knowledge as believed to be true by someone. This bogus objectivity is expressed in Bertrand Russell's definition of truth as the correspondence between a person's beliefs and the actual facts. This definition is futile since there is no way of knowing what the actual facts are except by the activity of knowing subjects. The definition implies a standpoint outside of the real human situation of knowing subjects—and no such standpoint is available.[51]

---

[47]Lesslie Newbigin, *Truth to Tell: The Gospel as Public Truth* (Grand Rapids, Mich.: Eerdmans, 1991), p. 64.

[48]Lesslie Newbigen, *The Gospel in a Pluralist Society* (Grand Rapids, Mich.: Eerdmans, 1989), p. 23.

[49]Ibid., p. 22

[50]Kenneson, "There Is No Such Thing," footnote 15, pp. 226-27.

[51]Newbigen, *Gospel in a Pluralist Society*, p. 22.

As I argued in chapter four, Russell distinguishes objective reality from true belief (or knowledge of objective reality), which corresponds to that reality. Of course, there is no way of *knowing* the facts except as they are known by knowing subjects. To know is precisely to know the objective facts as a knowing subject. Newbigin sounds quite postmodern in denying that there is a standpoint outside the human situation (what Kenneson refers to as "the view from nowhere") that would somehow be necessary for Russell's view of truth to hold. But Russell's definition of truth does not require access to a standpoint unavailable to humans. It simply requires that, for a belief to be true, it must linguistically represent some *part* of reality *accurately*, from a perspective, not without any perspective.

Newbigin thinks this "definition of truth" cannot be used to test our own "perceptions of truth, since there is no way in which I can stand outside my own perception of the facts." Further, one cannot say one believes something and also say that reality differs from my belief.[52] This, I believe, confuses the definition of truth with the tests for, or verification, of truth. Truth *is* defined as correspondence to reality, whether or not anyone *knows* a particular reality or not. For instance, there are a certain number of dust particles on the moon (or hairs on my head) at any given time, but no human knows what the numbers are. However, it is possible in many cases to perform tests to see if one's beliefs match reality. For instance, William Willimon claimed that Jesus never asked people to agree with him. We showed from Scripture that this is false. Willimon's statement does not agree with reality.

Second, Newbigin argues against traditional apologetics, largely on the basis of his use of some philosophical themes found in Michael Polanyi and Alasdair MacIntyre. I will not critique these profound and complex writers directly but rather assess Newbigin's concerns about apologetics that draw on their thinking.

Like postmodernists, Newbigin emphasizes the dominance of perspectives and interpretations over verifiable facts. For instance, he says that "the simple truth is that the resurrection [of Christ] cannot be ac-

---

[52]Ibid.

commodated in any way of understanding the world except one of which it is the starting point."[53] If Newbigin means that we must let the gospel story of Easter speak for itself without revising it along secular lines, his point stands.[54] But his comment seems to also imply that we cannot use any intellectual means outside of the proclamation of the resurrection itself to vindicate its truth to unbelievers. He calls the resurrection "a starting point."[55] If so, this means that we have to believe in a worldview with the resurrection at its center in order to believe in the resurrection. Quite so (in a tautological sense), but what do we say to the non-Christian doubter or the Christian suffering uncertainties? Just believe? Why should anyone believe in Christ's resurrection in the first place? Newbigin says that making the resurrection a starting point gives us a "whole new way of understanding our human experience" that makes more sense than "the reigning plausibility structure."[56] However, the resurrection itself is accepted "on faith," as is the creation of the universe.[57] They are both equally "mysterious to human reason."[58]

There is a better way to argue. If we build a good philosophical case for theism, miracles become *possible* since a supernatural Creator exists. Even the secular postmodernist Jean Baudrillard understands this logic: "The insurance against death is to have been created *ex nihilo*, which keeps open the possibility of an equally miraculous resurrection."[59] Having argued for the Creator, we are then in the position to present the historical evidence for the resurrection of Christ as an *actual* miracle (which implies our own future resurrection). One need not begin the argument from *Christian* theism in order to argue for the resurrection of Christ or human immortality. (That, in fact, would beg the question.)

---

[53]Ibid., p. 11.
[54]This issue was the context of his statement, but his statement has implications beyond just this application.
[55]Newbigin, *Gospel in a Pluralist Society*, p. 12.
[56]Ibid.
[57]Ibid.
[58]Ibid., p. 11.
[59]Jean Baudrillard, *The Perfect Crime*, trans. Chris Turner (New York: Verso, 1996), p. 23.

Rather, one may move apologetically from a generic, philosophically established monotheism[60] to Christian theism through the use of historical evidences.[61] The resurrection, a miraculous event in history, need not be accepted on blind faith without accompanying evidence.

Although Newbigin believes that the resurrection occurred in objective space-time history (it is not merely a social construction), he does not, it seems, allow for historical evidence to count for its existence epistemologically. In this he is insulating the Christian worldview from external confirmation, from empirical evidence. In this, his epistemology somewhat resembles that of postmodernists who speak of "heterogeneous languages games" (Lyotard) and incomparable "final vocabularies" (Rorty). Newbigin takes Christianity to be "true for everyone" (unlike postmodernists), but he appears to not leave much room for arguing this case logically across traditions and worldviews because he appears to find no common ground from which to argue for the truth of Christianity. He claims that the long tradition of apologetics in the church is misguided in its attempt to demonstrate the reasonableness of the Christian faith. This is because the Christian worldview "cannot possibly be accommodated within any plausibility structure except one of which it is the cornerstone."[62] Further, "there is no disembodied reason which can act as impartial umpire between rival claims."[63] He has also claimed that there is no way to demonstrate that "a worldview which sees ultimate reality as in some sense personal" is superior to "a worldview which sees ultimate reality as impersonal." This is because there "is no principle more fundamental than either of these views and by which one could, therefore, adjudicate between them."[64]

---

[60]See, for example, Craig, *Reasonable Faith,* chap. 3; Moreland, *Scaling the Secular City,* chaps. 1-4.

[61]See Corduan, *No Doubt About It,* pp. 146-64; Moreland, *Scaling the Secular City,* chaps. 5-6.

[62]Lesslie Newbigin, *Proper Confidence: Faith, Doubt, and Uncertainty in Christian Discipleship* (Grand Rapids, Mich.: Eerdmans, 1995), p. 93.

[63]Newbigin, *Gospel in a Pluralist Society,* p. 57.

[64]Newbigin, *Proper Confidence,* pp. 13-14. For an argument that a personal view of ultimate reality is rationally and morally superior to an impersonal one, see Douglas Groothuis, *Confronting the New Age* (Downers Grove, Ill.: InterVarsity Press, 1988), pp. 106-26.

A fuller analysis of a proper apologetic method awaits our next chapter, but suffice to say that Newbigin fails to distinguish the common canons of logic and evidence from non-Christian plausibility structures. Newbigin is right to affirm that the apologist must not truncate the gospel by making it fit into fallen patterns of thinking or ungodly cultural trends, but one may appeal to the light of conscience and reason available to all people made in the image and likeness of God who live within the revelation of creation (Gen 1:26; Ps 19; Acts 14:17; Rom 1—2). Our reasoning is never "disembodied," because we reason as flesh and blood creatures within particular cultures. However, the basic principles of logic—such as the law of noncontradiction and the law of excluded middle—are universally true and applicable within and between worldviews.

Newbigin's argument may boil down to the idea that all religious worldviews involve faith and that the naturalistic (or nonreligious) worldview is not entailed by pure reason and objective evidence. Naturalists, as well as Christians and other believers, see the world from a perspective that they bring to the world. This is an important point for deflating the supposed superiority of *secular reason* over *religious faith*, but stopping at this point deprives the Christian worldview of the philosophical power to marshal significant evidence and arguments for its own objective truth. Although Newbigin makes some telling points against ethical relativism and non-Christian theories of religious pluralism,[65] his own view of Christianity seems ill-equipped to handle adequately the postmodern relativist challenge. He tends to conflate apologetics with proclamation and the evangelistic influence of Christian community.

> The proper form of apologetics is the preaching of the gospel itself and the demonstration—which is not merely or primarily a matter of words—that it does provide the best foundation for a way of grasping and dealing with the mystery of our existence in this universe.[66]

> How is it that the gospel should be credible, that people should come to

---

[65]See Newbigin, *Gospel in a Pluralist Society*, pp. 155-70.
[66]Newbigin, *Proper Confidence*, p. 94.

believe that the power which has the last word in human affairs is represented by a man hanging on a cross? I am suggesting that the *only* answer,
the *only* hermeneutic of the gospel, is a congregation of men and women
who believe it and live by it.[67]

However, biblical preaching is powerful for those ready to believe,
but skeptics, agnostics, atheists and those in other religions often need
to find sufficient reasons why they should embrace the Christian message—although people sometimes do come to faith through preaching
with little or no antecedent apologetical preparation. God is free to
work in any way that honors truth.[68] It is true that all those outside the
Christian faith need to perceive its reality in the everyday lives of Christians, but it is difficult to see how Newbigin's "apologetic" can provide
"the *best* foundation for a way of grasping and dealing with the mystery of our existence," when he has, I believe, ruled out apologetically
fruitful common ground and evidential support for Christian faith outside of proclamation and community. Furthermore, any number of non-
Christian religious communities proclaim their version of "the truth"
and attempt to live it out. Christians need something beyond this. Like
Paul, the great apologist, we should present cogently a faith that is both
"true and reasonable" (Acts 26:25).

By disallowing any external confirmation of the Christian worldview as objectively true and reasonable, Newbigin makes the notions of
truth and rationality intrinsic to each worldview itself. Concerning the
historical events crucial to Christianity, he says that we have no access
to "'what really happened' apart from any tradition of rational discourse, and there is no external criterion by which we can decide in advance which tradition is the one to be the reliable one."[69]

It is a truism that we find Christian truth claims within the Christian
tradition, Marxist truth claims within the Marxist tradition and Islamic
truth claims within the Islamic tradition; but the pivotal issue is the
truth-value of these truth claims and their credibility. The appeal to tra-

---

[67]Newbigin, *Gospel in a Pluralist Society*, p. 227; emphasis mine.
[68]Consider Pascal's discussion of this in Blaise Pascal, *Pensees*, ed. Alban Krailsheimer
(New York: Penguin, 1966), 381/286, p. 139; 382/287, pp. 138-39.
[69]Newbigin, *Gospel in a Pluralist Society*, p. 77.

dition against objective truth simply begs the question of the truthfulness or falsity of the traditions themselves. Newbigin tries to defend himself from relativism or subjectivism by saying that we are responsible for what tradition we choose, and that we make this decision with "universal intent" (Polyani's phrase). This means we are

> bound to publish it, to commend it to others, and to seek to show in the practice of life today that is the rational tradition which is giving greater coherence and intelligibility to all experience than any other tradition.[70]

Yet to publicly display one's belief does not make it objective or rational. All world religions and major worldviews do that in various ways. Moreover, it is impossible—not just difficult—to show that ours is the best "rational tradition" if rationality has been relativized to various communities and if there is no way to adjudicate disputes by appealing to objective reality or universal principles of logic. Newbigin seems to realize this (at least partially) when he claims that "the tradition is not ultimate; it is subject to the test of adequacy to the realities which it seeks to grasp."[71] But given what he has said elsewhere, there remains no way to test a tradition against reality, since all interpretations of reality are tradition-bound and culture-bound. This would also invalidate making the resurrection a "starting point" for a better explanation of human experience, since human experience itself can only be understood within disparate traditions and cultures. Newbigin, I maintain, cannot have it both ways. Because of his logical inconsistencies and his downplaying or dismissing of traditional apologetics, Newbigin's approach cannot provide an adequate apologetic response to truth decay.[72]

Toward a Better Way

Our analysis of the apologetic proposals of Willimon, Kenneson and Newbigin reveals that postmodernist ideas have affected Christian

---

[70]Ibid.; see also p. 22.

[71]Ibid., p. 55.

[72]See Winfried Corduan, "Ambivalent Truth: A Response to Lesslie Newbigin," *Philosophia Christi* 20, no. 1 (1997): 29-40. This is a critique of *Gospel in a Pluralist Society*. I found Corduan's critique to be helpful in my assessment of Newbigin.

apologetics in profound and unfavorable ways. The result is either the end of apologetics or its enfeeblement. Where apologetics founders, the church loses its intellectual witness to the objective truth of the gospel; truth ceases to be compelling and meekly recedes into the background. Therefore, we must find a better way to respond to postmodern conditions, to refute the thinking of postmodernists and to defend the objective and life-changing truth of Christian faith. Pascal set an apologetic agenda in the seventeenth century that honored both truth and sensitivity to the spirit of the time. It should be ours as well.

> Men despise religion. They hate it and are afraid it may be true. The cure of this is first to show that religion is not contrary to reason, but worthy of reverence and respect.
> Next make it attractive, make good men wish it were true, and then show that it is.
> Worthy of reverence because it really understands human nature. Attractive because it promises true good.[73]

To this constructive apologetic task we turn in the following chapter.

---

[73]Pascal, *Pensees*, 12/187, p. 34.

7

APOLOGETICS FOR
POSTMODERNS

If a Christian apologist of postmodernist stripe were to stand on our equivalent of Mars Hill today, he or she might say something to this effect, something quite different in spirit from the apostle Paul's original address (Acts 17:16-31).

People of Postmodernity, I can see you speak in many language games and are interested in diverse spiritualities. I have observed your pluralistic religious discourse and the fact that you use many final vocabularies. I have seen your celebration of the death of objective truth and the eclipse of metanarratives, and I declare to you that you are right. As one of your own has said, "We are suspicious of all metanarratives." What you have already said, I will reaffirm to you with a slightly different spin.

We have left modernity behind as a bad dream. We deny its rationalism, objectivism and intellectual arrogance. Instead of this, we affirm the Christian community, which professes that God is the strand that unites our web of belief. We have our own manner of interpreting the world and using language that we call you to adopt for yourself. We give you no argument for the existence of God, since natural theology is simply rationalistic hubris. We are not interested in metaphysics but in discipleship.

For us, Jesus is Lord. That is how we speak. We act that way, too; it's important to us. And although we cannot appeal to any evidence outside our own communal beliefs and tradition, we believe that God is in control of our narrative. We ask you to join our language game. Please. Since it is impossible to give you any independent evidence for our use of language, or to appeal to hard facts, we simply declare this to be our truth. It can become your truth as well, if you join up. Jesus does not call you to believe propositions but to follow him. You really can't understand what we're talking about until you join up. But after that, it will be much clearer. Trust us. In our way of speaking, God is calling everyone every-where to change his or her language game, to appropriate a new dis-course and to redescribe reality one more time. We speak such that the resurrection of Jesus is the crucial item in our final vocabulary. We hope you will learn to speak this way, as well.

Having criticized the postmodernizing tendencies of three Christian writers in the previous chapter, the inadequacies of the above approach should be readily recognizable. It has no apologetic nerve; it is sapped of argumentative and evidential support; it has nothing unique or even provocative to say to postmoderns. If so, how ought we to communi-cate the Christian message to those imbued with postmodernist beliefs?

Biblical Apologetics: Arguing Truth in the Marketplace

Scripture makes a distinction between the proclamation of the gospel, the defense of the gospel and the communal manifestation of the gospel. Christians who subscribe to postmodernist ideas absorb the defense of the gospel into proclamation and manifestation, given their views on lan-guage, truth and rationality. However, F. F. Bruce's classic book *The Defense of the Gospel in the New Testament* thoroughly demonstrates the early church's passionate apologetic impetus. He notes that "Christian witness in the New Testament called repeatedly for the *defense* of the gos-pel against opposition of many kinds—religious, cultural and political."[1] Bruce observes that when Paul speaks of himself as imprisoned "for the

---

[1]F. F. Bruce, *The Defense of the Gospel in the New Testament* (Grand Rapids, Mich.: Eerd-mans, 1977), p. vii.

defense of the gospel" and when Peter speaks of being "prepared to make a defense to any one who calls you to account for the hope that is in you," the Greek word is *"apologia,* from which we derive the words 'apology,' 'apologist' and 'apologetic.'"[2] The apologetic emphasis in the New Testament inspired the "age of the apologists" in the second century A.D., when Christian intellectuals began to fight back against false charges and repression. For writers such as Justin Martyr and others,

> Christianity . . . is the final and true religion, by contrast to the imperfection of Judaism and the error of paganism. Not only does Christianity provide the proper fulfillment of that earlier revelation of God given through the prophets of Israel . . . it also supplies the answer to the quests and aspirations expressed in the philosophies and cults of the other nations. It was divinely intended from the beginning to be a universal religion.[3]

It is still intended to be a "universal religion," even in a day when universality is equated with antiquated or even dangerous metanarratives of totality and hegemony. An apologetic for the people of postmodernity must place the concept of truth at the center of all its endeavors. The term *truth* is so subject to abuse, dilution and distortion, it is incumbent that apologists define and illustrate the term, and engage postmoderns according to it. As I mentioned in earlier chapters, biblical truth is, as Schaeffer nicely put it, "true to what is"; it matches reality and it calls us to embrace God's reality with all of our beings. It is also revealed, objective, absolute, universal, antithetical, systemic and momentous, and it has intrinsic value.

The Hidden Dangers of Relevance

Because of the postmodernist redescription of truth, apologists must be wary of working to make the Christian message relevant to the felt needs of non-Christians. What is relevant to those enmeshed in postmodernity is not, typically, the biblical view of truth or biblical truths themselves. Our operative term ought to be *engagement,*

---

[2]Ibid.
[3]Ibid.

not relevance. The performer Madonna is the apex of relevance to many postmoderns, but the protean princess of sexual seduction offers Christians nothing positive from which to draw for evangelistic or apologetic endeavor. Rather, we must dynamically engage the thinking of postmoderns with intelligence, sensitivity and courage.[4]

As Douglas Webster notes, our situation often demands that we "renegotiate the presuppositions" of our audience and not cater to its truth-decaying tendencies.[5] When people are asking the wrong questions, or not asking questions at all, Christians need to introduce new concepts and suggest new ways of thinking. This means that we must reorient the discourse toward the nature of truth and the truths of reality, and away from human constructions, personal preferences and tribal leanings. Thomas Merton speaks of the insecurity of "being afraid to ask the right questions—because they might turn out to have no answer." This results in a sad condition of "huddling together in the pale light of an insufficient answer to a question we are afraid to ask."[6] Christians must shine the bright light of truth by raising penetrating questions and giving satisfying answers. When words are cheap and float weightlessly over a wasteland of artificiality and cultural triviality, followers of Jesus must utter and write words of weight and significance—words that point to the unshakable but approachable truths of the kingdom of God. Webster's comments on pastors and theologians also applies to apologists:

> Jesus plunged his audience into truth too deep for humanistic consumption. The ocean of God's truth can be overwhelming apart from the grace of God. But ocean depth has always characterized God's Spirit-filled pastors and theologians. Augustine, Luther, Calvin and Edwards preached the Word of God with a sense of power and mystery. They did not inter-

----

[4]On engagement in preaching, see Richard John Neuhaus, *Freedom for Ministry* (Grand Rapids, Mich.: Eerdmans, 1992), pp. 166-67.
[5]Douglas Webster, *Selling Jesus: What's Wrong with Marketing the Church* (Downers Grove, Ill.: InterVarsity Press, 1992), p. 67. Webster is discussing Jesus' interaction with the rich young ruler in Mark 10.
[6]Thomas Merton, *No Man Is an Island* (Garden City, N.Y.: Image Books, 1967), p. 10.

rupt the momentum of the truth with endearing human-interest stories and tension-releasing humor. They were seriously intense about proclaiming the Word of God.[7]

At the same time we must appeal to areas of common ground and common grace. The postmodern condition may induce a kind of value vertigo, a disorientation regarding matters that matter. The often heard, flippant response, "Whatever . . ." uttered with a smirk and a slouch, does not slake the thirst of the soul for something beyond itself. "Whatever" is never enough when it comes to issues of forever, and ultimate concerns. Postmodernity, given its endorsement of religious pluralism and its rejection of the Enlightenment's rationalism, tends to be more interested in "spiritualities." This provides a point of contact, since the gospel clearly addresses the realities of the inner person. However, we must move from self-styled spiritualities to a Christ-centered spirituality, a spiritual way of being oriented to Christ as "the way and the truth and the life" (Jn 14:6), the singular source for spiritual regeneration, sustenance and direction (1 Tim 2:5).

True Spirituality: Truth for the Soul

The postmodern temptation, as mentioned in chapter one, is to entice souls to create a self-styled spirituality of one's own or to revert to the spiritual tradition of one's ethnic or racial group without a concern for objective truth or rationality. In a pluralistic setting, people are exposed to all manners of religious teaching and may mix-and-match elements. Someone raised as a Buddhist may date a Jewish person and begin to enjoy the ceremonies at the temple. Or a nominal Christian may be impressed with the religious devotion of his Muslim coworker, who stops for prayer several times during a workday, and so want to know more about Islam. Or one can try to be nonjudgmental and simply appreciate various religious traditions without worrying much about the truth question.

To offset these tendencies a Christian apologetic should emphasize spirituality as set within a framework of objective truth. Otherwise,

---

[7]Webster, *Selling Jesus*, pp. 108-9.

Christian spirituality will be seen as simply another pragmatic, relative, subjective option. God will be trivialized by being reduced to a mere means to avert boredom, create excitement, enhance self-image or give some order and sanity to family life. Furthermore, no major religious tradition—whether Buddhist, Hindu, Islamic or Jewish—has ever presented its doctrines as social constructions or as mere psychological aids to a more satisfying life. They have always been presented as truths concerning the ultimate reality and how we ought to relate to that reality. Scholar of religions Huston Smith, who is not an evangelical, rightly notes that "religions are worldviews or metanarratives—inclusive posits concerning the ultimate nature of things."[8] That is, religions make claims that include all of reality; therefore, they also exclude claims that contradict their assertions.

In our pluralistic and postmodern context, it is helpful to articulate Christian truth claims in relation to opposing views—not to be contentious but to clarify what is being put forth and what is not. Any truth claim negates every proposition that denies it. This is the logic of antithesis, as discussed in chapter three. For instance, if Jesus is God incarnate, then he is not (1) a mere prophet of Allah (Islam), (2) a misguided reformer (Judaism), (3) an avatar of Brahman (Hinduism), (4) a manifestation of God (Baha'i Faith), (5) a God-realized guru (New Age), (6) an inspired but not divine social prophet (theological liberalism), and so on.

C. S. Lewis made the claims of Jesus Christ stand out in clear relief in his essay "What Are We to Make of Jesus Christ?" Speaking of Christ's unique claims to deity, he argued:

> There is no half-way house and there is no parallel in other religions. If you had gone to Buddha and asked him "Are you the son of Bramah?" he would have said, "My son, you are still in the value of illusion." If you had gone to Socrates and asked, "Are you Zeus?" he would have laughed at you. If you had gone to Mohammed and asked, "Are you Allah?" he would first have rent his clothes and then cut your head off. If you had

---

[8]Huston Smith, "Postmodernism and the World's Religions," in *The Truth About Truth*, ed. Walter Truett Anderson (New York: G. P. Putnam's Sons, 1995), p. 209.

asked Confucius, "Are you Heaven?", I think he would have probably replied, "Remarks which are not in accordance with nature are in bad taste." The idea of a great moral teacher saying what Christ said is out of the question. In my opinion, the only person who can say that sort of thing is either God or a complete lunatic suffering from that form of delusion which undermines the whole mind of man.[9]

Consider the reality of antithesis concerning God. If God is a personal being who exists eternally as three equal persons (the Father, Son and Holy Spirit), then divine reality is not (1) one in a unitarian sense (Islam, Judaism or Unitarianism), (2) an impersonal-amoral consciousness (some versions of Hinduism, Buddhism and New Age thinking), (3) nonexistent (Theraveda Buddhism, Jainism and secular forms of atheism), (4) many gods (Mormonism, Shinto and other forms of polytheism, animism), and so on. Given the confusions of postmodernity, much work must be done on the level of enunciating the very claims Christians believe, even before specifically defending those claims as true.

Steve Turner's satirical "Creed," which summarizes the perplexities of postmodern perspectives, makes this point well:

We believe that all religions are basically the same
at least the one that we read was.
They all believe in love and goodness
They only differ on matters of
creation sin heaven hell God and salvation.

Having made Christianity's irreducible and nonnegotiable truth claims as clear as possible, apologists should engage in both negative and positive apologetic efforts. Negative apologetics can be taken to mean two things: deflecting criticism of the Christian worldview and philosophically criticizing non-Christian worldviews. Positive apologetics has to do with giving evidence and arguments for core Christian claims. Both are strategic in the postmodern context.

In the next chapter we will address the notion that metanarratives intrinsically oppress outsiders. That is the case for some worldviews

---

[9]C. S. Lewis, *God in the Dock: Essays on Theology and Ethics*, ed. Walter Hooper (Grand Rapids, Mich.: Eerdmans, 1970), pp. 157-58.

(such as Marxist Leninism) but not for Christianity rightly understood, which is a faith rooted in God's love, grace and justice. This contrast should be made clear to postmodernists who suspect that all comprehensive views are latently totalitarian.

As I have emphasized earlier, claiming that the Christian viewpoint is true does not imply that any Christian's knowledge is comprehensive or perfect. The absoluteness of truth does not imply the absoluteness of our human knowledge. Nevertheless, God ordains that we use "jars of clay" to present the gospel to a lost world (2 Cor 4:7). As Richard John Neuhaus put it, "God's truth is strong enough to survive its passage through you and me."[10]

Exposing Postmodernist Nihilism

Negative apologetics entails zeroing in on the defects of the postmodernist way of thinking. Chesterton captured the activity of exposing philosophical error brilliantly in his novel *The Man Who Was Thursday,* where a character describes the "work of the philosophical policeman" who

> is at once bolder and more subtle than that of the ordinary detective. The ordinary detective goes to pot-houses to arrest thieves; we go to artistic tea-parties to detect pessimists. The ordinary detective discovers from a ledger or a diary that a crime has been committed. We have to trace the origin of those dreadful thoughts that drive men on at least to intellectual fanaticism and intellectual crime.[11]

One salient element in challenging postmodernism is to demonstrate that with respect to ethics and meaning in life, it reduces to nihilism. While existentialism was a kind of revolt against nihilism, whereby the individual self valiantly created (or tried to create) personal meaning in a meaningless world,[12] postmodernism shuns such heroism and simply accepts the free play of culture without too much seriousness. Baudrillard describes postmodernism like this:

---

[10]Neuhaus, *Freedom for Ministry,* p. 168.

[11]G. K. Chesterton, *The Man Who Was Thursday* (New York: G. P. Putnam's Sons, 1908), p. 42.

[12]For an excellent treatment of existentialism, see James W. Sire, *The Universe Next Door,* 3rd ed. (Downers Grove, Ill.: InterVarsity Press, 1997), pp. 94-117.

The characteristic of a universe where there are no more definitions possible. . . . One is no longer in a history of art or a history of forms. They have been deconstructed, destroyed. In reality, there is no more reference to forms. It has all been done. The extreme limit of these possibilities has been reached. It has destroyed itself. It has deconstructed its entire universe. So all that are left are pieces. All that remains to be done is to play with the pieces. Playing with the pieces—that is postmodern.[13]

Baudrillard is being characteristically cryptic, but the gist is that reality has lost its form, its meaning, its significance and its intelligibility. A thoroughly deconstructed universe is not a uni-verse but a plura-verse or multi-verse, which resists comprehension and cohesion and offers only chaos. When everything is deconstructed, no original remains. Everything is disconnected, fragmented and blown into a billion pieces—with which we can play. It is as if a stained glass window, which offered a pictorial message of a reality beyond itself when illuminated by the sun, were shattered into countless fragments, which a bemused onlooker is now rearranging into every pattern but its lost original.

Postmodernity may look and feel that way, at least when one is divorced from the supernatural revelation proffered through Christ and the Scriptures. But the "play" of the postmodern, in Baudrillard's sense, is hardly enjoyable or even recreational. It cannot re-create. Playing only has meaning in relation to non-playful activities (such as work or sleep), which serve to offset or bracket it. Play has historically been associated with joy or even ecstasy, wherein a kind of transcendence is experienced. Play may create an openness to a dimension of enjoyment outside the boundaries of the mundane. Peter Berger has even developed an argument for God and the supernatural from the social fact of play.[14] The nature of play evokes a kind of timelessness and innocence that Berger takes to be a "signal of transcendence" even within the es-

---

[13]Jean Baudrillard, "Interview: Game with Vestiges," *On the Beach* 5 (winter 1984): 24; quoted in Douglas Kellner, *Media Culture: Cultural Studies, Identity and Politics Between the Modern and the Postmodern* (New York: Routledge, 1995), p. 329. See also Richard Keyes, *Chameleon Christianity: Moving Beyond Safety and Conformity* (Grand Rapids, Mich.: Baker, 1999), p. 61.

[14]Peter Berger, *A Rumor of Angels: Modern Society and the Rediscovery of the Supernatural*, 2nd ed. (New York: Doubleday, 1990), pp. 65-68.

sential patterns of human culture.[15] C. S. Lewis also argued that experiences of deep "joy" indicate a reality beyond the material, to which our souls are sometimes exposed and in which they gratefully delight.[16]

But for the "saturated self" of postmodernism, the mundane, while multiform, is all that remains. One may rearrange the debris in any number of contingent ways, but there is no original order and no image that reflects a reality outside of itself. It is self-referring all the way down, over and over again. These fragments are not pieces of a puzzle, but puzzling pieces inducing an irreducible bafflement that can only succumb to a resignation, an exhaustion, in which all is tolerated because nothing is worthy of allegiance. Dorothy L. Sayers identified this tendency before the ascension of postmodernism:

> In the world it calls itself Tolerance; but in hell it is called Despair. It is the accomplice of the other sins and their worst punishment. It is the sin which believes nothing, cares for nothing, seeks to know nothing, interferes with nothing, enjoys nothing, loves nothing, hates nothing, finds purpose in nothing, lives for nothing, and only remains alive because there is nothing it would die for.[17]

The apologist for Christ must seize on the dizzying meaninglessness of postmodernism and name it for what it is—nihilism, a nihilism that naturally induces the kind of sloth that Sayers condemned as sin. This nihilism encompasses ethics, purpose and personal identity in its merciless grasp. Playing with fragments is no play at all, but a mere diversion from the loss of meaning, a vanity. Vanity takes many forms, especially in an entertainment-saturated day, but at the end of the day—or when the power goes out—nothing remains but nothing.

This condition is unlivable—if taken seriously. The structure of human action presupposes goals and goods that are intrinsic, what Charles Taylor calls "hyper-goods" or ultimate goods. These goods are

---

[15]Ibid., p. 59.

[16]See C. S. Lewis, *The Weight of Glory and Other Addresses*, rev. ed. (New York: Macmillan, 1965), pp. 3-19.

[17]Dorothy Sayers, *Christian Letters to a Post-Christian World* (Grand Rapids, Mich.: Eerdmans, 1969), xi, p. 4; quoted in Richard Keyes, *True Heroism* (Colorado Springs, Colo.: NavPress, 1995), p. 135.

not in service of something else but good in their own right and cannot be explained in terms of what is nonmoral. Hyper-goods are "goods which not only are incomparably more important than others but provide the standpoint from which these must be weighed, judged, decided about."[18] These hyper-goods constitute our moral being; they cannot be dismissed without extreme self-deception and logical contradiction, as when someone says: "There is no moral law; and you'd better believe it for your own good." Even the most blatant of postmodernists—such as Rorty, who sees truth as what his peers let him get away with saying[19]—still feels moral outrage at things like female genital mutilation and slavery in Sudan and elsewhere.[20]

If evil is deconstructed into incommensurate language games, perspectives and final vocabularies, no evil remains—but the evil of its attempted banishment and the haunting impression that something is deeply amiss. At the other end, when all objective beauty—that which inspires praise and respect—is similarly deconstructed into meaninglessly collocations of fragments, one's sense of elation at a Bach pipe organ recital or a John Coltrane soprano saxophone solo becomes merely emotive—without transcendence, without objective value.[21] Moral heroism is dissolved in the same postmodernist solvents. The "heroes" (never forget the quotation marks; without them, postmodernism dies of overexposure) are debunked as opportunists with a savvy for public relations.[22] Virtues such as courage, prudence and humility are not things in themselves to be praised in those who bear them, but fronts, mere facades, rooted not in character but in conventions, which are rooted in cultures, which are rooted in . . . themselves. This means that virtues are rooted nowhere and in nothing; they float everywhere at random, but are sometimes mistaken for items of objective value. It is all explained

---

[18]Charles Taylor, *Sources of the Self* (Cambridge, Mass.: Harvard University Press, 1989), p. 63; see pp. 63-73 for a developed discussion.

[19]Richard Rorty, *Philosophy and the Mirror of Nature* (New York: Princeton University Press, 1979), p. 176. See Alvin Plantinga, *Warranted Christian Belief* (New York: Oxford University Press, 2000), pp. 429-36.

[20]Rorty's views on ethics are taken up in detail in the next chapter.

[21]I discuss artistic beauty and truth in relation to postmodernism in chapter ten.

[22]For a biblical view of heroism, see Keys, *True Heroism*.

away, with a wink and a smirk and a shrug. As C. S. Lewis put it in 1944, when one sees through everything, there is nothing left to see.

> You cannot go on "explaining away" for ever: you will find that you have explained explanation itself away. You cannot go on "seeing through" things for ever. The whole point of seeing through something is to see something through it. It is good that the window should be transparent, because the tree or garden beyond it is opaque. How if you saw through the garden too? It is no use trying to "see through" first principles. If you see through everything, then everything is transparent. But a wholly transparent world is an invisible world. To "see through" all things is the same as not to see.[23]

A reflective account of the human condition requires that we praise the good, condemn the evil and the ugly, and seek purpose and value in our activities. First principles remain, despite stupefactions and deconstructions and redescriptions. The Christian worldview explains this fact handily. We are meaning-seeking beings, because we were created to exist within the meaning of God's universe. But as fallen creatures east of Eden, our quest for meaning goes awry as we try to erase the divine from the landscape, deface the divine through caricature, or simply escape our hungers and dissatisfactions through diversions.

Postmodern Diversions and the Testimony of Human Need

Blaise Pascal goes to great lengths to expose the diverse diversions that prohibit people from seeking truth in matters of ultimate significance. He argues that diversions insinuate that humans seek out various activities in order to deny their misery and their need for God. Their very escape from God testifies to their need of God. For Pascal in the seventeenth century, diversion consisted of hunting, games and other amusements. The repertoire of diversion was infinitesimal compared with what is available in the postmodern world, whether in cyberspace—CD-ROM games, various fantasy environments, video games, e-mail, chat rooms—or on television, at the movies, at amusement parks or any number of other means of omnipresent entertainment. Nevertheless,

---

[23]C. S. Lewis, *The Abolition of Man* (New York: Macmillan, 1975), pp. 86-87.

the human psychology of diversion remains the same. Diversion consoles us in the face of our miseries. Yet, paradoxically, it becomes the worst of our miseries because it hinders us from thinking about our true condition and deceives us into believing that we are in no danger of being destroyed. If not for diversion, we would "be bored, and boredom would drive us to seek some more solid means of escape, but diversion passes our time and brings us imperceptibly to our death."[24]

Diversion serves to distract humans from a plight too terrible to stare in the face, namely, our mortality, finitude and sinfulness. Pascal unmasks diversion for what it is—an attempt to escape reality, and an indication of something unstable and strange in the human condition. Interest in, and addiction to, entertainment is more than silly or frivolous. It is revelatory of a moral and spiritual malaise begging for an explanation. Our condition is "inconstancy, boredom, anxiety."[25] Humans face an incorrigible mortality that drives us to distractions designed to overcome the inevitable by means of the impossible: finding satisfaction and release through empty activity that masquerades as worthwhile.

> Man is obviously made for thinking. Therein lies all his dignity and his merit; and his whole duty is to think as he ought. Now the order of thought is to begin with ourselves, and with our author and our end.
>
> Now what does the world think about? Never about that, but about dancing, playing the lute, singing, writing verse, tilting at the ring, etc., and fighting, becoming king, without thinking what it means to be a king or to be a man.[26]

Diversions would not be blameworthy if they were recognized as such: trivial or otherwise distracting activities engaged in to occasionally avoid the harsh and unhappy realities of human life. However, self-deception also comes into play. In the end "we run heedlessly into the abyss after putting something in front of us to stop us seeing it."[27] Ac-

---

[24]Blaise Pascal, *Pensees*, ed. Alban Krailsheimer (New York: Penguin, 1966), 414/171, p. 148.
[25]Ibid., 24/127, p. 36.
[26]Ibid., 620/146, p. 235.
[27]Ibid., 166/183, p. 82.

cording to Pascal, this condition illustrates the corruption of human nature. Humans are strangely not at home in their universe. They are
scarcely content to sit quietly in their own rooms. "If our condition
were truly happy we should feel no need to divert ourselves from
thinking about it."[28]

Pascal says "there was once in man a true happiness, of which all
that now remains is the empty print and trace," which he "tries in vain
to fill with everything around him, seeking in things that are not there
the help he cannot find in those that are." This, however, is futile because an "infinite abyss can be filled only with an infinite and immuta-
ble object; in other words by God himself."[29] "Grace fills empty spaces,"
according to Simone Weil, "but it can only enter where there is a void to
receive it, and it is grace itself which makes this void."[30] Ecclesiastes
adds that God has put eternity into the human heart (3:11).

The compulsive search for diversion is often an attempt to escape the
wretchedness of life. We have great difficulty being quiet in our own
rooms, even when the television or color computer screen offers an
overabundance of possible stimulations and simulations. Postmodern
souls adrift from Christ are restless; they seek solace in diversion instead of satisfaction in truth. As Pascal said, "Our nature consists in
movement; absolute rest is death."[31]

The postmodern condition is one of oversaturation and overstimula-
tion, which caters to our propensity to divert ourselves from higher realities. In such a culture as this, the Christian apologist should not
shrink back from explaining the stakes involved concerning the truth of
the gospel. We are not merely manipulating religious symbols or outlining pragmatic preferences. One cannot medicate one's worries forever.
A day of reckoning awaits us all. As Pascal warned, "Between us and
heaven and hell there is only this life, the most fragile thing in the
world."[32] This fragility should drive us to our knees, not deeper into

---

[28]Ibid., 70/165b, p. 48.
[29]Ibid., 148/429, p. 75.
[30]Simone Weil, *Gravity and Grace* (New York: Routledge, 1992), p. 10.
[31]Pascal, *Pensees*, 641/129, p. 238.
[32]Ibid., 152/213, p. 81. I have altered the translation slightly to make it clearer.

more diversions. These truths offer hope but also hurt our hubris.

Despite the supposed playfulness of postmodernism and its endless diversions, the inevitability of death remains a reminder of our fragile lot after the Fall. Pascal's parable painfully captures this:

> Imagine a number of men in chains, all under sentence of death, some of whom are each day butchered in the sight of the others; those remaining see their own condition in that of their fellows, and looking at each other with grief and despair await their turn. This is an image of the human condition.[33]

Christian defenders of the faith in postmodern times need to communicate the realities of what truth is, and to contend against the nihilism of postmodernism and it multiplicity of diversions. They must also appeal to right reason in the quest for truth. While I cannot offer a complete apologetic method here, I will outline several points contested by those who embrace aspects of postmodernist thinking. We begin with foundations.

Rudiments of Apologetic Method

Foundationalism is a kind of theory of knowledge that holds that some truths serve as the basis for other truths, that we build on the more certain items of our knowledge. Postmodernists reject foundationalism in favor of some kind of pragmatism or coherence view of truth.[34] They argue that there are no indubitable truths from which we argue, no set of beliefs that we can call everyone to affirm and from which we can build an argument for the Christian worldview. Postmodernists typically lump together all types of foundationalism as versions of Descartes's project and think they have thereby destroyed it all. But this is naive and false.

The kind of foundationalism necessary to apologetics need not be Cartesian through and through. There is no reason to claim that all our beliefs can be deductively proven from indubitable first principles, or

---

[33]Ibid., 434/199, p.165.
[34]It is granted that some thinkers who are not postmodern also reject foundationalism. I critique the coherence and pragmatic views of truth in chapter four.

that all our beliefs must be of necessary truths (a triangle has three sides) or be based on empirical evidence (the earth is round). Some beliefs are "properly basic," in that they are not logical necessities, but neither are they proven on the basis of other things more certainly known. One candidate for a properly basic belief is "there is a real past." One cannot marshal evidence for this; it is a presupposition of normal thought. An extreme skeptic could doubt it by claiming we are somehow deceived into thinking there is a past when there is not, by virtue of a malfunctioning brain or a powerful malevolent being who always deceives us. While this is a logically possible state of affairs, there is no positive reason to believe it. However, there is no reason to reject basic beliefs as long as they are not contradicted by empirical evidence, intrinsically illogical or out of alignment with things that we know.[35]

What is essential to foundationalism is simply that some core of beliefs do serve as first principles; they are not derived from other beliefs, and they are not relative to cultures or individuals. The basic defect of nonfoundationalist views is that they make worldviews relative to communities and thus not open to independent assessment according to universal rational principles. Without some foundations for knowledge, crosscultural apologetics loses its rational power.[36] A foundationalism for apologetics will, minimally, affirm two broad principles.

1. There are essential truths of logic that are necessary for all intelligible thought and rational discourse, Christian or otherwise. These are not contextually derived or person-relative. They are intrinsic to the rational nature God has granted us. The law of noncontradiction and excluded middle—which I discussed earlier—are included in this foun-

---

[35]The debate over the nature and scope of basic beliefs is quite involved. Alvin Plantinga has been very influential in this debate, although I don't agree with all of his views on the matter. See Alvin Plantinga, *The Analytical Theist: An Alvin Plantinga Reader*, ed. James F. Sennett (Grand Rapids, Mich.: Eerdmans, 1998), pp. 97-209. For Pascal's comments on what are now called basic beliefs, see *Pensees*, 110/282, p. 58; 131/434, pp. 62-66.

[36]For a good summary of the recent debate over foundationalism and a brief defense of foundationalism, see Paul K. Moser, "Foundationalism," in *The Cambridge Dictionary of Philosophy*, ed. Robert Audi (New York: Cambridge University Press, 1995), pp. 276-78.

dation.[37] Any worldview should be tested by these criteria. If a worldview contradicts itself (by affirming one thing and denying the same thing) or fails to be consistent with external facts of history, the cosmos, morality or common human experience, it is false.[38]

2. There are also basic forms of reasoning that are nonnegotiable and are universally valid; they are not matters of contingent social construction or personal taste. Arthur Holmes puts it well, "Good logic is one of God's good gifts, and it is essential to thinking in this and any world."[39] For instance, the principle of *modus ponens* says: If p, then q; p; therefore, q. This form of reasoning has been known and used by various peoples at various times, because it is universally valid. The Australian aborigine rightly thinks, *If I shoot the poison dart into the animal, it will die. I hit the animal with the dart. Therefore, it will die.* The postmodern American rightly thinks, *If I fail to file my income tax, the IRS will be after me. I forgot to file my taxes. Therefore, the IRS will be after me.* Both are appealing to the same foundational form of right reasoning.

Or consider the principle of *modus tolens*: If p, then q; not q; therefore, not p. A French painter thinks, *If I am to learn to paint in the surrealistic style, then I must immerse myself in studying the surrealist style. I will not study the surrealists. Therefore, I will never learn to paint in the surrealist style.* The Bible says, "If one is born again, one will love Christian brothers and sisters." If you observe someone who, while claiming to be a Christian, does not love Christians, you may infer that this person is not born again (see 1 Jn 3:11-24). Both the artist and the apostle are using the same form of reasoning. There is nothing contextual or relative about it. The apostle does not use some special "religious logic." These

---

[37]I also include the related principles of identity and bivalence.

[38]On testing religious worldviews by criteria, see Harold Netland, *Dissonant Voices: Religious Pluralism and the Question of Truth* (1991; reprint, Vancouver, B.C.: Regent College Publishing, 1997), pp. 151-95; Keith E. Yandell, *Christianity and Philosophy* (Grand Rapids, Mich.: Eerdmans, 1984), pp. 272-89; Gordon R. Lewis, "An Integrative Method of Justifying Religious Assertions," in *Evangelical Apologetics*, ed. Michael Bauman, David Hall and Robert Newman (Camp Hill, Penn: Christian Publications, 1996), pp. 69-88; and more generally, Sire, *Universe Next Door*.

[39]Arthur Holmes, *Contours of a Worldview* (Grand Rapids, Mich.: Eerdmans, 1983), p. 131.

forms are foundational to argument and knowledge, postmodernism to the contrary.[40]

The importance of these two points is that although Christianity does make many truth claims that are unique to the Christian faith—such as, Jesus rose from the dead, God is triune and so on—an apologetic for the objective, absolute and universal truth of Christianity employs logical criteria that are not relative to or limited to Christianity. Otherwise, the Christian faith would be intellectually insulated and apologetics rendered impossible.[41]

Christian truth is public truth—truth for the marketplace that can be assessed according to universal criteria by any thinking person who is willing to consider it openly, seriously and humbly (see Mt 7:7). This is what Paul declared on Mars Hill before the non-Christian thinkers of his day (Acts 17:22-31). Unlike the postmodernist version I gave at the beginning of this chapter, Paul affirmed the following propositions:

1. Athenian religion is objectively inadequate because it lacks Christ (vv. 22-23).

2. God is the Creator of all and cannot be reduced to idols. The Athenians' idolatrous worship is false before the fact of God (vv. 24-25).

3. God is the sovereign source of every human being and has marked out each one's habitation and place in history (v. 26).

4. God did this so that people would seek him and perhaps find him (v. 27).

5. A non-Christian Greek thinker's writings expand on point 4 (v. 28).

6. Since we are God's creatures, God should not be depicted by an image made by human skill (v. 29). It fits neither God nor us.

7. God overlooked the race's previous ignorance, but now commands all people everywhere to repent (v. 30).

8. God has decreed a day when the world will be rightly judged by the risen Christ (v. 31).

---

[40]On the use of logical argument across religious traditions, see Paul Griffiths, *An Apology for Apologetics* (Maryknoll, N.Y.: Orbis, 1991).
[41]This concern was addressed in chapter six in relation to Lesslie Newbigin's claims.

9. God has proven point 8 for all people by raising Christ from the dead in history (v. 31).

Paul is setting forth claims concerning objective truths. These truths can be known by those who presently hold another worldview. He appeals to the objective evidence of Christ's resurrection from the dead as evidence available to convince these people. He does not encourage them to join his community or language game, redescribe life along his lines or accept Christianity because it has a tight web of belief. Public truth demands universal access—although we should not expect universal assent because of the darkness of unrepented sin (2 Cor 4:4). Throughout the book of Acts Paul engages in dialogue and dispute with unbelievers, both Jewish and Gentile. Never do we find him employing the strategies recommended by postmodernists of our day. That would have been intellectually suicidal and counterproductive to the cause. The same is true for us today because God's truth has not changed, and humans are still made in the image of God, corrupted by sin and redeemable though the work of Jesus Christ, God Incarnate.

Appeal to the Best Explanation

Within the kind of minimal foundationalism described above, the best way to defend the truth of Christ is by presenting the Christian vision as the most cogent explanation for a whole range of facts in accordance with the essential tenets of logic and criteria for evidence that are required for all critical thinking. This is sometimes called a cumulative case method or abductive argumentation. Christianity is presented as an explanatory hypothesis that best accounts for a wide range of facts about the universe, humans and history. (A less effective apologetic is deductive argumentation where conclusions supposedly follow with necessity from premises that everyone accepts.)[42]

In a cumulative case argument Christianity is presented as a full-

---

[42]On the limits of deduction in apologetics, see Winfried Corduan, *No Doubt About It: A Defense of Christianity* (Nashville: Broadman & Holman, 1997), pp. 50-54. On abductive or cumulative case explanation, see Basil Mitchell, *The Justification of Religious Belief* (New York: Oxford University Press, 1981); and Gordon Lewis, *Testing Christianity's Truth-Claims* (Chicago: Moody Press, 1976).

orbed worldview (or conceptual system) that best accounts for life in every dimension. Christian apologists need not ask people to take a blind leap of faith in the dark, or to play with a new language game to see if it helps them somehow, or to join a new community for the sake of joining a new community. We claim it is rational to hold Christian claims—more rational, in fact, than believing any other worldview. To make this kind of case with respect to postmodernism, we appeal to several areas.

1. The postmodernist worldview collapses in on itself with respect to being logically inconsistent, morally inadequate, and unable to identify and meet the deepest human needs (see 2 Cor 10:3-5). It is ultimately a house of cards.

2. The universe as a contingent and designed system is best explained by a noncontingent Creator, who depends on nothing outside himself (Acts 17:25) and who created the universe to operate in various goal-related ways. Living systems presuppose intelligent design and cannot be explained on the basis of merely chance and natural laws. Naturalism, the postmodernist default position, is not credible given the vast evidence for an intelligent Creator and Designer.

3. The only basis for an objective moral law is the existence of an objective moral lawgiver who is the source, standard, and stipulator of what is good for his creation and what brings honor to the Creator. Morality is far more than social construction or personal preference; it demands a transcendent and personal source and judge.

4. The Christian worldview best explains the human condition as that of "deposed royalty" (Pascal). We are not mere animals, nor are we gods. The evidence of history and psychology shows us to be unique in the universe, but also fatally flawed apart from the redeeming grace of God in Christ. We are great and we are depraved. Scripture accounts for this paradoxical polarity on the basis of our original creation in the image of God and our subsequent fall into sin. Pascal's apologetic insights on the explanatory value of Christian theism for anthropology are extremely pertinent for postmoderns grappling with the meaning of personal identity.[43]

---

[43]See Douglas Groothuis, "Deposed Royalty: Pascal's Anthropological Argument," *Journal of the Evangelical Theological Society* 41 no. 2 (1998): 297-312. This argument uses the abductive form of reasoning.

5. The various kinds of spiritual experiences of a personal and moral God, as recorded in the New Testament (Rev 1:12-17) and in Christian history and Old Testament figures (Is 6:1-8), cannot be explained away as delusions or myths. God has revealed himself to certain people directly and has provided a moral direction and inner experience not explicable in nontheistic ways.

6. Christianity makes a host of historical claims, culminating in the report that Jesus Christ rose from the dead. The study of history is not arbitrary or reducible to political or idiosyncratic methods, as postmodernists claim. A careful study of history shows that these claims are credible and cogent. An antisupernatural prejudice against miracle-claims should be ruled out, given the arguments for theism that make miracles possible and by virtue of the authentic nature of the scriptural documents. History matters for Christian theism.

7. Given his incomparable claims and credentials, Jesus' identity is best explained by the historic Christian claim that he was God incarnate. Other explanations—that he was a guru, a social reformer or an impostor—do not fit the facts. As God incarnate, Jesus is the only avenue of spiritual liberation and escape from divine judgment and, therefore, should be followed as Lord of the universe and of one's life.

Apologists should not only defend the rationality of Jesus as Lord but also encourage unbelievers to expose themselves to the Gospel narratives (about which many are ignorant). Here we find many unforgettable micronarratives inseparably wedded to the metanarrative of God's grand design for the universe, the Word become flesh for the purpose of personal and cosmic redemption (Jn 1:14). There is an apologetic force simply in the thoughtful reading of the accounts of Jesus' incomparable life, as I experienced myself in 1976. Questions regarding specific apologetic issues may be generated out of such exposure to the reliability of the Gospel accounts (see point 6), but direct exposure to the life of Christ through Scripture is in itself a powerful apologetic that must not be ignored by the apt apologist.[44]

8. Apologetic endeavors should make clear that Christianity is a high stakes situation prudentially: a matter of heaven or hell. If the gospel is

---

[44]My thanks to James Sire for asking me to flesh out this vital element of apologetics.

true and one rejects it, there are deleterious consequences in this life
and beyond. One forfeits fellowship with God and his followers on
earth, and inherits unending estrangement from God and all good beyond the grave. If the gospel is true and one accepts it, there are beneficial consequences in this life and beyond: fellowship with God and his
people as well as unending fellowship with God and all the redeemed
in the world to come. These prudential stakes often need to be made
clear to postmoderns, who are typically so satiated with stimuli and so
subjectivistic that they have become numb to matters of eternity. Apologists should invoke the resources of heaven and hell in order to demonstrate that one's response to truth has staggering consequences, and
that one must take Christ, the Judge of history, seriously.[45]

9. The Christian life centered on Jesus Christ—involving prayer,
worship, biblical knowledge and meditation, service, fellowship, evangelism and so on—provides the most compelling and engaging meaning for life available. Given the realism and hope that Scripture
supplies, a biblical way of life also promotes both personal and social
integrity, which avoids both utopianism and pessimism.

These nine considerations (and there are more) all decisively con-
verge on the objective truth of Christian theism: the triune God has created the universe and provides redemption and reconciliation through
Jesus Christ, the Messiah. Because of the resurgence of Christians involved in intellectual life, particularly philosophy, the Christian community has a treasury of resources from which to draw apologetically. It
is ironic and distressing that when Christian theism and evangelicalism
are coming out of a time of intellectual withdrawal and paralysis, many
Christian intellectuals intoxicated by postmodernism would deprive
the church of the solid apologetic resources that are readily available.
This should not be. Consider two examples of exemplary apologetics.

Two Apologetic Models

William Lane Craig is a prolific writer and speaker who holds earned

---

[45]On the prudential aspect to apologetics, see Douglas Groothuis, "Two Objections to
Pascal's Wager," *Religious Studies* 30 (1994): 479-86.

doctorates in philosophy (under John Hick) and theology (under Wolf-hart Pannenberg). While Craig publishes widely in the academic realm, he also writes at a popular level and engages in public debates with atheists, agnostics, Muslims, liberal Christians and others. These debates often draw hundreds of believers and unbelievers at college campuses and elsewhere. Craig is no postmodernist! If he were, he would not be defending the objective truth of Christianity rationally as he has done so well in so many venues. He employs arguments and evidence for the rationality of the Christian truth claim.[46]

Since the publication of his book *Darwin on Trial* in 1991, law professor Phillip Johnson has led a movement that intellectually challenges Darwinian naturalism by demonstrating its logical and evidential inadequacies.[47] He is mounting a credible attack against a leading ideological opponent of Christian theism today and defending the contention that the intelligent design of living systems is far more rational than mere evolution through natural laws and chance mutations.[48] Postmodernist strategies cannot avail in these environs; we need rational persuasion and shrewd strategy.[49]

There are many other Christians engaging the apologetic arena through public debates, editorials, letters to the editor, campus ministry, teaching in secular schools, writing books and articles in scholarly and popular circles, and more. The nerve of these ministries would be cut by the postmodernist ploys evaluated throughout this book. I can speak from fairly extensive experience in addressing secular university audiences that an emphasis on the objectivity and rationality of Christian truth will get a fair hearing when it is presented clearly, with passion and much prayer. There is no reason to change strategies now.[50]

---

[46]For his general apologetic approach, see William Lane Craig, *Reasonable Faith* (Wheaton, Ill.: Crossway, 1994).

[47]Phillip E. Johnson, *Darwin on Trial*, rev. ed. (Downers Grove, Ill.: InterVarsity Press, 1993).

[48]See William A. Dembski, ed., *Mere Creation: Science, Faith & Intelligent Design* (Downers Grove, Ill.: InterVarsity Press, 1998), and William A. Dembski, *Intelligent Design* (Downers Grove, Ill.: InterVarsity Press, 1999).

[49]I also discuss intelligent design in chapter four.

[50]Christian philosopher J. P. Moreland, who has spoken to many more such audiences than I have, concurred on this point in a conversation with me.

The Need for Objective Truth and Subjective Engagement

Apologists need to be sensitive to postmodern realities with respect to the subject addressed and the capacities of one's audience. Several decades ago an apologist could usually launch right into a defense of Christianity as objectively true and rational. Today, in many settings, particularly that of the secular university, one needs to defend the notions of objectivity and rationality themselves before employing them apologetically. I have argued that this can and should be done. Only then will the traditional apologetic arguments have much force. I do this myself when I speak to campus groups at secular institutions.

While apologetics needs to be *truth-centered*, it must also be *person-sensitive* and *culturally aware*. Unbelievers come to the table with a variety of issues, misconceptions and values that need to be discerned before for a fruitful apologetic encounter can occur. The truths for which we argue are not relative, but the level of knowledge of our hearers is relative and must be taken into account. An objectively good argument may ring hollow if it does not match the concerns of the hearer. Pascal understood the person-sensitivity of argumentation well.

> We think playing upon man is like playing upon an ordinary organ. It is indeed an organ, but strange, shifting and changeable. Those who only know how to play an ordinary organ would never be in tune on this one. You have to know where the keys are.[51]

David Clark's book *Dialogical Apologetics* addresses the issue of "knowing where the keys are" thoroughly and wisely. His thesis is that although solid arguments for Christian faith are available,

> apologetics . . . should not be understood as an attempt to develop a perfect system of assertion and argument that will prove faith once and for all. Rather, it is a strategy for presenting, in the course of a unique discussion with a particular audience, the sort of case that makes sense to those persons. In other words, apologetics is the reasoned defense of the Christian faith in the context of personal dialogue.[52]

---

[51]Pascal, *Pensees*, 56/181, p. 44.
[52]David K. Clark, *Dialogical Apologetics: A Person-Centered Approach to Christian Defense* (Grand Rapids, Mich.: Baker, 1993), p. 99.

This fits well with Arthur Holmes's insight that *metaphysical objectivity* is compatible with *epistemological subjectivity*. Objective reality exists in its own right apart from human knowers; it is metaphysically objective and representable through true statements. However, our knowledge of truth is influenced by a number of epistemologically subjective factors, such as our level of intelligence, background beliefs, personal interests and so on. The key error of the Enlightenment approach in this regard was not (as postmodernists maintain) a desire to discover objective truth but the assumption that subjectivity could be neutralized by one perfect method of rational knowing, which could be appropriated clinically by anyone so inclined.[53] This is an important distinction that many miss. Stanley Grenz, for example, sides with postmodernists against modernists by saying, "We must affirm with postmodern thinkers that knowledge—including knowledge of God—is not merely objective, not simply discovered by the neutral knowing self."[54] This seems to conflate "neutral" with "objective." No one is neutral, since we have a set of subjective dispositions and unique experiences. However, one may come to know objective truth if one sincerely applies the proper procedures of knowing.

Human knowing is a complex affair, involving the entire person over a lifetime. Nonetheless, the aim of knowing should be objective truth, subjectively interiorized and existentially engaged. Holmes puts it well:

> I can passionately believe in a certain objective reality without at all violating either my intellectual integrity or the universality of truth. I can believe in God, I can love my neighbor as myself, and I can accept a Christian world-view with all the subjective intensity of my being without compromising in the least the universal truth of theism, of Christian ethics, and of a Christian worldview. I believe all truth is God's truth, passionately, but that does not make it any less objectively real.[55]

---

[53]Arthur Holmes, *All Truth Is God's Truth* (Grand Rapids, Mich.: Eerdmans, 1977), pp. 6-7, 31-48.
[54]Stanley Grenz, *A Primer on Postmodernism* (Grand Rapids, Mich.: Eerdmans, 1996), p. 168.
[55]Holmes, *All Truth*, p. 6.

Still, subjectivity should be addressed carefully, given the subjectivism and relativism of the postmodern situation. It may have been wise in some ways for Kierkegaard to hyperbolically announce that "Truth is subjectivity," in nineteenth-century Denmark when the objective truth of Christianity was taken for granted and not subjectively engaged inwardly.[56] Such a strategy today would fail to affirm both metaphysical objectivity and epistemological subjectivity, since the scales have tipped in just the opposite direction in our postmodern situation. Countermanding truth decay requires highlighting and elucidating objective truth along with its subjective demands and its eternal benefits. Only the truth of Jesus Christ will set anyone free (Jn 8:31-32).

---

[56]On Kierkegaard's strategy, see Holmes, *All Truth*, pp. 43-48.

8

ETHICS WITHOUT REALITY, POSTMODERNIST STYLE

What remains of morality for postmodernism? How ought denizens of the postmodern condition conduct themselves morally regarding the perennial questions of the nature of the good life, the value of persons and the obligations of conscience? The answer depends on which postmodernist school or philosopher one is considering. Generally speaking, postmodernist ethics reject both the universalism of premodern ethics based on divine revelation and modernist ethical projects stemming from the ethical insights and principles of unaided human reason.

Some postmodernists may agree with Christians (and other theists) on certain ethical precepts, yet deny them any theological or metaphysical foundation. Richard Rorty, who describes himself as a "postmodernist bourgeois liberal," exemplifies such thinking. Having rejected the objective legitimacy of metanarratives (to use Lyotard's term) as offering transhistorical explanations for the self, God and social ordering, Rorty simply opts for the Western liberal tradition of ethics—without any metaphysical grounding in anything beyond itself. On this basis he says that he would honor the human rights of a wandering child who was "the remnant of a slaughtered nation whose temples have been razed and whose books have been burned."[1]

Christians would agree on the assumption that all human beings are made in the image and likeness of God and should be respected (Gen 1:26)—especially the most helpless of our race—because God calls us to preserve and conserve life (Ex 20:13). Not so for Rorty. Having thrown off any foundation for ethics based on the nature of persons or the reality of God, he simply says that "it is part of the tradition of *our* community that the human stranger from whom all dignity has been stripped is to be taken in, to be reclothed with dignity."[2] Rorty admits that according to his view, any sense of human dignity is culturally constructed through a tradition. It does not reside in the essence of humanity itself. Therefore, such an orphan from civilization would, strictly speaking, "have no share in human dignity," since she would be without any surrounding culture to provide it. But Rorty balks at this logical consequence and is glad for the "Jewish and Christian element in our tradition" that can be invoked by "freeloading atheists like myself."[3]

Nevertheless, Rorty reminds us an "ironist" does not claim that her "vocabulary is closer to reality than another, that it is in touch with a power not herself." Further, "anything can be made to look good or bad by being redescribed."[4] As a twentieth-century American, Rorty just happens to inherit an ethical tradition, largely based on Judeo-Christian concepts, that honors the alien and the stranger. This is just an accident of history, time and place. Gergen summarizes the basic postmodernist take on ethics: "For the postmodern there is no transcendent reality, rationality, or value system with which to rule between competitors."[5]

Of course, there is nothing in the nature of things to constrain a Rorty

---

[1]Richard Rorty, *Objectivity, Relativism, and Truth* (New York: Cambridge University Press, 1991), p. 201.
[2]Ibid., p. 202.
[3]Ibid.
[4]Richard Rorty, *Contingency, Irony, and Solidarity* (New York: Cambridge University Press, 1989), p. 73.
[5]Kenneth Gergen, *The Saturated Self* (New York: BasicBooks, 1991), p. 253.

or anyone else from simply ignoring—or torturing—such a cultureless child. A particularly clever "ironist" could simply "redescribe" the child—not as an orphan from civilization, an object of pity, but as a non-entity, something outside our community and thus worthless from our perspective. Rorty's agreement with a Christian conscience on this point is intrinsically whimsical, haphazard, arbitrary and contingent. Rorty on the one hand seems to admit this, but on the other hand he wants to live off the borrowed moral capital of a Judeo-Christian civilization despite the fact that he denies objective moral and spiritual truth, divine revelation and a determinate human nature possessing intrinsic moral and spiritual value.

Rorty and those influenced by him are working on the assumption that one *ought* to stay within one's moral tradition. There is no possible reason to do so, however, since placement within a particular culture has no inherent meaning or value or significance. Social constructions of value may coalesce and cohere within civilizations over time, but if their origin is merely within themselves, they have only the appearance of stability and legitimacy. It is all built on the shifting sands.

In an infamous passage Rorty says that "when the secret police come, when the torturers violate the innocent [even uprooted orphans?], there is nothing to be said to them of the form 'there is something within you which you are betraying . . . something beyond those [totalitarian] practices which condemns you.'"[6] This is because there "is nothing deep down inside us except what we have put there ourselves." All criteria, all standards and all argumentation are solely "obedience to our own conventions."[7]

Rorty tries to argue that his postmodernist position is not relativism, since he is not claiming that "every tradition is as rational or as moral as every other"—a claim that would be possible for a god who could survey them all.[8] He is maintaining only that we operate from within our own moral tradition and that we should not try to make metanarratival

---

[6]Richard Rorty, *Consequences of Pragmatism* (Minneapolis: University of Minnesota Press, 1982), p. xlii.

[7]Ibid.

[8]Rorty, *Objectivity, Relativism, and Truth*, p. 202.

assessments of other traditions. The ironist is "a nominalist and a historicist."[9] Our words cannot capture general or universal truths (moral or otherwise), and we are inextricably immersed in the language and thinking of our particular time in history. There are no ahistorical judgments between periods of history. Even in considering the Holocaust, we cannot appeal to moral truth beyond history and institutions.

> At times like that of Auschwitz, when history is in upheaval and traditional institutions and patterns of behavior are collapsing, we want something which stands beyond history and institutions. . . . I have been urging
> . . . that we try not to want something which stands beyond history and institutions.[10]

Our beliefs, according to Rorty, are "caused by nothing deeper than contingent historical circumstances."[11]

Protests notwithstanding, Rorty is still a relativist because he has no absolute, objective and universal standard for ethical evaluation. He need not claim that all traditions are equally rational or moral in order to affirm relativism. In fact, the concepts of rationality and morality fail to apply at all in his view, according to which they are contingent creations of disparate traditions with no moral or intellectual common ground. He is right to say that postmodernists are in no position—not having "the God's eye view"—to deem all cultures as created equal in rationality and morality. They are in no position to deem them as anything—moral or immoral or amoral. They have no eyes at all, let alone divine eyes. All they can say is "We do this and they do that."

Even though Rorty dissolves ethics into culture without remainder, he does possess and prescribe a metanarrative. First, he claims to be a "freeloading atheist"—a very telling admission of metaphysical guilt. As an atheist, he denies the objective existence of God. His universe is godless. This is far more than a cultural judgment; it is theological and cosmic in scope. Second, Rorty is also a confessed "*freeloading* atheist." A freeloader is one who takes advantage of something to which one has

---

9Rorty, *Contingency, Irony, and Solidarity*, p. 74.
10Ibid., p. 189.
11Ibid.

no right or privilege. A better word might be *parasite*, something that depends for its life on another entity without contributing anything positive to that entity. Rorty is admitting that his atheistic social constructivism or ironism does not warrant the existence of objective or universal human rights. Yet somehow he is drawn to altruism in the sad case of the abandoned orphan. Chalk it up to social influence and habituation. But the Christian knows better. The reality of Rorty's humanity (made in God's image with a conscience that recognizes moral value) pulls him in the right direction, while the logic of his postmodernism pulls him into the abyss. This tension is inescapable for such a position.[12]

Such tension is evident when Rorty admits that the ironist cannot move beyond "the language game of one's time." So she worries over "the possibility that she has been initiated into the wrong tribe, taught to play the wrong language game," such that she has been turned into "the wrong kind of human being." But the "criteria of wrongness" is unavailable to her, so she remembers her "rootlessness" by "consistently using terms like 'Weltanschauung,' 'perspective,' 'dialectic,' 'conceptual framework,' 'historical epoch,' 'language game,' 'redescription,' 'vocabulary,' and 'irony.'"[13]

Rorty is right that ethical reflection is contextual or embedded within a culture and a tradition. This is a truism with little philosophical force in itself. As philosopher Nicholas Reschler points out, our pyramids have a vertex at the top just as those of the ancient Egyptians; two shekels plus two shekels equals four shekels for Babylonians as well as for us; the interior angles of a plane triangle equal 180 degrees both for Euclid and for us.

> The fact that the affirmation of a fact must proceed from within a historio-cultural setting does not mean that the correctness and appropriateness of what is said will be restricted to such a setting. The fact that we make our

---

[12]On this humanistic dynamic, see Francis A. Schaeffer, *The God Who Is There*, 30th anniv. ed. (Downers Grove, Ill.: InterVarsity Press, 1998), pp. 147-54. See also Patrick Glynn, *God: The Evidence: The Reconciliation of Faith and Reason in a Postsecular World* (Rocklin, Calif.: Prima Publishing, 1997), pp. 140-48.

[13]Rorty, *Contingency, Irony, and Soldarity*, p. 75.

assertions within time does not prevent us from asserting timeless truths.[14]

The moral statement "All innocent orphans should be treated with dignity" is not culture-bound any more than are mathematical or geographical truths. Surely the burden of proof is on anyone who would assert otherwise, and Rorty gives us no reason to do so. The Judeo-Christian tradition, on which Rorty supposedly takes his stand, never considered such statements as self-generated, cultural creations but rather as reflecting objective moral truths—verities of the moral order based on the Law Giver. For Rorty to shear this tradition of its philosophical basis—by abandoning its theistic metanarrative in favor of atheism—is to strip it bare of its moral force as well.

Reification and Ethics

Rorty's rejection of moral foundations is typical of postmodern ethics. To ground one's moral positions in anything deeper than the vicissitudes of culture is to commit the error of reification—which consists in taking something that is constructed and contingent as being discovered and necessary. As Berger and Luckmann put it:

> Reification is the apprehension of human phenomenon as if they were things, that is, in non-human or possibly suprahuman terms. Another way of saying this is that reification is the apprehension of the products of human activity *as if* they were something else than human products—such as facts of nature, results of cosmic laws, or manifestations of divine will.[15]

For instance, if I insist that heterosexual monogamy is the one right way for sexual intimacy, then, according to postmodernism, I have fallen into reification—regardless of what I claim as the basis for my belief, whether natural law, Islamic law or biblical principle. This sup-

---

[14]Nicholas Rescher, *Objectivity: The Demands of Impersonal Reason* (Notre Dame, Ind.: University of Notre Dame Press, 1997), p. 61.

[15]Peter Berger and Thomas Luckmann, "The Dehumanized World," in *The Truth About Truth*, ed. Walter Truett Anderson (New York: G. P. Putnam's Sons, 1995), p. 36.

posed error is also known as moral realism: the belief that we can know objective moral principles that apply in reality. For the postmodernist, any community can set up norms for behavior. This is fine. The mistake is to reify or absolutize those norms and inflict them on other communities outside of their domain. The postmodernist position is one of moral nonrealism: the belief that there is no moral reality to be known apart from the cultures that create them. Philosopher Charles Taylor summarizes Rorty's take on it:

> Rorty offers a great leap into non-realism: where there have hitherto been thought to be facts or truths-of-the-matter, there turn out to be only rival languages, between which we end up plumping, if we do, because in some way one works better for us than the others.[16]

Postmodernist nonrealism differs from some earlier forms of relativism. Whereas an existentialist will say to the Christian, "You are too restrictive on sexual ethics! You must allow each person to determine sexual behavior through his or her own authentic choices—and nothing more," the postmodernist will say, "Christian ethics is fine for the Christian community. However, do not try to make them applicable outside of your community. Each community determines its own ways." One may keep Christian morals so long as they are demystified and disinfected of any residual absolutism.

Postmodernists opt for a thoroughly contextualized ethic partially because they fear the restrictive reign of metanarratives and their objective viewpoints. Full-orbed worldviews that make absolute claims about nature, humanity, God and ethics are, to use their jargon, "totalistic" and "hegemonic" and, therefore, dangerous. Reification on this scale leads to dehumanization and oppression. Gergen represents this position by saying that "totalizing discourses" must

> truncate, oppress, and obliterate alternative forms of social life. . . . To be convinced of the "truth" of a discourse is to find the alternatives foolish or

---

[16]Charles Taylor, "Rorty in the Epistemological Tradition," in *Reading Rorty*, ed. Alan R. Malachowski (Oxford: Basil Blackwell, 1990), p. 258; quoted in James Sire, *The Universe Next Door: A Basic Worldview Catalog*, 3rd ed. (Downers Grove, Ill.: InterVarsity Press, 1997), p. 188.

fatuous—to slander or silence the outside. . . . When convinced of the truth or right of a given worldview, a culture has only two significant options: totalitarian control of the opposition or annihilation of it.[17]

This critique, often voiced loudly by sundry postmodernists, is akin to condemning all medicine because some medications prove lethal or to damning all automobiles since so many occupants die in accidents. Not all metanarratives are of a piece. Postmodernism confuses a general category with some of degenerate members of that category. In so doing, it creates a straw man fallacy. Certainly, Marxist-Leninism is a metanarrative that leaves little room for dissent, freedom of speech, or political diversity. The Gulag is always more prominent than free elections or human rights. Marxists have traditionally attacked the motives of their opponents as bourgeois or reactionary rather than to engage their arguments rationally. Similarly, militantly Islamic states such as Iran and Iraq leave little freedom for religious pluralism or public debate on religious matters. Opposition is often annihilated or silenced. Christian believers are persecuted for their faith by various totalitarian states around the world, all of which claim that it is in the best interest of society to do so.

Communism has been responsible for upwards of one hundred million deaths in the twentieth century. The Marxist-Leninist and Islamic worldviews have led to much moral mischief, to put it mildly. Traditional Islam oppresses women and leaves little room for religious liberty. However, their fatal flaw does not inhere in their being metanarratives that make comprehensive claims about objective reality. (Even postmodernists do that in different ways, despite themselves.) Their moral error is attributable to their particular philosophical and theological falsehoods, not to the fact that they claim to be true.

The Christian worldview makes comprehensive truth claims, as we have seen in chapter three. It is incorrigibly a metanarrative: God's grand story about creation, the Fall, redemption and glorification. However, followers of Christ are never called to annihilate or silence their opposition. On the contrary, the Great Commission is premised on

---

[17]Gergen, *Saturated Self*, p. 252.

persuasion, not coercion; on argument, not propaganda; on evidence, not intimidation (Mt 28:18-20). Those commissioned are to teach the nations and make "disciples," not to make slaves. Peter calls believers to give unbelievers solid reasons for their faith, and to do this with gentleness and respect (1 Pet 3:15-17). Paul engaged unbelievers, both Jew and Gentile, in dialogue and debate throughout the book of Acts. He did not denounce them through diatribes or threaten them with recriminations.

Moreover, although Christians claim that the Bible gives us an accurate and sufficient revelation on all that it addresses (2 Tim 3:15-17; 2 Pet 1:20-21, 3:16), they should never claim to have totally mastered that holy book so as to be beyond correction or without need of more light from the Holy Spirit concerning ethics or theology. Even the apostle Paul confessed that "we see but a poor reflection as in a mirror" and that we now know only in part (1 Cor 13:12). Yet despite our myopia and dyslexia, the light dawns and moral truth may be known. "There may yet be more truth to break forth from God's word" as the saying goes.

The model of social involvement for the community of Jesus is to be salt and light (Mt 5:13-16), to preserve and further goodness, and to illuminate one's environment with truth. This involves loving our neighbors, loving even our enemies and praying for them—not preying on them (Mt 5:43-48). It embraces the blessedness of poverty, meekness, mourning, moral hunger, mercy, purity, peacemaking and even persecution on account of the righteousness of Christ (Mt 5:3-12). Arrogance is neither a gift nor a fruit of the Holy Spirit. The biblical metanarrative gives place to the downtrodden, the lost, the least and the forgotten (Mt 25:31-46). Jesus preached concern for the poor and proclaimed their liberation (Lk 4:18-19). Disciples of Jesus play leading roles in a great cosmic drama, narrated by the Creator himself. Their roles, however, are not scripted for destroying dissent, enforcing conversion through the sword, or turning a deaf ear to objections to their beliefs. Christian faith, at its best and truest, has always tackled the great intellectual, moral and social issues of the day with humility, passion, intelligence and grace. Consider carefully William Wilberforce (1759-1833), the chief architect and activist of the peaceful abolition of slavery in England.

Wilberforce: Against the World, for the World

Against all odds, against almost all of England, and seemingly ill fit for the daunting task, Wilberforce mounted a principled attack on the trading of human souls for slave labor. In 1787, Wilberforce—a small, physically unattractive man whose evangelical faith was not in political favor—proposed the abolition of slave trade to the Houses of Parliament. He later told the House of Commons:

> So enormous, so dreadful, so irremediable did the Trade's wickedness appear that my own mind was completely made up for Abolition. Let the consequences be what they would, I from this time determined that I would never rest until I had effected its abolition.[18]

A few months after his challenge to the political order, he famously wrote in his journal, "God Almighty has set before me two great objects, the suppression of the Slave Trade and the Reformation of Manners."[19] Despite a frail constitution and relentless opposition, Wilberforce worked for fifty years before his vision became a reality. Human beings would no longer be bought and sold like chattel by the British Empire. The slave trade was stopped in England in 1807. Only shortly before his death in 1833, a bill was passed forbidding slavery throughout the vast expanse of British colonies, to be effective as of 1834. This moral reformation transpired without bloody revolution or a civil war. Moral persuasion, over time, won the day and freed the slaves. The effect of the British Empire's abolition inspired abolition throughout the Western world.[20] The able historian of race, Thomas Sowell, one not prone to overstatement, writes that this "achievement was one of the most revolutionary in the history of the human race."[21]

According to Rorty's terms, Wilberforce was "a metaphysician" in that he believed that "there is a single permanent reality to be found be-

---

[18]Quoted in Os Guinness, *The Call: Finding and Fulfilling the Central Purpose of Your Life* (Nashville: Word, 1998), p. 27.
[19]Ibid.
[20]See Thomas Sowell, *Race and Culture* (New York: BasicBooks, 1994), pp. 211-12.
[21]Ibid., p. 211.

hind the many temporary appearances."[22] He was an "essentialist," someone who thinks that there are "intrinsic, context-independent" realities.[23] These benighted folks, according to Rorty,

> believe that there are, out there in the world, real essences which it is our duty to discover and which are disposed to assist in their own discovery. They do not believe that anything can be made to look good or bad by being redescribed—or, if they do, they deplore this fact and cling to the idea that reality will help us resist such seductions.[24]

Indeed, as Christians Wilberforce and his cohorts in the "Clapham Sect" believed that all human beings have an essence that makes them human in every historical and social context, irrespective of how they may be described or redescribed. They are God's creatures, whether African or British. This is reality. Wilberforce earnestly endeavored for fifty years against the redescription of humans as subhumans, as subservient to economic imperatives and the forces of British tradition and honor. Wilberforce won his battle, despite intense opposition, because he believed reality was on his side. The "little parliamentarian" believed that his language concerning the slave trade was not merely a new vocabulary that had a dialectical effect on his hearers. He was convinced that his words about the evil of slavery and the virtue of abolition, grounded in his painstaking research, corresponded to an objective moral reality—a reality far larger than social convention, established vocabularies and economic exigencies.

The Rortyian ironist, who confesses no transcendent moral principles, could have agreed with the Ottoman sultan who impatiently demurred when challenged by the British to end the Ottoman Empire's slave trade. The first response of the sultan was relayed by the British ambassador. He expressed

> extreme astonishment accompanied with a smile at a proposition for destroying an institution closely inter-woven with the frame of society in his country, and intimately connected with the law and with the habits

---

[22]Rorty, *Contingency, Irony, and Solidarity*, p. 74.
[23]Rorty, *Objectivity, Relativism, and Truth*, p. 99.
[24]Ibid., pp. 102-3.

and even the religion of all classes, from the Sultan himself on down to the lowest peasant.[25]

Although he did not use the term, Wilberforce's assessment of slavery was that it was a *reification*. Slavery was deemed by many at the time as a given of nature, something built into the fabric of things. Aristotle and many others believed that some people were slaves by nature and existed to serve their superiors. This was not a contingent social arrangement of power but integral to the world as we know it. However, as Wilberforce and other abolitionists proved, invoking the concept of reification is only helpful when it is contrasted with its opposite—objective realities. We know slavery to be a mere reification (however socially embedded) because we know the transcultural reality that human beings are essentially worthy of respect; they are not objects fit to be bought and sold. The reification of slavery as a fixed institution was unjust because justice itself is not a reification but an objective verity that places demands upon us as moral agents.

Value Creation: Rorty and Nietzsche

Rorty and his postmodernist cohorts would have us abandon such a "spirit of seriousness" (as Nietzsche put it) and moral gravity. Philosophers, according to Rorty, should engage in "light-minded aestheticism."[26] While other philosophers and moralists take the notion of moral truth and obligation seriously, Rortyians should "josh them out of the habit"[27] of such premodernist and modernist sobriety and cajole them into approaching moral issues more playfully. In other words, we must abandon the courtroom of truth for the carnival of redescription and recontextualization. Rorty goes so far as to say that philosophy can no longer exist as a discipline in its own right, since it has no access to universally valid principles of reason or objective truth.[28] Gertrude

---

[25]Quoted in Sowell, *Race and Culture*, p. 212.

[26]Rorty, *Objectivity, Relativism, and Truth*, p. 193.

[27]Ibid.

[28]See Richard Rorty, *Essays on Heidegger and Others*, Philosophical Papers 2 (Cambridge: Cambridge University Press, 1991), p. 86.

Himmelfarb aptly observes: "Rorty would abolish philosophy by abolishing reality itself, which is nothing more than the arbitrary construct of the philosopher."[29]

Despite the light-hearted approach to morality Rorty seems more serious about making sure that ironists carve out an existence that is truly their own, innovative as opposed to traditional. The ironist wants to use language not to express truth, moral or otherwise (which doesn't exist anyway), but "to make something that never had been dreamed of before." Fearing not being original, the ironist wants to stand with Nietzsche and say of one's life, "Thus I willed it!" Rorty says the ironist is

> trying to get out from under inherited contingencies and make his own contingencies, get out from under an old final vocabulary and fashion one which will be all his own. The generic trait of ironists is that they do not hope to have their doubts about their final vocabularies settled by something larger than themselves. This means that their criterion for resolving doubts, their criterion of private perfection, is autonomy rather than affiliation to a power other than themselves. "[30]

He will not be judged by history or even his own standards. "The judge the ironist has in mind is himself."[31]

Rorty's goal fits the description of the ungodliness and chaos during the time of the Judges: "In those days Israel had no king; everyone did as they saw fit" (Judg 21:25). It also echoes the cry of Zarathustra, who speaks for Nietzsche's atheistic conclusions:

> Verily men gave themselves all their good and evil. Verily, they did not take it, they did not find it, nor did it come to them as a voice from heaven. Only man placed values in things to preserve himself—he alone created a meaning for things, a human meaning. Therefore he calls himself "man," which means: the esteemer.
>
> To esteem is to create: hear this you creators! Esteeming itself is of all esteemed things the most estimable treasure. Through esteeming alone is

---

[29]Gertrude Himmelfarb, *On Looking into the Abyss: Untimely Thoughts on Culture and Society* (New York: Vintage, 1994), p. 14.
[30]Rorty, *Contingency, Irony, and Solidarity*, p. 97.
[31]Ibid.

there value: and without esteeming, the nut of existence would be hollow. Hear this you creators![32]

Nietzsche's mouthpiece, Zarathustra, is prophetic, oracular and insistent in style, while Rorty is cool, rather detached—and, of course, ironic. Nevertheless, their messages are almost identical with respect to value-creation.[33] Humans are not bound to an objective moral order. All values (or vocabularies for Rorty, given his linguistic turn) are human without remainder. The Nietzschean Superman or Rortyian ironist self-consciously and without objective criteria selects values creatively, not reactively. Nietzsche also proclaimed through his character, Zarathustra: "He, however, has discovered himself who says, 'this is my good and evil'; with that he has reduced to silence the mole and dwarf who say, 'good for all, evil for all.'"[34] (One not-so-minor detail is that while Rorty views women and men as equally good candidates for ironism, Nietzsche limited the Superman role to men.)

Both Nietzsche's thundering pronouncements and Rorty's relaxed but radical ruminations share the same essential philosophical defect. Creatures of mere chance contingency, citizens of an atheistic world without purpose, meaning or value, cannot truly create anything original or uniquely theirs, however vigorously they may "redescribe" or "esteem." The Rortyian anti-essentialist believes that we are historically conditioned "all the way down."[35] We have no identifiable soul or self to stand out from the conditioning environment. Neuhaus offers a penetrating criticism:

> While he seems to know that even the "self" is itself socially constructed, Rorty's project of self-creation is aimed at denying or overcoming what he knows. Put differently, the project is one of overcoming the self, including what has gone into the making of the self, which leaves, precisely, noth-

---

[32]Friedrich Nietzsche, *Thus Spoke Zarathustra* in *The Portable Nietzsche*, ed. Walter Kauffman (New York: Viking, 1968), p. 171.

[33]This is not to say that Rorty and Nietzsche's positive ethical programs were identical; they were not. Nietzsche, for instance, hated democracy, while Rorty defends it (however inadequate his reasoning may be).

[34]Nietzsche, *Thus Spoke Zarathustra*, p. 306.

[35]Rorty, *Contingency, Irony, and Solidarity*, p. 99.

ing. . . . Since even the most original self is but the more-or-less novel reconfiguration of inherited vocabularies, the overcoming of that self must finally mean the destruction of the self.[36]

Rorty's attempt to bless the ironist's life by uttering the Nietzschean benediction, "Thus I willed it," is like trying to build a ladder of water, to use Cornelius Van Til's phrase. It terminates in a will worship that is, ultimately, the worship of nothing. Nothing is sacred. As a nominalist, the ironist cannot use words to capture general or universal truths never before known; words are mere things with no connection to a reality outside themselves. As a historicist, the ironist cannot transcend the ways of thinking and being dictated by one's historical situation. History happens to us, we cannot shape history. Nothing real remains to sponsor any significant individuality or creativity.

Love also evaporates for the postmodernist ironist. Since we cannot know reality as it is, we cannot love anything because it is worthy to be loved or deserving of our love or ought to be loved. Love is merely a product of arbitrary will, as is all else for the contingent self fighting to transcend its contingency through creating new vocabularies. As Neuhaus notes:

> nothing approximating unconditional love is possible. Nothing is loved for itself except the self; there is no good beyond the self, never mind a summum bonum; all is instrumental to self-creation. A self that has only instrumental relations to other selves would seem, however, to be a pitiably shriveled self.[37]

In other words, other selves are not centers of irreducible value and meaning in their own right, as Christianity teaches. For that matter, one's own self is deflated as well, since it is has no real nature that can be known, nor can it claim objective value in relation to others. We are not part of a community of embodied souls. As a socially constructed self, I confer meaning on whatever and whomever I wish. And others do this with respect to me as well. The human other is not a person with irreducibly objective value; it, therefore, places no obligation upon me.

---

[36]Richard John Neuhaus, "Joshing Richard Rorty," *First Things*, December 1990, p. 22.
[37]Ibid.

In the end, Rorty's version of postmodernist ethics is reduced to joshing about what it cannot rationally defend. Ironists have no ground on which to stand. Their moral pronouncements cannot have any prescriptive force beyond their own wills, conventions and constructions.

Foucault on Human Nature

Michel Foucault also rejects any human essence from which to theorize or moralize:

> To all those who still wish to think about man, about his reign or his liberation, to all those who still ask themselves questions about what man is in his essence, to all those who take him as their starting-point in their attempts to reach truth . . . to all these warped and twisted forms of reflection we can answer only with a philosophical laugh—which means, to a certain extent, a silent one.[38]

To understand humans as having a set of rights and obligations, we must assume what Foucault denies: a human nature. Despite Foucault's critique of the idea of a human nature, his writings reveal a kind of ethical concern for the marginalized and oppressed, those who have been defined or categorized as deviant, insane or abnormal by established institutions. He writes of the repressive practices of insane asylums, yet has no moral basis from which to condemn them as repressive. William Placher observes that

> Foucault attacks the very idea of standards of "good" and "true" because they can serve to support systems of repression. But the moral force of his attack depends on our recognition that such repression is a bad thing. That in turn seems to require some standard by which we can judge that freedom is better than repression—really better, objectively better—just the kind of argument Foucault set out to undermine.[39]

Foucault, like so many postmodernists, is operating on borrowed

---

[38]Michel Foucault, *The Order of Things: An Archeology of the Human Sciences* (New York: Random House-Pantheon, 1971), pp. 342-43; quoted in Stanley Grenz, *A Primer on Postmodernism* (Grand Rapids, Mich.: Eerdmans, 1996), p. 131.

[39]William C. Placher, *Unapologetic Theology: A Christian Voice in a Pluralistic Conversation* (Louisville: Westminster John Knox, 1989), p. 94.

intellectual capital, which he can never repay given the impoverishment of his worldview. Ironically, Foucault himself worked for prison reform.[40]

As an active homosexual who died of AIDS, Foucault doubtless experienced the condition of the outsider. As an anarchist, Foucault made the individual's freedom to maximize pleasure the highest good and was fearful that "society constitutes a conspiracy to stifle one's own longings for self-expression." He "agonized profoundly over the question of whether rape should be regulated by penal justice" because he believed that law equaled oppression and lawlessness meant freedom.[41] His final writings made clear his ethical concern to lay out "alternative forms of existence" by liberating "human beings from contingent conceptual constraints masked as unsurpassable a priori limits."[42]

The logic of Foucault's presuppositions forced him to wrestle with a proposition that is self-evident: rape is immoral violence and exploitation of the highest magnitude. No "alternative form of existence" can overthrow that. But without an objective moral order such self-evident truth is beyond philosophical reach. Foucault contradicts himself by granting some kind of individual right to pleasurable self-expression, some goodness in the liberation of the marginalized. This hangs firmly in midair, however, since human nature is only, in the final analysis, a reification—a social construct of relatively recent origin. As Stanley Grenz rightly says, "Postmoderns like Foucault no longer engage in a quest for an independent self, a given reality governed by lawlike regularities."[43] Why pit the contrarian, libertine self against the establishment or pit the outcast against the orthodox? Why choose sides at all when both sides are only fortuitous constructs through and through? There is no reason for this choice—outside of whimsy, which is really

[40]Gary Gutting, "Michel Foucault," in *Routledge Encyclopedia of Philosophy*, ed. Edward Craig (New York: Routledge, 1998), 3:709.

[41]Ronald Beiner, "Foucault's Hyper Liberalism," *Critical Review*, summer 1995, pp. 353-54; quoted in Sire, *Universe Next Door*, p. 183.

[42]Gary Gutting, "Michel Foucault," *The Cambridge Dictionary of Philosophy*, ed. Robert Audi (New York: Cambridge University Press, 1995), p. 276.

[43]Grenz, *Primer on Postmodernism*, p. 128.

no reason at all but simply unreason. For Foucault, God is eliminated, human nature is annulled, ethics is eroded; only madness and anarchy remain.[44]

Exploring Otherness

Foucault's purported concern for the powerless—the underdog, the stranger and the alien—is impaled on his own assumptions. Yet many postmodernists continue to speak of breaking from the modernist metanarrative of reason, progress and science in order to disclose the realities of those outside the orthodoxies of the Western world. They speak of "otherness" or "alterity" as breaking in on the ruins of modernity. This is often linked with the idea of entering a postcolonial period in which formerly colonized nations attempt to regain their native voices after long periods of suffering under military and intellectual imperialism. Women are sometimes included in this category as well.[45] Edward Said put it well in noting that those of the Western world need to recognize the

> right of formerly un- or misrepresented human groups to speak for and represent themselves in domains defined, politically and intellectually, as normally excluding them, usurping their signifying and representing function, over-riding their historical reality.[46]

This is a legitimate concern if one's worldview can account for otherness in an ethically and intellectually satisfying manner. The postmodernist perspective on this raises important—and often neglected—questions but fails to provide a satisfying framework for answering them.

Jean-Francios Lyotard, in his rejection of metanarratives, opts for heterogeneous language games instead. Each group structures reality

[44]See Francis Schaeffer's prescient comments on Foucault in *Escape from Reason* (Downers Grove, Ill.: InterVarsity Press, 1969), pp. 69-71.
[45]This will be addressed in chapter nine.
[46]Edward Said, "Orientalism Reconsidered," in *Literature, Politics and Theory: Papers from the Essex Conference, 1976-1984*, ed. Francis Barker et al. (London: Methuen, 1986), p. 212; quoted in Steven Connor, *Postmodernist Culture: An Introduction to Theories of the Contemporary*, 2nd ed. (New York: Blackwell, 1997), p. 264.

according to its own unique speaking and knowing. No one system can impose its views of reality upon another one. The resulting plurality of value, perspectives and practices cannot be unified under a universal category. To do so would be to totalize the discourse and therefore marginalize those outside of one's language game. We are left with a decentered openness instead of a closed system of rationality.[47]

Sadly, however, this push to reinvigorate the other and to compensate for previous exploitation and suppression only ends up silencing the other once again. By dispensing with totalizing metanarratives, postmodernism is left without the conceptual resources to understand the voice of the other at all. There is no human nature, language is merely a social construction unrelated to objective reality, and there is no God-given meaning or value in the world. Therefore, various cultures and kinds of people become opaque to one other—monads of otherness, as it were. The postmodernist idea of "difference" divides and polarizes. Finkielkraut zeros in on this problem for the postmodernist:

> Instead of the collective me [of modernism], without hesitation they took the side of the non-me, of the proscribed, the excluded, the outsider. Wanting to rehabilitate the foreigner, they abolished any sense of commonality among people.[48]

Finkielkraut continues by noting that these thinkers "carry differences to the absolute extreme, and in the name of multiplicity of specific causalities destroy any possibility of a natural or cultural community among peoples."[49] This kind of thinking is represented in slogans such as, "It's a black thing. You wouldn't understand" or "Men just don't get it." Racial, cultural and gender differences do make a difference and do make communication difficult at times. Nonetheless, any philosophy that renders mutual understanding between these groups impossible has done nothing to reconcile them or to lessen alienation and misunderstandings.

---

[47]Steven Connor, *Postmodernist Culture: An Introduction to Theories of the Contemporary*, 2nd ed. (New York: Blackwell, 1997), p. 263.

[48]Alain Finkielkraut, *The Defeat of the Mind* (New York: Columbia University Press, 1995), p. 66.

[49]Ibid., p. 79.

Worse yet, if metanarratives are jettisoned at the expense of a universal ethic of respect for humans *qua* humans, there is no reason even to attempt to honor or listen to members of other groups. We must simply revert to our local narratives, whatever they may be. Grand systems of objective justice, universal human rights and crosscultural values are annulled in principle. This contextualized view of otherness, as Keith Yandell notes, "takes the particularities its supporters supposedly prize and turns them into isolating disabilities."[50] Civil, national and tribal disputes remain just that—disputes, without any hope of appealing to common ground ethically. The postmodernist rejection of totality undercuts dialogue and amplifies distrust. It also tends to excuse people from working for any global goals, given their penchant to "discard the idea of totality in a rush of holophobia."[51] Connor claims that postmodernists have shown how metanarratives can be oppressive by falsely claiming totality and universality for their views, but the postmodernists

> nowhere build convincingly into an argument against the desire for a universal application of the principles of freedom and justice. Indeed, when inspected closely, ißt becomes apparent that the postmodern critique of unjust and oppressive systems of universality implicitly depends for its force upon the assumption of the universal right of all not to be treated unjustly and oppressively—otherwise, who would care whether metanarratives were false or not, oppressive or not, and what reason might there be for their abandonment when they no longer compelled assent.[52]

Connor goes on to say that the elimination of "the horizon of universal value" entails either a "might is right" ethic or "the sunny complacency of pragmatism," which simply resorts to the values one finds congenial, since nothing beyond them is available.[53] The latter option

---

[50]Keith E. Yandell, "Modernism, Post-Modernism, and the Minimalist Canons of Common Grace," *Christians Scholars Review* 27, no. 1 (1997): 25.

[51]Terry Eagleton, *The Illusions of Postmodernism* (Cambridge, Mass.: Blackwell, 1996), p. 9. Eagleton's point is sound, but I reject his neo-Marxist metanarrative.

[52]Connor, *Postmodernist Culture*, p. 276.

[53]Ibid.

singles out Rorty, for one, although Connor does not name him.

Not only does ethics need a "horizon of universal value," which postmodernism has blotted out, it needs a foundation for objective moral value, moral obligation, moral law and moral community between individuals, races and cultures. It is one thing to decry the postmodern rejection of an objective moral order; it is quite another to give a compelling case for the existence of such a reality at all.

Paul Ramsey spells out this problem when he writes of the digression from the notion of inalienable rights endowed by our Creator, as expressed in the Declaration of Independence, to the Charter of Human Rights of the United Nations, which is content to affirm that these rights "have simply been endowed upon many—presumably by nothing and no one at all! Derived from the fullness of nonentity, suspended from vacancy, grounded in the grandeur of nothing, it is no wonder that human rights are fast running out."[54] Merely *asserting* a moral horizon does not *establish* it intellectually.

The answer to this problem cannot be found in reverting to some rationalistic, modernist morality that attempts to anchor ethics in mere moral sentiment or universal imperatives without a Lawgiver. These notions take aspects of the Christian understanding of ethics and split them off from their proper home, thus resulting in an amputated ethics that cannot not carry the load of moral reality. Only the God of the Scripture provides a source of moral authority and obligation, standards for ethical endeavor, the incentive and power for character, and a moral community of truth, which respects transcendent realities.

Coming to Terms with the Lawgiver

Despite their theorizing, postmodernists such as Rorty and Foucault still retain some sense of objective right and wrong. Foucault worked for prison reform, and Rorty supports democracy as the fairest system of government. A close reading even of postmodernist ethics reveals some understanding of ethical principles that transcend the merely cul-

---

[54]Paul Ramsey, *Nine Modern Moralists* (Englewood Cliffs, N.J.: Prentice-Hall, 1962), p. 24.

tural. These are buried beneath much verbiage and muddled with contradictions about relativity and contingency, but they can be unearthed.
This evidences the reality of a natural, moral law built into the human
soul. As Paul taught, God's law is written on our hearts, our consciences bearing witness to it (Rom 2:14-15) even despite the fact that
we may be suppressing much of the truth in unrighteousness (Rom
1:18). According to natural law theorist J. Budziszewski, these moral
truths "constitute the deep structure of our minds. That means that so
long as we have a mind, we can't not know them."[55] Nevertheless,
humans are quite good at denial.

The postmodernists who attempt to eject themselves out of the domain of natural law find themselves in a dilemma. On the one hand,
they want autonomy from God and moral law; on the other, they still
intuit standards of morality beyond themselves. As autonomous from
God, they realize that objective moral truth is impossible; as creatures
made in God's image, they realize objective moral truth is inescapable.
Legal scholar Arthur Leff captures this well: "What we want, heaven
help us, is simultaneously to be perfectly ruled and perfectly free, that
is, at the same time to discover the right and the good and to create it."[56]

If we insist on no transcendent Word concerning the right and the
good, all our words finally ring hollow; they are subject to the rejoinder
"says who?" because they are created by merely finite and fickle beings.
Every ethical evaluation can be refuted by some other evaluation if the
evaluators have no warrant beyond themselves. But our sense of the
natural law is that it is binding upon the conscience, that it stipulates
behavior, that it reveals normative realities, that it is not optional or
constructed. As Leff states it:

> If the evaluation is to be beyond question, then the evaluator and its eval-
> uative process must be similarly insulated. If it is to fulfill its role, the

---

[55]J. Budziszewski, "Escape from Nihilism," *Re:Generation Quarterly* 4, no. 1 (1998): 14.
See also his *Written on the Heart* (Downers Grove, Ill.: InterVarsity Press, 1997); and
George Grant, *Philosophy in the Mass Age*, ed. William Christian (1959; reprint, Toronto: University of Toronto Press, 1996), pp. 26-37.
[56]Arthur Allen Leff, "Unspeakable Ethics, Unnatural Law," *Duke Law Journal*, December 1979, p. 1129.

evaluator must be the unjudged judge, the unruled legislator, the premise maker who rests on no premises, the uncreated creator of value.[57]

Such a reality would have to be a personal being, according to Leff. He skillfully argues that every merely human system, every contingent social construction of ethics, is susceptible to the "grand sez who," if God is not invoked as the ultimate evaluator, the One whose words constitute moral truth. Whether one appeals to standing law, the autonomous wills of individuals, collective happiness or to a particular Constitution, the question of the ultimate warrant for the good and the right is begged. Why should a given legal system be endorsed? Why should selves ("godlets," as Leff calls them) legislate morality, and how can they relate to each other morally without any principle beyond themselves? Why should we seek the greatest happiness for the greatest number? What makes the Constitution the proper glue for our society? Says who?

Leff correctly observes that

> a statement of the form "you ought to do X," "it is right to do X," or "X is good" will establish oughtness, rightness, or goodness only if there is a set of rules that gives the speaker the power totally to determine the question [of moral foundations]. But this is precisely the question of who has the power to set such rules for validating evaluations that is the central problem of ethics and . . . of legal theory. There is no one who can be said a priori to have that power unless the question being posed is also being begged.
>
> Except, as noted, God. It *necessarily* follows that the pronouncements of an omniscient, omnipotent and infinitely good being are always true and effectual. When God says, "Let there be light," there is light. And when He sees that it is good, good is what it is.[58]

In other words, God, and God alone, certifies and establishes an objective moral order, which is necessary for orienting ourselves ethically in ways that transcend matters of mere legality, opinion and culture. God's commands, based on God's unchangingly good character, deter-

---

[57]Ibid., p. 1230.
[58]Ibid., p. 1232.

mine morality—a morality that fits the universe and the human beings
that God brought forth in his image for the purpose of serving the Creator.[59] Moreover, God in Christ incarnated perfect goodness and holiness to give us a model for virtue. God also granted us divine forgiveness and the strength for moral reform and godly community through
Jesus' saving death and triumphant resurrection.

Leff sadly never resolves his dilemma: God or nihilism. He does not
profess belief in God, although his entire argument sharply points in
just that direction. The coda to Leff's profound article forcefully exhib-
its the crushing results of ethics without God. Only if ethics were something transcendent could law be based on more than human
arrangements and therefore be authoritative.

Nevertheless:

> Napalming babies is bad.
> Starving the poor is wicked.
> Buying and selling each other is wicked.
> Those who stood up to and died resisting Hitler, Stalin, Amin, and Pol
> Pot—and General Custer too—have earned salvation.
> Those who acquiesced deserve to be damned.
> There is in the world such a thing as evil.
> [All together now:] Sez who?
> God help us.[60]

The living and speaking God can split open the doors of the postmodernist prison of socially constructed ethics and articulate the resounding words of moral truth. God may indeed help us. But we must
listen to God speak. We must have ears to hear if truth decay is to be reversed in our postmodern world.

---

[59]For some rich philosophical argumentation on this point, see James G. Hanik and
Gary R. Mar, "What Euthyphro Couldn't Have Said," *Faith and Philosophy* 4, no. 3,
(1987): 241-61.

[60]Leff, "Unspeakable Ethics, Unnatural Law," p. 1249; bracketed material in the original.

9

RACE, GENDER &
POSTMODERNISM

The postmodernist destabilization and redescription of truth often poses as a
form of liberation from racial and gender oppression. "Truth," postmodernists claim, has been used to subjugate women and minorities by
muting and marginalizing them according to categories that are really
no more than reifications or social fictions. According to Foucault:

> [that] which categorizes the individual . . . attaches him to [an] identity,
> imposes a law of truth on him which he must recognize and which others
> have to recognize in him. . . . [This] is a form of power which makes indi-
> viduals subjects.[1]

This superimposition of categories is what made blacks slaves, what
made women second-rate citizens in a man's world, what fueled white
imperialism worldwide for centuries and what continues to hinder
many minorities and women from appropriate social attainment. This
purported "law of truth" stigmatizes homosexuals, lesbians and bisex-

---

[1]Michel Foucault, *The Subject and Power*; quoted in Kenneth Gergen, *The Saturated Self*
(New York: HarperCollins, 1991), p. 95.

uals as "abnormal," "deviant" and "sinful." Zymunt Bauman tersely states what he takes to be the essential fault of this kind of thinking to be: "The target of certainty and of absolute truth was indistinguishable from the crusading spirit and the project of domination."[2] The idea of a fixed truth about race and gender is the culprit, the engine of domination. As William Simon put it:

> A quest for some seemingly permanent objective guide to human uses of gender tends to reveal little more than a history of historically specific human uses. The quest for a comprehensive species-wide "truth" only reveals a rapidly expanding pluralization of gender "truths."[3]

In the shadow of rigid and oppressive gender stereotypes and in the presence of various liberation movements striving to give voice to the concerns of the sexually marginalized, postmodernists believe that a new model of gender must be forged, one that realizes that "*gender identity* is not so much a thing as a continuing process of negotiation—not only between the individual and the world, but also between different constructions of the self."[4] Anderson claims that the global women's movement is powerful precisely because it has made "one of the most fundamental and revolutionary discoveries people have ever made: That any society's customs are constructions of reality." Since they were invented under various conditions, they can be reinvented when the time comes.[5] Women's gender identities are a process of construction and deconstruction, invention and reinvention, with little if any mooring to transcultural realities. Anderson grants that there are certain *sexual* givens of the male and female body, but norms of behavior and interpretations of sexual identity are matters of socially constructed *gender*.[6] The culture gives and the culture takes away; nothing is perma-

---

[2]Zymunt Bauman, "Postmodernity, or Living with Ambivalence," in *A Postmodern Reader*, ed. Joseph Natoli and Linda Hutcheon (New York: State University of New York Press, 1993), p. 11.
[3]William Simon, "The Postmodernization of Sex and Gender," in *The Truth About Truth*, ed. Walter Truett Anderson (New York: G. P. Putnam 's Sons, 1995), p. 157.
[4]Ibid.
[5]Walter Truett Anderson, *The Future of the Self: Inventing the Postmodern Person* (New York: Jeremy Tarch/Putnam, 1997), p. 60.
[6]Ibid., p. 62.

nent. "For the postmodernist, there is no true self."[7]

These postmodernist claims are daunting issues because of their complexity and consequence. In this chapter I will consider how the postmodernist view of race and gender is at odds with the biblical account of truth. However, I will also argue that the concept of reification, or social construction, can be a useful conceptual tool for analysis from a Christian perspective. Christians have too often succumbed to the worship of ideological idols, or reifications, which have put women and minorities into false and constricting molds not justified by Scripture.

Truth, Race and Gender

Everyone should celebrate the fact that women and ethnic minorities are finding a more confident and courageous voice in Western cultures. Scripture affirms that all people are equally made in the image and likeness of God (Gen 1:26), that God is no respecter of persons (Acts 10:34), that God deeply cares about those who have been oppressed and abandoned (Jas 1:27), that Jesus' disciples should not show favoritism (2:1), and that the gospel message must be brought to people of every racial and ethnic group (Mt 28:18-20; Acts 1:8-9). However, giving voice to people who have been silenced or muffled does not entail that they will always speak the truth. Both oppressed and oppressors are, in the biblical vision, sinners in need of forgiveness and intellectual/moral reorientation by the Word and the Spirit. We all need large transfusions of objective truth from God to offset our proclivities to self-justification, exoneration, blame-shifting, stereotyping and so on. But an objective orientation to truth is a vanishing value in postmodernity.

Thomas Sowell, a wise and rigorous social analyst, comments on the fact that readers thanked columnist Anna Quindlin for "speaking our truth" on a particular matter. "However lofty and vaguely poetic such words may seem, the cold fact is that the truth cannot become private property without losing its whole meaning." This is because truth "is honored precisely for its value in *interpersonal* communication." If we

---

[7]Walter Truett Anderson, "Four Different Ways to Be Absolutely Right," in *The Truth About Truth*, ed. Walter Truett Anderson (New York: G. P. Putnam's Sons, 1995), p. 114.

relativize truth to individuals or special interest groups, we would be more honest "to stop using the word or the concept and recognize that nobody's words could be relied upon anymore."[8] By making truth the particular possession of oppressed groups, we insinuate that "we should arbitrarily single out some group for different standards, according to the fashions of the times."[9] When truth is reduced to a fashion statement, it has no binding force or persuasive power. The apprehension of truth decays when relativized to certain culturally anointed groups; only a pathetic plenitude of opinions remains.

No one owns or controls *truth*, although *opinion* is shaped in many ways. Sowell cites John Adams's comment: "Facts are stubborn things; and whatever may be our wishes, our inclinations, or the dictates of our passions, they cannot alter the state of facts and evidence."[10] Truth is neither pigmented nor gendered. There is no "black truth" or "white truth" or "red truth" or "gay truth" or "women's truth" or "male truth." Truth is a property of only those statements, propositions and beliefs that match objective reality; it matters not who utters them, where they are uttered or why they are uttered. The real questions of moral order fall along these lines: Who is speaking the truth? What are the social and ethical consequences of truth and of falsity? What rights do all people deserve? How should particular groups be treated with love and justice? Everyone deserves to be heard; sadly, society has not always allowed women and minorities that voice, despite their First Amendment rights. Yet not all voices speak truthfully or reasonably. We must distinguish between the importance of free voices and truthful speech.

Arthur Schlesinger, a well-respected senior historian, worries that groups who have not been adequately recognized in history tend to engage in "compensatory history" in order to get even for past of-

---

[8]Thomas Sowell, *The Vision of the Anointed: Self-Congratulation as a Basis of Social Policy* (New York: HarperCollins, 1995), p. 98.

[9]Ibid., p. 99.

[10]John Adams, *John Adams: A Biography in His Own Words*, ed. James Bishop Peabody (New York: Newsweek, 1973), pp. 121-22; quoted in Sowell, *Vision of the Anointed*, p. 64.

fenses at the expense of objectivity and constructive dialogue. One writer he cites, John Henrik Clarke, claims that "African scholars are the final authority on Africa," as if pigment and culture dictated truth.[11] This is as wrong as saying that American scholars are the final authority on America. Some multicultural curricula approach history "not as an intellectual discipline but rather as a social and psychological therapy whose primary purpose is to raise the self-esteem of children from minority groups."[12] The question of objective truth takes a backseat to narratives that supposedly empower beleaguered groups. But only the truth will ever set anyone free, not compensatory constructions lacking factual foundation and rational support.

Historian Gertrude Himmelfarb notes that the postmodernist writing of history makes it "an instrument for the struggle to power." The postmodernist "historian . . . is the bearer of the class/race/gender 'war'—or, rather 'wars.'"[13] When history is used as a weapon to counterbalance past evils (real or supposed), it fails to focus on a real past and, instead, constructs a useable past for present political and cultural purposes. However, two wrongs don't make a right; and two lies don't make a truth. Postmodernist history-writing results in a quandary; when the quest for objectivity is lost, and everyone is writing from a specific racial/ethnic/gender perspective radically different from and incommensurate with other perspectives, fairness and justice—professed postmodernist values—are necessarily ruled out.

Ironically, the postmodernist attempt to give a voice to the marginalized results in incompatible perspectives that marginalize other perspectives. As Himmelfarb notes, all "the ethnic, racial, religious, sexual, national, ideological, and other characteristics that distinguish people"

---

[11]Arthur Schlessinger, *The Disuniting of America* (New York; W.W. Norton, 1991), p. 70.
[12]Ibid., p. 68. For a thorough assessment of Afrocentrism, see Dinesh D'Souza, *The End of Racism* (New York: Free Press, 1995), pp. 337-39, 360-80, 396-97, 421-26, 469. For a Christian perspective that differs somewhat from D'Souza, see Glenn Usry and Craig S. Keener, *Black Man's Religion: Can Christianity Be Afrocentric?* (Downers Grove, Ill.: InterVarsity Press, 1996).
[13]Gertrude Himmelfarb, *On Looking into the Abyss* (New York: Vintage, 1994), pp. 153-54.

are rendered divisive and serve only to politicize history. The "pernicious effect" of postmodernist history is to

> demean and dehumanize the people who are the subjects of history. To
> pluralize and particularize history to the point where people have no his-
> tory in common is to deny the common humanity of all people, whether
> their sex, race, class, religion. It is also to trivialize history by so fragment-
> ing it that it lacks all coherence and focus, all sense of continuity—indeed
> all meaning.[14]

Postmodernists typically take this consequence as good, since it
brings down "the 'totalizing,' 'universalizing,' 'logocentric,' 'phallocen-
tric' history that is said to be the great evil of modernity."[15] However,
racial, gender and ethnic fragmentation can hardly encourage mutual
understanding, reconciliation and civility that is so needed in our increasingly pluralistic, confusing and antagonistic world.

Without the concept of a knowable objective truth concerning a reality independent of our biases, ignorance and prejudices, history becomes a wax nose that can be twisted in any direction without regard
for proper method, objective facts or implications. All that remains is
partisanship, ideology, power mongering, image manipulation, name
calling, propaganda and subversion. These are not the essential elements of equitable gender and racial relations.

It is beyond question that power and prejudice can and do corrupt
our understanding of the truth about race and gender. They can even silence the voices of the oppressed and rob them of comfort, as the ancient Preacher noted:

> I looked and saw all the oppression that was taking place under the sun:
> I saw the tears of the oppressed—
> and they have no comforter;
> power was on the side of their oppressors—
> and they have no comforter. (Eccles 4:1)

Postmodernists face a daunting dilemma when it comes to matters of

---

[14]Ibid., p. 154.
[15]Ibid., p. 155.

race and gender, given their views of truth and the self. On the one hand, postmodernists make truth the possession of various groups, fracturing truth into ethnic and gender conclaves.[16] On the other hand, postmodernists reject all forms of "essentialism," the notion that there is an essential or given identity that is fundamental to any individual or social group. All identity, whether individual or collective, is contingently constructed and is not rooted in any objective reality beyond culture.

Anderson explains that the efforts of "earnest liberals" to preserve the distinct identity of various ethnic groups "are biased in favor of an idea of the naturalness and timelessness of those cultures, blinkered against recognizing them as inventions that have been turned into things by the process of reification."[17] Postmodernists cast off all essentialist notions. Rather, identity (along with every other abstract value or concept) is socially constructed by specific cultures and communities. Since any person normally moves in and out of a number of subcultures every day, postmodernist identity is not determined either by the individual or the group. Instead, identity is indeterminate and protean, and the postmodernist self is really much more *self*-involved than involved with any one social group. Thus postmodernism scuttles objective truth and furthers the fragmentation of individuals and communities that began with modernity.[18]

Scriptural Truth on Race and Gender

Christians should rise to the postmodernist occasion by articulating and incarnating a theology of race and gender equal to the task of creating a climate for rational discourse, civil exchange and social justice. Without attempting to resolve the debates on affirmative action, the strengths and weaknesses of multiculturalism, and other highly charged political issues, I will give the rudiments of a biblical theology of race, gender and justice that honors individual uniqueness, ethnic and gender identity, and objective truth. All three are indispensable.

---

[16]See Gene Edward Veith Jr., *Postmodern Times: A Christian Guide to Contemporary Thought and Culture* (Wheaton, Ill.: Crossway, 1994), pp. 142-56.

[17]Anderson, *Truth About Truth*, p. 58.

[18]This paragraph was written by Rebecca Merrill Groothuis.

The biblical metanarrative begins with God creating the universe by his Word (Gen 1:1; Heb 1:2-3; 1 Jn 1:1-3). The world is the expression of God's power and design. The Creator recognized the prehuman world to be good and deemed humans, who were made in his image and likeness, to be "very good" (Gen 1:26, 31). The first man and woman are the parents of us all, both in their original goodness and in their original sin. This couple was charged to procreate, to care for creation and to cultivate it under God's guidance. However, both heeded the serpent's lie that the way of disobedience and autonomy was better than the way of obedience and blessing under God. This resulted in the fall of humans from their original state of goodness and social harmony. The world "east of Eden" is riddled with gender, racial and class hostilities that are rooted not in God's original design for human flourishing but in human rebellion (Gen 3; Rom 3).

Humans of both genders and all races are equally sinful as well as equally created in God's image. Sin takes different forms in different cultures at different times, but women and men of all races all "fall short of the glory of God" (Rom 3:23). Genesis 3:16 teaches that after the Fall, man will "rule over" woman. This is not God's moral command but a consequence of sin having poisoned the world through human rebellion against God's character and commands. It is a description of the coarse contours of an alienated world in crying need of healing grace.

God has not placed one race above any other race. The supposed "curse of Ham" as applied to blacks has no basis in Scripture but was derived from a text used out of context as a pretext for racism against blacks (Gen 9:18-27). In his Mars Hill address, Paul states that from the first human, God "made all the nations, that they should inhabit the whole world; and he determined the times set for them and the exact places where they should live." God did not make one nation superior to another. God's purpose was that they "would seek him and perhaps reach out for him and find him, though he is not far from each one of us" (Acts 17:26-27). God's election of the people of Israel was not because of their race or their strength or wisdom, but by God's grace alone, and through them all the nations of the world were to be blessed (Gen 12:1-3).

God's redemptive plan brought Jesus to this sin-stained, tear-soaked, blood-caked planet to reconcile creatures to the Creator and to reconcile them one to another. The drama of the gospel's liberation began with the Jews but quickly moved out to embrace the world. Jesus instructed his disciples to receive the Holy Spirit's power and to be his "witnesses in Jerusalem, and in all Judea and Samaria, and to the ends of the earth" (Acts 1:8). The inclusion of Samaria is significant, since the Jews historically took the Samaritans to be racially and religiously contemptible. These barriers had already come down in Jesus' ministry (Jn 4) and had to be cleared away completely for the gospel to prosper. Patterns of prejudice and bigotry had to be broken. Jews and all Gentiles can find unity through the work of Jesus Christ (Acts 10; Eph 2:11-22).

Moreover, men and women are released from the old social structures of domination and subservience through the life, death and resurrection of the divine Messiah. Jesus said that his followers are not to dominate each other (as did the Gentiles) but rather to serve one another (Mt 20:25-26). He scandalized the establishment of his day through his respect for women demonstrated in many circumstances. Dorothy Sayers captures this poignantly:

> Perhaps it is no wonder that women were first at the Cradle and last at the Cross. They had never known a man like this Man—there never has been such another. A prophet and teacher who never nagged at them, never faltered or coaxed or patronized; who never made jokes about them, never treated them either as "the women, God help us!" or "The Ladies, God bless them!"; who rebuked without querulousness and praised without condescension; who took their questions and arguments seriously; who never mapped out their sphere for them, never urged them to be feminine or jeered at them for being female; who had no ax to grind and no uneasy male dignity to defend; who took them as he found them and was completely unself-conscious. There is no act, no sermon, no parable in the whole Gospel that borrows its pungency from female perversity; nobody could possibly guess from the words and deeds of Jesus that there was anything "funny" about woman's nature.[19]

---

[19]Dorothy L. Sayers, *Are Women Human?* (Grand Rapids, Mich.: Eerdmans, 1971), p. 47. For an in-depth treatment of the Gospel material on how Jesus treated women, see Millard Erickson, *The Word Became Flesh: An Incarnational Christology* (Grand Rapids, Mich.: Baker, 1991), pp. 577-93.

The promise of the kingdom involves both men and women filled with the Spirit and serving Christ (Acts 2:17-18; see also Joel 2:28-32). The new covenant, unlike the old, allows for no principled privileging of men over women as part of God's spiritual order. Paul enunciates this in his charter of Christian freedom for all peoples and both sexes. Here he speaks not merely of salvation but of one's spiritual prerogatives and responsibilities in Christ:[20]

> You are all children of God through faith in Christ Jesus, for all of you who were baptized into Christ have clothed yourselves with Christ. There is neither Jew nor Greek, slave nor free, male nor female, for you are all one in Christ Jesus. If you belong to Christ, then you are Abraham's seed, and heirs according to the promise. (Gal 3:26-28)

Colorizing Church History

Sadly, the voices of women and minorities have not always been heard in the Western Christian tradition. The oneness in Christ emphasized by Paul has often been neglected. This injustice should be rectified. Christians should not reject all multicultural concerns in an effort to guard against the "politically correct" ideology of postmodernists who abandon objective truth and paint Christianity as inherently oppressive and hegemonic. In 1992 historian Ruth Tucker wrote a provocative essay for *Christianity Today* called "Colorizing Church History: A History that Ignores Women and Minorities Is a Poor Reflection of Our Christian Heritage." Without challenging the notions of objective truth, rationality or the need for impartial evidence, Tucker asks why our accounts of church history are dominated by white men when, in fact, God has powerfully used women and people of other races to propagate, defend and apply the gospel through the centuries.

Tucker notes that God often uses the weak and small things of the world for great purposes (Mt 20:26; 1 Cor 1:27-28). Thus Christians should recognize that "a history that focuses on those with prestige and

---

[20]For an elaboration on this vital point, see Rebecca Merrill Groothuis, *Good News for Women: A Biblical Picture of Gender Equality* (Grand Rapids, Mich.: Baker, 1997), pp. 19-39.

position is not the fullest reflection of our Christian heritage—in that it is out of step with how God works in the world."[21] She tries to rectify this somewhat by telling of Katherine Zell's forgotten role in the Reformation. Although excluded from the clergy, she preached in the streets of Strasbourg, wrote tracts, supervised a large refugee program, edited a hymnbook and took a stand for religious toleration among orthodox Christians, even the often despised Anabaptists.[22] Zell was not as influential as Luther or Calvin or other male reformers, whose gender gave them opportunities unavailable to women of the time. However, "her ministry of servanthood—as Jesus defined servanthood—is worthy of recognition, and her stand against religious intolerance ought to serve as a model for Christians today."[23]

Our understanding of church history, and of all history, influences our views of ourselves and others. We are historical beings who need heroes to emulate (Heb 11). Those struggling for recognition and opportunity need strong role models such as Zell for inspiration. Tucker alerts us that "the standard list of great nineteenth century American revivalists invariably leaves off men and women of color."[24] We hear much of Charles Finney's influence but little of John Jasper, his African American contemporary. Both had dramatic adult conversions, ministered for over half a century and were recognized as powerful preachers who drew enthusiastic crowds. Jasper began a church in Richmond, Virginia, with nine members, which grew to over two thousand. Although he was a "great humanitarian and defender of the Bible . . . his story has been lost in obscurity."[25]

Tucker also writes of Samson Occum, a preacher and evangelist who ministered for over forty years in eighteenth-century New England and New York. He studied at a school that later became Dartmouth, ministered in England and published a hymnal for his people. Why have we not heard more of him? Why is he omitted from Sydney Ahlstrom's

---

[21]Ruth Tucker, "Colorizing Church History," *Christianity Today*, July 20, 1992, p. 20.
[22]Ibid., pp. 21-22.
[23]Ibid., p. 22.
[24]Ibid.
[25]Ibid.

well-respected work *A Religious History of the American People*? Occum
was a Mohegan Indian.[26]

Tucker issues this clarion challenge:

> We need to re-examine the lens we use to view church history. Like the
> writers of Scripture, we need to focus on the significance of women,
> minorities, and those of various cultures. Only by using this more inclu-
> sive lens will we have any hope of seeing the full spectacle of what God is
> accomplishing on earth through his church—and any hope of seeing him,
> and each other, more clearly.[27]

Tucker does not advocate a quota system for church history or a
compensatory model that vilifies previous heroes (typically white
males) to make room for new (nonwhite) ones. Rather, "Church history
must be told anew—not to satisfy certain interest groups, but to capture
the whole picture of the church and to listen to voices that have traditionally not been heard."[28]

Truth Known and Shared Across Cultures

While we must retain the doctrines of biblical inspiration and the objective meaning of biblical texts, Christians ought to open up the discourse
on theology, biblical studies, apologetics and ethics to the global Christian community, male and female. The body of Christ is multicolored,
multiethnic and made up of both sexes. God is a global God, disclosing
insights and teaching lessons to Christians around the world. The postmodern condition of expanded communications and travel allows us
greater access to this rainbow of truth given to the church worldwide.
There is nothing postmodernist about pursuing all of God's truth, as it
is reflected through different peoples in different places.

Standard theological works should not be dispensed with because
they are typically written by white, European males. (Augustine, however, was from North Africa, and may have had dark skin.) Nor should
minority voices always trump received opinion, simply because they

---

[26]Ibid., p. 23.
[27]Ibid.
[28]Ibid.

are minority voices. We don't need a Hispanic theology, an African American theology, an Asian-American theology as separate fields of study, any more than we need a white theology. True theology is the corpus of God's truth that is true for all, engaging for all and needed by all. Christians should practice theology by discerning the proper application of God's objective, universal and absolute truth to their particular cultural situation. Rather than *any* ethnocentric or male-centered or female-centered reading of Scripture, we need a theo-centric reading of Scripture that discerns how God's universal truth applies to all people and all cultures.[29]

Women and people of color will often will bring different questions to the text of Scripture and, therefore, find truths neglected or minimized by others. These truths are not constructed but discovered. Nevertheless, we are all Christians who open the same Bible and bow before the same universal Lord. The "black perspective" or the "Native American perspective" or the "Asian perspective," is, of course, experienced within particular cultures, but if these perspectives lay claim to truth at all, they can and should be presented to and known by others outside of these cultures. This may be difficult and require time and patience, but if truth is truly truth, the enterprise is possible and worthwhile.

Keith Yandell convincingly argues against the claim that knowledge is only contextual and local and not universal or commonly shared:

> The questions to ask are questions about how the perspective of one context allows its inhabitants to see accurately a common world better than do those in other contexts, and how it prevents its inhabitants from accurately seeing a common world as well as those who do inhabit other contexts. . . . But those questions assume a knowledge that is not merely contextual, local and particular. No knowledge is *intrinsically* local; all is potentially universal.[30]

---

[29]Against the charge that the Bible is written from a male perspective, see Rebecca Merrill Groothuis, *Women Caught in the Conflict: The Culture War Between Traditionalism and Feminism* (Eugene, Ore.: Wipf and Stock, 1997; orig. pub. 1994), pp. 103-8.

[30]Keith E. Yandell, "Modernism, Post-Modernism, and the Minimal Canons of Common Grace," *Christian Scholars Review* 27, no. 1 (1997): 25.

Dorothy Sayers makes the helpful distinction between special *knowledge* and special *ability* with respect to "the woman's point of view." In areas where women have knowledge not typically—or ever—held by men, their "point of view" is uniquely valuable. Sayers notes that since some women know more about children than most men, their opinion *as women* is valuable but only in the same way that a coal miner's opinion on coal-mining and a physician's opinion on disease is valuable. It is because they have special knowledge. But there are other matters where "the woman's point of view" has no value or does not even exist, since the particularities of being female are irrelevant. There is no "woman's point of view" on Greek grammar or logic or the art of writing a detective story.[31]

However, if a woman derives an insight from Scripture that would normally be difficult for men to perceive, this insight would be true whether received by a woman or a man. For instance, the *Study Bible for Women* contains an insightful sidebar about the "crisis pregnancy" of Mary, which elaborates on facets of her condition that most men would never consider—such as her fears, her need for friendship and so on.[32] Although it is more likely for an attentive woman—especially one who has experienced a crisis pregnancy—to discover these truths, if a woman *knows* these truths of Scripture, it means that her belief corresponds to what the sacred text teaches (which itself is an accurate report of what happened in history). Although men and women may have, in some cases, different ways of coming to know certain things, there is no "female truth" as opposed to "male truth." If any man or any woman *knows* anything, he or she must know something that is *true*, something that matches up with objective reality. Truth itself is not gendered; truth answers to reality.

Postmodernism and Ethnocentrism

This principle of seeking objective truth about race and gender should

---

[31]Dorothy L. Sayers, *Are Women Human?* (Grand Rapids, Mich.: Eerdmans, 1971), p. 30.

[32]Catherine Clark Kroeger, commentary on Luke 1, *Study Bible for Women*, (Grand Rapids, Mich.: Baker, 1995), pp. 121-22.

be applied more broadly to all of cultural history. Keith Windshuttle, an Australian historian and author of *The Killing of History*, a critique of postmodernist trends in history-writing, nonetheless recognizes that in his nation the "Aboriginal perspective, and the often shocking and disgraceful story of how Aborigines were treated, was omitted entirely" from history-writing until 1970. He does not question "whether the views of this repressed 'other' should return or be revived." The question is whether the tools of traditional historiography need to be thrown out in order to do so.[33] Windshuttle thinks not and argues against the assumptions of postmodernist historians, which, he claims, work against any hope for understanding between groups or for building a more just social order.

Postmodernists reject history-writing based on observation and inductive argument as Enlightenment modernism. They also embrace relativism concerning truth and knowledge, and most deny that anything can be known with certainty. Each culture creates its own truth. Most deny that humans can "gain any direct contact with or access to reality." Instead, "we are locked within a closed system of language and culture, which refers not beyond our minds to an outside world but only inwardly to itself."[34] With these assumptions locked in place, any meaningful communication between, say, Aborigines and white Australians or white Americans and Native Americans would be impossible in principle. Each culture creates truth through its language, and language cannot refer to extralinguistic realities. The Enlightenment vision of rational observation and inductive argument is merely a cultural prejudice that sheds no light on other cultures' histories. Yet without at least a partially knowable past as part of our common discourse, neither repentance nor restoration is possible. Ludwig Wittgenstein's epigram is telling: "Only someone who can reflect on the past can repent."[35]

---

[33]Keith Windshuttle, *The Killing of History: How Literary Critics and Social Theorists Are Murdering Our Past* (New York: Free Press, 1996), p. 35.

[34]Ibid., p. 36.

[35]Ludwig Wittgenstein, *Zettle*, ed. G. E. M. Anscombe and G. H. Wright (Berkeley: University of California Press, 1967), 519, 91e.

Terry Eagleton observes that the "postmodernist 'anti-ethnocen-trism'" ironically rebounds into ethnocentrism since it "leaves our own culture conveniently insulated from anyone else's culture. All those anti-Western bleatings from the so-called third world may be safely ignored, since they are interpreting our conduct in terms quite irrelevant to us."[36] This makes moral discourse across cultures unattainable. The problem ramifies even within pluralistic cultures, where diverse ethnic and racial groups coexist within a common legal framework and geographic area. For instance, in America, a Laotian Hmong man in his thirties kidnaps a seventeen-year-old woman as part of the accepted marriage-by-capture practice of the Hmongs.[37] This forces the post-modernist into a sharp dilemma. The traditional Hmong culture endorses this overtly patriarchal abduction as a binding marriage; the American legal system considers kidnapping a crime and not the equivalent of matrimony. Who is right? Whose law should obtain?

The Christian view provides the moral assessment that avoids both the errors of ethnocentrism and postmodernism. The Hmong people are made in the image and likeness of God and are eligible for redemption in Christ, but they are just as subject to sin as any other group. Given that patriarchal abuses flow from the disorder of the Fall (Gen 3:16), every culture is adversely affected by such abuses, and every Christian needs to work for equal dignity and respect for women and men. The Christian condemns the traditional Hmong practice on the basis of the woman's created dignity as a person with human rights granted by God. Kidnapping under the Old Testament law was a capital offense (Ex 21:16; Deut 24:7); the creation order for marriage is mutual care and concern in a voluntary, one-flesh relationship (Gen 2:20-25); marriage should involve mutual submission, respect and love (1 Cor 7:1-7; Eph 5:21-33).

---

[36]Terry Eagleton, *The Illusions of Postmodernism* (Cambridge, Mass.: Blackwell, 1996), p. 124.
[37]This is a true story related to me by a Hmong student at Denver Seminary in 1997. The abductions can sometimes also involve rape. This is cited in Daniel A. Farber and Suzanna Sherry, *Beyond All Reason: The Radical Assault on Truth in American Law* (New York: Oxford University Press, 1997), p. 106.

One can denounce the Hmong practice as the worst sort of misogyny, not because of any prejudice against Asians but because of God's objective and crosscultural standards. In fact, Hmong people who are Christians should oppose this practice. Similarly, Christians should oppose female genital mutilation, abortion on demand, institutionalized poverty, racism and slavery wherever they occur because they hold every culture accountable to God, especially their own.

Using one's own culture as the final standard is idolatry. Even the ancient Jews, who were graciously selected by God from among all the peoples of the earth, could not invoke their ethnicity to justify themselves or excuse their sins. On the other hand, not recognizing the gifts God has given one's own culture is sinful ingratitude. Each culture is a complicated mixture of common grace, sin and special grace. The wheat will grow with the tares until the final harvest (Mt 13:24-30). The moral assessment of practices enshrined in other racial groups is not necessarily racist or ethnocentric. Charles Taylor makes this clear:

> When we stand with the moral outlook of universal and equal respect, we don't consider its condemnation of slavery, widow-burning, human sacrifice, or female circumcision only as expressions of our way of being, inviting a reciprocal and equally valid condemnation of our free labor, widow-remarriage, bloodless sacrifice, and sex equality from the societies where these strange practices flourish. . . . The moral outlook makes wider claims, and this by its very nature. For it engenders a pitiless criticism of all those beliefs and practices within our society which fail to meet the standard of universal respect.[38]

The standard of universal respect is no mere reification, social construct or final vocabulary. We cannot alter it any more than we can create it or destroy it. The standard requires a standard stipulator, who established the moral law over all nations, peoples and for all time.[39]

The Christian insistence on the reality of an objective moral standard applicable to all people does not preclude a development over time of a

---

[38]Charles Taylor, *Sources of the Self: The Making of the Modern Identity* (Cambridge, Mass.: Harvard University Press, 1989), pp. 67-68.
[39]See chapter eight for a discussion of the theistic grounding for morality.

culture's or individual's knowledge of moral truth, with respect to gender and race. Sadly, American Christians were divided over the legitimacy of slavery for far too long, with each side invoking Scripture for support. Christians also opposed women's suffrage, supposedly on biblical grounds.[40] But in both cases the interpreters were in error, not the Scriptures. As has been often said, "There may yet be more light to break forth from God's word."

Are Egalitarians Postmodernists?

Some have claimed that those who reject a gender-based hierarchy of authority and who hold to the full equality of men and women in marriage, the church and society have capitulated to the postmodernist sensibility that texts can be deconstructed to mean things radically different from their originally intended meanings. Since the traditional view has been that the biblical text says that women must submit to their husbands unilaterally (i.e., in ways that husbands do not reciprocate) and that women should not be allowed to serve in the highest positions of leadership in the church, deviation from this view is deemed a concession to postmodernist ideas; Scripture "clearly teaches" otherwise. It is feared that some evangelicals have allowed "women's experience" to pollute their understanding of the sacred text. The question as to whether the traditionalist view has correctly discerned the objective meaning of the biblical text often is not seriously considered for these reasons.

Those who make these charges typically categorize belief in biblical equality with all manner of deviations from orthodoxy. So, Robertson McQuilken and Bradford Mullen claim that

> we are challenged by fellow evangelicals to give up Adam and Eve, role distinctions in marriage, limitations on divorce, exclusively heterosexual unions, hell, faith in Jesus Christ as the only way to acceptance with God and—most pivotal—an inerrant Bible.[41]

---

[40]On this see Rebecca Merrill Groothuis, *Women Caught in the Conflict*, pp. 39-40.
[41]Robertson McQuilkin and Bradford Mullen, "The Impact of Postmodern Thinking on Evangelical Hermeneutics," *Journal of the Evangelical Theological Society* 40, no. 1 (1997): 72.

They also accuse egalitarians of "tortuous hermeneutics" in their defense of egalitarian marriage from Ephesians 5 and claim that the "cultural form of husband/wife, parent/child, master/servant relationships are part of the mandate in that passage and indeed define the principle of 'being subject to one another' enunciated as a preamble."[42] Evidently, according to these traditionalists, the authoritarian, patriarchal customs of ancient Greco-Roman societies—including the absolute rule of the wife by the husband and the ownership of the slave by the master—are divinely mandated for all time, and are to be seen as inherent to and compatible with the principle of mutual submission that the passage also mandates. This reading of the text is not only rather "tortuous" itself but would universally sanction slavery as well as wives' unilateral submission to husbands, which were the *cultural forms*, after all. (This was the argument of Christian slave owners before the Civil War.) Moreover, evangelical egalitarians do not "give up role distinctions in marriage," since they affirm heterosexual monogamy and all its sexual distinctions.

Yet the authors fail even to address such responses to their position, thinking they have dismissed the alternative view as merely tortuous, postmodernist hermeneutics. In this they commit the fallacy of guilt by association. This certainly inhibits healthy debate.[43]

The debate on gender roles is very complex, and I cannot settle it all here. My point is that although one *may* embrace egalitarianism for postmodernist reasons (as we will see below), a strong biblical case can be made for gender equality that keeps the notions of biblical inerrancy, objective truth, universal rationality and authorial intent firmly in place. This is significant to understand because Christians often become unfair in labeling egalitarian believers as sub-Christian or even anti-Christian in this respect.

Derrida to the Rescue?
Before addressing the specific charges by traditionalists, I want to con-

---

[42]Ibid., p. 81.
[43]For an evangelical interpretation of Ephesians 5 that relies on no postmodernist assumptions and that explains and defends egalitarian marriage, see Rebecca Merrill Groothuis, *Good News for Women*, pp. 145-58, 164-70.

sider an example of ill-advised postmodernist influence on the gender controversy. In critiquing the views of gender held by J. I. Packer, egalitarian Curt Purcell argues that Packer's belief in the inherent, objective meaning of Scripture is unwarranted. Purcell claims that, on the contrary, all language is equivocal and no language is univocal. "An irreducible moment of equivocity lies at the heart of all language, ever forcing us to decide how words with which we are confronted fit into the context in which we encounter them."[44] He then quotes a passage from Derrida to make his point: "If, in fact, equivocity is always irreducible, that is because words and language in general are not and cannot be absolute objects. They do not possess any resistant and permanent identity that is absolutely their own."[45] The last two sentences quoted by Purcell trail off into unintelligibility (as does much of Derrida), so I do not cite them.[46]

To enlist Derrida for the cause of biblical equality is both unnecessary and self-destructive. Derrida removes any objective meaning from texts; their meaning is forever indeterminate. This view would render the concept of Scriptural *authority* void. If something is to have authority it must be in the intellectual position to demand and receive obedience. The author's voice must be heard for there to be authority. If a text is intrinsically and irreducibly equivocal, its meaning is unavailable and its interpreters can never be judged rationally against the one meaning of the text itself. The author vanishes, and readers are left adrift. Since Scripture is God's inspired word (2 Tim 3:16; 2 Pet 1:20-21), it *does* pos-

---

[44]Curt Purcell, "J. I. Packer and the Logic of Patriarchy," *Priscilla Papers*, 11, no. 1 (1997): 12.

[45]Jacques Derrida, *Edmund Husserl's Origin of Geometry: An Introduction*, trans. John P. Leavy Jr. (Stony Brook, N.Y.: Nicholas Hays, 1978; Lincoln: University of Nebraska Press, Bison Books, 1989), p. 104; quoted in Purcell, "J. I. Packer and the Logic," p. 12.

[46]Purcell, "J. I. Packer and the Logic," p. 12. They read: "They have their linguistic being from an intention which traverses them as mediations. The 'same' word is always 'other' according to the always different intentional acts which thereby make a word significative," This passage may be trying to prove Derrida's point about the unintelligibility of texts! I assume he has one meaning in mind, but has difficulty expressing it coherently. Foucault once accused Derrida of writing obscurely and then of attacking people for misinterpreting him. See Himmelfarb, *On Looking into the Abyss*, p. 159.

sess a "permanent identity that is absolutely its own." The divine Author employed human authors to make truth known. Our concern is how to interpret rightly and truly the objective meaning of the text, to discern how it coheres with the rest of Scripture and how the text applies to us today.

A difficulty in interpreting a particular text such as 1 Timothy 2:8-15 (concerning the place of women in the church) implies nothing about the text itself being equivocal. Paul, under infallible divine inspiration, had something definite in mind for his original readers, and that principle applies to us today, however different our cultural and ecclesiastical situation might be from that of the early church at Ephesus. What Paul meant, and what his words mean for us, is a matter of intense debate. Egalitarians find a principle concerning the inadvisability of women *in that church* teaching and having authority over men, because of some factor not inherent to their gender—such as ignorance or false doctrine. Traditionalists find a crosscultural principle of male spiritual authority. Egalitarians disagree, since we find women in God-ordained leadership over men throughout Scripture. God would not break his own rules.[47]

Peter did warn that some of Paul's writings were difficult to understand, but he affirmed that they were still inspired Scripture and that some had misinterpreted them to their own destruction (2 Pet 3:16; see also Jer 8:8). The very concept of a misinterpretation necessarily assumes an objective and determinate meaning that has been violated by bad faith or poor reasoning of some kind. Both the egalitarian and traditionalist interpretations cannot be correct; one has missed Paul's original and intended meaning (which is singular, not plural). However, this does not make the egalitarian view postmodernist, since most evangelical egalitarians reach their conclusions by using essentially the same exegetical methods as traditionalists. Egalitarians maintain that certain cultural prejudices have hindered traditionalists from seeing the theological, exegetical and logical evidence against male authority and for biblical equality. The situation should not be viewed as a hopeless

---

[47]For a discussion of this issue, see Rebecca Merrill Groothuis, *Good News for Women*, pp. 209-30.

power struggle, since God's word is "living and active" to accomplish its purposes in the long run (Heb 4:12; see also Is 55:10-11).

In some limited cases, a particular section of Scripture may be interpreted in two opposing ways, each of which is equally rational, given the knowledge available at the time.[48] That is, interpretation A and interpretation B may end up being exegetically equal; both can be rationally accepted by informed, wise and godly people, and no third interpretation seems plausible. In this case, "It could go either way." But it *is* either one way or the other, not both and not neither (unless a better interpretation C is found later). Even when an interpretation is difficult, some interpretations can be ruled out. Whatever Paul meant by being "baptized for the dead" (1 Cor 15:29), and this is much disputed, he did not mean that we should perform proxy baptisms that somehow apply salvation to those now dead, as the Mormons teach; for this would contradict clear teaching elsewhere in Scripture on the need to find salvation before death (e.g., Mt 25:46; Heb 9:27).[49]

These issues in interpretation stem not from the text itself being equivocal (many texts that seem obscure to us were perfectly clear to the original recipients) but from *our* interpretational limitations. The meaning of the text remains unequivocal in itself, and with new arguments and discoveries the equivocity of our understanding of the text may be cleared up or at least reduced. The reduction or elimination of ambiguity and unclarity in our understanding of Scripture should be the goal of biblical interpretation. This, however, is *not* Derrida's point. His view in the passage quoted is that word meanings are inevitably and always equivocal; such a view must be rejected as destructive to biblical authority, to sound exegesis. As Carl Henry notes, "In the absence of an objective textual meaning, no valid choice is possible between two or more conflicting interpretations."[50] The result is "hermeneutical nihilism."[51]

---

[48]I do not take this to be the case with 1 Timothy 2:8-15, since I believe the traditionalist view is much less plausible than the best egalitarian interpretations.

[49]On baptism for the dead, see David A. Reed and John R. Farkas, *Mormons Answered Verse by Verse* (Grand Rapids, Mich.: Baker, 1992), pp. 85-87.

[50]Carl F. H. Henry, *God, Revelation, and Authority* (Waco, Tex.: Word, 1979), 4:305.

[51]Ibid., 4:296-315.

The purpose of biblical interpretation is to *discover* the text's meaning, not to *supply* or *construct* a meaning for the text.

Ironically, Derrida has attacked his critics, such as John Searle, for misinterpreting and misrepresenting his own work. Apparently, Derrida's intended meaning took on an objective identity, which he expected his readers to ascertain. He even claimed that his point should have been clear and obvious to Searle![52] Millard Erickson notes that this is "an incredibly nondeconstructionist nonpostmodern response for someone who maintains that the meaning of a text is not in the author's intention, but in what the reader finds it saying to him or her."[53] In response to a deconstructionist reading of Scripture, D. A. Carson explains that there is always "a link between text and authorial intent. I have never read a deconstructionist who would be pleased if a reviewer misinterpreted his or her work: thus *in practice* deconstructionists implicitly link their own texts with their own intentions."[54] If so, why should we exempt the biblical text—or any other text—from this commonsensical and eminently logical approach?

Why Egalitarianism Need Not Be Postmodernist

The above postmodernist-leaning defense of egalitarianism does not exhaust the field of possibilities. I disagree with Packer's conclusions on gender restrictions. However, I find no need to invoke notions of the intrinsic equivocacy of texts or to conscript Derrida to the cause. Theologically, I agree with Packer's views of divine inspiration, the objective meaning of biblical texts and the classical method of biblical interpretation.

The charge that biblical egalitarians are crypto-postmodernists rests on a few incorrect assumptions; by identifying them, we can clear up some confusion so that a fair debate may ensue.

1. Egalitarians are accused of simply copying postmodern secular cul-

---

[52]Jacques Derrida, "Limited, Inc., abc," *Glyph* 2 (1977): 162-254; cited in Millard Erickson, *Postmodernizing the Faith: Evangelical Responses to the Challenge of Postmodernism* (Grand Rapids, Mich.: Baker, 1998), p. 156.

[53]Erickson, *Postmodernizing*, p. 156.

[54]D. A. Carson, *The Gagging of God: Christianity Confronts Pluralism* (Grand Rapids, Mich.: Baker, 1996), p. 103. For an excellent discussion of postmodernist ideas on hermeneutics, see Carson, pp. 93-140.

ture and twisting the Bible to mean what they want it to mean. This begs the question as to what the Scriptures actually teach. Egalitarians are asking for an alternative analysis of the ancient text, not an updated or edited Bible. The assumption that egalitarianism is postmodernist also commits the genetic fallacy that by discrediting the source of an idea, one discredits the idea itself. But even if some Christians have been challenged to rethink what Scripture teaches on gender because of feminist insights from secular culture (although much of secular feminism is patently unbiblical and rejected by evangelical egalitarians), it does not follow that Scripture itself opposes every aspect of feminism. Many evangelicals and fundamentalists, such as Jerry Falwell, initially rejected the civil rights movement as unbiblical and merely worldly, only to later realize that white Christians should have supported its nonviolent expressions all along, precisely because that was the biblical thing to do.

2. The charge is made that egalitarians make their own experience or beliefs the final authority over Scripture. Since they have felt uncomfortable with traditional gender roles, they have misinterpreted the Bible accordingly. One's experience certainly affects how one comes to Scripture, but it does not determine how Scripture comes to one. Many egalitarians, such as my wife and I, were at first reluctant to embrace egalitarianism, because we were not sure it was biblical. Early on we were rightly taught that we should put Scripture above experience. Therefore, we had to be thoroughly convinced theologically and exegetically before we could change our minds. Many other cases also follow this pattern. This is not a postmodernist matter of an individual or a community freely choosing a lifestyle without any objective criteria or concern for objective truth and rationality.

3. Some also argue that egalitarians deconstruct gender roles and engage in a postmodernist construction of gender without objective constraints. This is why McQuilkin and Mullen put egalitarianism in the same category as accepting homosexual unions, denying hell and so on.[55]

It is true that egalitarians believe that many of the traditionalist

---

[55]For the record, I (an egalitarian) have written a piece defending the doctrine of a literal hell (Mt 25:46). See Douglas Groothuis, "What About Hell?" *Christian Research Journal*, winter 1997, pp. 8ff.

views on gender are social reifications and are not rooted in God's created order or kingdom realities. For instance, if traditionalists take God to be male in some spiritual sense (and not all do), this is a reification, since God is beyond gender and sexuality.[56] If traditionalists take maleness to mean superiority to femaleness with respect to leadership in the home and the church, egalitarians believe that they have taken a contingent social structure and absolutized it. Scripture is filled with examples of powerful women leaders (such as Deborah and other Old Testament prophetesses, and female prophets and leaders in the early church),[57] and the New Testament teaches mutual submission and reciprocal love in marriage (1 Cor 7:4; Eph 5:21-33; 1 Pet 3:7).[58]

Egalitarians agree that God has framed our sexuality according to his wisdom. This means that heterosexual, monogamous marriage is the moral norm and the standard crossculturally (Gen 2). Fornication, adultery and homosexual relations are intrinsically sinful and must be avoided (Ex 20:14; Rom 1:18-27; Eph 5:3-5). Children should be prized and not aborted for personal preference or career advancement.[59] However, egalitarians believe that the structure for marriage and ministry is not provided by male hierarchy but by Christian love (1 Cor 13), the principles of the Sermon on the Mount (Mt 5—7), and the Ten Commandments (Ex 20:1-17). These are sufficient standards for friendship and leadership in marriage, the family and the church. There is nothing postmodernist here. Further, biblical egalitarianism does not undermine "role distinctions" in marriage; the distinctions are real where they touch on sexual relations. Everything is not up for grabs if some of the traditional gender roles are challenged.

4. Many also assert that egalitarians relativize biblical passages

---

[56]See Groothuis, *Good News for Women*, pp. 91-117.

[57]Ibid., pp. 189-201.

[58]The NIV and NIVI translations do not reflect the issue of mutual authority in 1 Corinthians 7:4 as well as do the NASB, NRSV and the KJV.

[59]For an argument that liberalized abortion is antiwomen and antifeminist, see Rebecca Merrill Groothuis, *Women Caught in the Conflict*, pp. 75-87; and Rebecca Merrill Grothuis, "Where Do We Go from Here? A Pro-life Call to Arms," in Douglas Groothuis, *Christianity That Counts: Being a Christian in a Non-Christian World* (Grand Rapids, Mich.: Baker, 1994), pp. 106-16.

about the submission of women by making them "merely cultural"; they make postmodern culture normative and deny "the clear teaching of Scripture." Hermeneutically, all Christians must fathom how ancient commands obtain today. Paul said to greet one another with "a holy kiss," that women should wear veils in church and that slaves should submit to their masters. Christians today understand the cultural context of these commands, without rejecting them as uninspired. The operative question in understanding such texts is, "What is the principle behind the commands and how do we obey it today?"

Yes, Paul told the Corinthian church that women were not to speak in their worship service (1 Cor 14:34-35). Does that mean women should not speak in churches today? The answer to this question requires an understanding of the cultural context of the Corinthian church. Egalitarians believe that "the universal principle behind Paul's words is not the permanent silencing and subordinating of women in the church, but the curtailing of practices that disrupt the flow and order of the public assembly of believers."[60]

The above response to these four assumptions only touches the tip of the iceberg. For an in-depth treatment of the historical, cultural, exegetical and theological issues involved, the work of Rebecca Merrill Groothuis should be consulted, as well as other evangelical egalitarians.[61] The divide between postmodernism and biblical egalitarianism is wide, far wider than the divide between evangelical traditionalists and evangelical egalitarians.[62]

Beyond Reification and into Postmodernist Chaos

Those postmodernists who take *all* gender identity to be mere reification sometimes confuse their lawlessness with liberation. Maureen

---

[60]Groothuis, *Good News for Women*, p. 203.

[61]See Groothuis, *Women Caught in the Conflict*; and her *Good News for Women*; Craig Keener, *Paul, Women, and Wives* (Peabody, Mass.: Hendrickson, 1992); and Mary Stewart Van Leeuwen, *Gender and Grace* (Downers Grove, Ill.: InterVarsity Press, 1992).

[62]See Groothuis, *Women Caught in the Conflict*, pp. 89-108. Careful readers will not find any postmodernist philosophical assumptions in her defense of biblical egalitarianism.

O'Hara claims that a constructivist view of gender ought not lead to despair but "an enormous sense of relief, hope, and responsibility," because

> the idea that each of us recreates reality with each encounter fills me with wondrous hope, empowerment and community connection. If there is no absolute truth "out there" to create pristine "expert systems" that can somehow solve our problems mathematically . . . then we are called to a new kind of community. If I can make culture I must act responsibly. If I can only ever be part of the creation I must act humbly.[63]

Exuberant academic prose does not justify non sequiturs. If there is no "absolute truth out there," then there is no possibility of responsibility or community or humility. These concepts imply that we are moral agents who owe allegiance to an authority beyond ourselves and that we ought to act in certain ways in relating to one another. O'Hara's postmodernist constructivism eliminates the categories of moral authority and accountability entirely. Her hope is emptiness constructed upon emptiness—all the way down. This is what Francis Schaeffer called "semantic mysticism": authors use words with positive connotations that their own worldview cannot rationally accommodate. This is done to mask their worldview's philosophical malignancies.[64]

A Better Way Forward
The biblical metanarrative supplies us with form and freedom for women and men of various races and ethnic extractions. We can live out our micronarratives and personal pilgrimages as gendered and racial beings within the all-encompassing metanarrative of God's providence. This is possible through the direction provided by Scripture, by the encouragement of the community of faith and according to the guidance of the Holy Spirit.

Rather than making our differences our starting point, we should

---

[63]Maureen O'Hara, "Constructing Emancipatory Realities," in *Truth About Truth*, p. 155.
[64]Francis A. Schaeffer, *The God Who Is There*, 30th anniv. ed. (Downers Grove, Ill.: InterVarsity Press, 1998), pp. 76-93.

emphasize that we are first and foremost creatures before the face of our Creator. Christians, in addition, are all redeemed people in Christ. As Paul exclaimed, all of our cultural background, ethnic inheritance and even our gender pales in comparison with the wonder of knowing Christ (Phil 3:1-11; Gal 3:26-28). Glenn Loury, an African American economist and writer, gets to the heart of the issue:

> Who am I, then? Foremost, I am a child of God, created in his image, imbued with his spirit, endowed with his gifts, set free by his grace. The most important challenges and opportunities that confront me derive not from my racial condition, but rather from my human condition. I am a husband, a father, a son, a teacher, an intellectual, a Christian, a citizen. In none of these roles is my race irrelevant, but neither can racial identity alone provide much guidance for my quest to discharge these responsibilities adequately.[65]

Instead of stereotyping others (or even ourselves) by race or gender, Christians should "let God be God" as he demonstrates his unshakable kingdom through the marvelous diversity of his one redeemed people, the body of Christ (1 Cor 12:12-31). As these kingdom realities are demonstrated, the hollowness of postmodernist posturings can be exposed in the light of something far greater.[66]

---

[65]Glenn Loury, *One by One from the Inside Out: Essays and Reviews on Race and Responsibility in America* (New York: Free Press, 1995), pp. 7-8.
[66]My thanks go to Rebecca Merrill Groothuis for her invaluable and insightful assistance with this chapter.

10

TRUE BEAUTY
The Challenge to Postmoderism

A thin but sharp wedge of truth decay into Christian circles is the postmodern-
ist notion that art does not express objective value, that it cannot be
evaluated or rated on the basis of aesthetic properties and values that
transcend subjective taste, preference and cultural fashion. Beauty and
ugliness and all the territory in between are *only* in the eye of the
beholder. The postmodernist twist on this idea is that the eye of the
beholder dissolves into the social and cultural conditions that make the
perceiver of art who she is. Any artistic creation or evaluation can be
deconstructed into various contingent social elements such as class,
gender, race and historical epoch.

The consequence is that art cannot convey objective truth, although
it can express styles, emotions, political passions and ever-shifting cultural trends. Therefore, the postmodernist dismisses the traditional
stratification of culture into high, folk and low (or pop) culture. A paradigm of the traditional view is Matthew Arnold's nineteenth-century
definition of culture (the good kind) as "the best that has been known
and said in the world." Reference to "the best" involves an objective

standard of evaluation; it assumes there is good, better, best, as well as outright bad.

Although we profitably could fix our attention on how postmodernism affects other areas of life such as education, science, business or politics, I will consider art because it is a dimension of life that is experienced by everyone but seldom reflected upon in much depth. Christians should be different in this. Art can profoundly shape our worldviews and sensibilities without our knowing its persuasive power. Moreover, when the postmodernist rejection of objective aesthetic standards and values takes root, it easily washes over into moral standards and values as well. If all art is equal and beyond normative evaluation, who is to draw fixed boundaries on behavior either? Therefore, this chapter will assess the postmodernist rejection of objective aesthetic realities, instead of outlining various theories of postmodernist aesthetics. Along the way we will examine several examples of and issues in postmodernist art.[1]

Art: By What Standard?

Dominating all of postmodern culture, Christian and otherwise, is the common but pernicious notion that artistic endeavor cannot be judged objectively. The non-Christian angle was expressed by musician Brian Eno, who rejects "the traditional classical view" that "art objects are containers of some kind of aesthetic value" derived from an outside source such as God or the Muse that is, in turn, "radiated back out to those who beheld" the art object. Instead, Eno adopts the postmodernist perspective "that cultural objects have no notable identity outside of that which we confer upon them. . . . Their value is entirely a product of the interaction that we have with them."[2]

> Things become artworks not because they contain value, but because we're prepared to see them as artworks, to allow ourselves to have art

---

[1]For details on postmodernist art, see Gene Edward Veith Jr., *Postmodern Times: A Christian Critique of Contemporary Thought and Culture* (Wheaton, Ill.: Crossway, 1994), pp. 93-149; and Steven Connor, *Postmodernist Culture: An Introduction to Theories of the Contemporary*, 2nd ed. (Cambridge, Mass.: Blackwell, 1997), pp. 74-223.

[2]"Gossip as Philosophy," interview with Brian Eno, *Wired*, May 1995, p. 207.

experiences from them, before them, to frame them in contexts that confer value on them.[3]

Eno's comments echo the perspective that roused C. S. Lewis's classic defense of objective moral law, *The Abolition of Man*. Lewis wisely observed the close connection between aesthetic relativism and moral relativism, and so begins his book by assessing an aesthetic judgment, not a moral one. Lewis refers to two writers who "deconstruct" (to use a postmodernist word) Samuel Coleridge's judgment that one person's assessment of a waterfall as "sublime" was superior to another's perspective that it was merely "pretty." The writers claim that, "When the man said That is sublime, he appeared to be making a remark about the waterfall. . . . Actually. . . he was not making a remark about the waterfall, but a remark about his own feelings."[4] In other words, we err when we attribute objective aesthetic properties to objects of nature (or culture), because we are really only speaking of our own inner states. "We appear to be saying something very important about something: and actually we are only saying something about our own feelings."[5]

Sublimity is only a human projection. It is not something to discover in the outside world, let alone a gift from the Creator—whether in a waterfall, a symphony or a tenor saxophone solo. Although Lewis's interlocutors predated postmodernism, their approach chimes in with its themes because much of modernism and virtually all of postmodernism is relativistic on ethics and aesthetics.[6] The culture's aesthetic evaluations have been altered to accommodate the deconstructions of those who see through so many things.

Similarly, Roger Rollin celebrates the death of Good Taste (the ability to discern objective aesthetic value according to reliable criteria) and

---

[3]Ibid.
[4]C. S. Lewis, *The Abolition of Man* (1944; reprint, New York: Simon & Schuster, 1966), p. 18. Lewis calls the book *The Green Book* and identifies the authors as Gauis and Titius, but these are not the real names.
[5]Ibid.
[6]For more on the relationship between modernism and postmodernism, see chapter two.

the resultant abandonment of any sense of aesthetic hierarchy. For him, "condemnations of popular culture and its study on the basis of aesthetic evaluation—'You mean you study that junk?'—are misguided."[7] We are beyond distinguishing junk from jewels, or seeking a few jewels in the junk. There are neither pearls to protect from swine nor swine to trample pearls. All aesthetic hierarchy is dismantled.

In this vein, postmodernists take up the study of popular culture—often under the banner of "cultural studies"—by analyzing such things as comic strips, soap operas, soap boxes, toys and tabloids with all the seriousness once reserved for classics in literature, painting and cinema. Rollin typifies postmodernist tastes when he decries the ranking of cultural artifacts according to Good Taste as "aesthetic imperialism."[8] Such traditional art criticism really tells us more about the critics themselves than about what they study. Moreover, "all culture is consumer culture—made to be used—and inherently evanescent, having its truest existence in its consumption."[9] Thus all culture—from Kleenex boxes to clarinet solos—is collapsed into that which is used, and used up, without invoking the aristocratic categories of value or virtue, which are mere pretexts for cultural hegemony. Kitsch is ennobled, consumer culture is sanctified, high culture is cut down to size, and the notion of cultural stratification according to intrinsic aesthetic value is committed to the flames. Alain Finkielkraut aptly speaks of postmodern thought as engaging in "a joyous confusion that elevates every practice to the ranks of great human creations."[10]

Postmodernist enemies of Good Taste also deftly utilize the uniquely American weakness of suspending one's critical faculties any time the word "democracy" is invoked. Anyone who sets up a spectrum of value between high culture and low culture is, horror of horrors, being "undemocratic." Such an attitude betrays everything wonderful and

---

[7]Roger B. Rollin, "Popular Culture and the Death of 'Good Taste,'" *National Forum* 74, no. 4 (1994): 13.
[8]Ibid., p. 15.
[9]Ibid., p. 17.
[10]Alain Finkielkraut, *The Defeat of the Mind* (New York: Columbia University Press, 1995), p. 114.

distinctive about America. Ray B. Browne waxes patriotic when he claims:

> In the United States, popular culture is presumably the voice of democracy—what makes America the country that she is. It is, to paraphrase Lincoln's Gettysburg Address, culture "of the people, by the people, for the people." As such it thus becomes America's statement of humanity.[11]

Such sensibilities are not limited to America, however. Those seeking to create a museum of George Frederick Handel's one-time residence in London found that the late rock guitarist Jimi Hendrix (d. 1970) once lived in the house next door. While Hendrix fans wanted a commemorative blue plaque placed on his former residence, a spokesman from the Handel House Trust deemed that "quite inappropriate," given the unbecoming comparison. The spokesman for the Hendrix estate dismissed this reluctance as "a certain musical snobbery."[12] Handel must not trump Hendrix in postmodernity.

One is tempted to leave things with C. S. Lewis's biting comment that it should not be the business of the church

> to greatly co-operate with the modern State in appeasing inferiority complexes and encouraging the natural man's instinctive hatred of excellence. Democracy is all very well as a political device. It must not intrude into the spiritual, or even the aesthetic world."[13]

However, an examination of postmodernist perspectives on art must take us deeper than a snappy quote, for much is at stake—the truth of beauty and the beauty of truth. A unified Christian vision for life—incorporating the good, the true and the beautiful—is up for grabs in postmodernity. This was aptly articulated by Francis Schaeffer: "Christ is the Lord of our whole life and the Christ life would produce not only

---

[11]Ray B. Browne, "Culture 'of the People, by the People, for the People,'" *National Forum* 74, no. 4 (1994): 11.

[12]"Handel and Hendrix Make Poor Neighbors," *Rocky Mountain News*, March 23, 1995.

[13]C. S. Lewis, "On Church Music," *Christian Reflections* (Grand Rapids, Mich.: Eerdmans, 1956), p. 98.

truth—flaming truth—but also beauty."[14]

Problems and Issues in Postmodern Art

Theories of art and artistic works are legion and often complex, and post-modernist ideas of art are not all of a piece. Some artists do not subscribe to postmodernism as a destructive philosophy but employ postmodern ideas in an attempt to overcome some of the limitations of the modernist tradition in art that emphasized abstract form over particularities of style and ornamentation. For instance, the modernist international style of architecture eliminated references to previous styles and aimed at a universal and impersonal ethos where "form follows function." The stark skyscrapers erected before about 1970 in New York City tell this story. By contrast, some postmodern architecture attempts to establish connections with previous historical styles, abandoning cool abstraction for references to real history. Ornamentation is restored and function is augmented by aesthetic richness. However, the references to history may be more artificial than authentic because "in our posthistoric condition," history is often reduced to a "quote from old movies in a theme park ride."[15]

An example of constructive postmodern sensibilities can be found in some recent music. The globalization of cultures has allowed for much cross-pollination between musical styles in the last several decades, some of which represents innovation and excellence. One musical group, Bela Fleck and the Flecktones, has combined folk, bluegrass and jazz into a winning synthesis without cheapening any of the distinct genres or crassly playing for strange, offbeat effects. The Flecktones' music is complex, innovative and at times humorous, and displays virtuosity in composition and in performance. Are they "postmodern"? Yes, in some ways, since they transcend modernist categories; however, they do so in a manner than is not nihilistic, ugly, prefabricated or trivial.[16]

---

[14]Francis A. Schaeffer, *Art and the Bible* (Downers Grove, Ill.: InterVarsity Press, 1973), p. 31.
[15]William Irwin Thompson, *The American Replacement of Nature: The Everyday Acts and Outrageous Evolution of Economic Life* (New York: Doubleday, 1991), p. 10.
[16]On postmodernism in jazz, see Ted Gioia, *The History of Jazz* (New York: Oxford University Press, 1997), pp. 355-64, 376, 381, 383.

But not all innovations are improvements. There are a few recurring postmodernist ideas that reinforce truth decay instead of creatively responding to the impersonal abstractions of modernism in art. Much postmodern music is mere mass-marketed pastiche with concern for neither truth nor beauty. These developments should alert the Christian. As Christian educator Frank Gaebelein put it, "Art that distorts the truth is no more pleasing to God than any other kind of untruth," because "the God of all truth looks for integrity in artistic expression as well as in theology."[17] How does postmodernism threaten truth in art?

First, for postmodernists, art must be freed from the impossible burden (imposed upon it in premodern and modern forms) to mean or represent one thing and to conform to received standards. If reality itself is incoherent, ad hoc and unknowable, art can have no stable framework or foundation from which to proceed. Postmodern pluralism has produced a great profusion of styles and forms, with no coherence in sight. Instead of sorting through the plethora of possibilities in order to find integrity and discover a hierarchy of artistic goods, postmodernist style emphasizes pastiche over pattern and amalgamation over arrangement. Derrida claims that the form of postmodernist discourse is the collage, which has no unified meaning or singular reference. Contemporary art, with its welter of conflicting meanings and images, gives us "a signification which could be neither univocal nor stable."[18] Artistic signs—whether printed words or painted images or recorded sounds—no longer connect with anything signified, anything outside of themselves. Signs are wrenched from signification, and art is divorced from objective truth and meaning. As English critic D. S. Savage put it, "Art is speech, and speech is ultimately impossible where there is no absolute existential relation to truth."[19] Postmodernist art, then, becomes mute with respect to truth.

Baudrillard elaborates on this problem with respect to the death of artistic standards of truth:

---

[17]Frank E. Gaebelein, *The Christian, the Arts, and the Truth: Regaining the Vision of Greatness*, ed. D. Bruce Lockerbie (Portland, Ore.: Multnomah Press, 1985), p. 52.

[18]Veith, *Postmodern Times*, p. 98.

[19]D. S. Savage, *The Withered Branch*; cited in Iris Murdoch, *Sartre: Romantic Rationalist* (New York: Viking Press, 1987; orig. pub., 1953), p. 74.

In the aesthetic realm of today there is no longer any God to recognize his own. Or, to use a different metaphor, there is no gold standard of aesthetic judgement or pleasure. The situation resembles that of a currency which may not be exchanged: it can only float, its only reference itself, impossible to convert into real value or wealth.[20]

He further speaks of the inertia or stasis of the art world, which displays a kind of exhaustion, "something that can no longer transcend itself and has therefore turned in upon itself, merely repeating itself at a faster and faster rate."[21] This paralysis of self-reference is evidenced by the endless cinematic remakes of low-culture television shows such as *Flintstones, The Brady Bunch, Lost in Space* and *Batman,* and by sequels and prequels of hit movies ad infinitum, ad nauseum.

Postmodernist art aspires no longer to represent or express the essence or nature of anything but rather to exhibit diversity, multiplicity, plurality and aimless fecundity. Modernism aspired to be deep; postmodernism forsakes the depths for the play of surfaces. Terry Eagleton notes that the postmodernist "stance towards cultural tradition is one of irreverent pastiche, and its contrived depthlessness undermines all metaphysical solemnities, sometimes by a brutal aesthetics of squalor and shock."[22]

Second, postmodernist art finds no need for rationality in expression; the meaning of an artwork need not be fixed or even discernible. Since reality is indeterminate and unknowable, there is no truth to be captured by art and, therefore, no reason to be rational in attempting the impossible. Rationality, after all, is merely a pretense for domination. Logocentricism, as Derrida and others have claimed, must be overthrown, and art is one means by which to destabilize and even topple the government of reason and the imperialism of logic. MTV, a prime cultural engine of postmodernist sensibilities, assaults the sense of rational narrative and analysis with its incessant, rapid-fire jump

---

[20]Jean Baudrillard, *The Transparency of Evil: Essays on Extreme Phenomena,* trans. James Benedict (New York: Verso, 1990), pp. 14-15.

[21]Ibid., p. 14.

[22]Terry Eagleton, "Awakening from Modernity," *Times Literary Supplement,* February 20, 1987.

cuts and incandescent incoherence, thus glorifying the visually visceral at the expense of the cerebral. As Kaplan astutely put it:

> MTV refuses any clear recognition of previously sacred aesthetic bound-aries; images from German Expressionism, French Surrealism, and Dada-ism . . . are mixed together with those pillaged from the noir, gangster, and horror films, in such a way as to obliterate differences.[23]

Coherence is the calculated casualty when eclecticism loses any uni-fying center or defining circumference. Linear presentations cease to ex-ist, and whirl reigns. This creates an environment in which the ascertaining of truth becomes a herculean task, which is rarely at-tempted, seldom achieved and never encouraged. Postmodernist art does not cease to communicate a worldview, however chaotically it may be presented. It communicates a chaotic worldview in which meaning is mangled, value is vaporized, significance is shattered, and apathy is deified. Those who never read a postmodernist author will be affected by postmodernist themes in art. As Schaeffer pointed out, "Art forms add strength to the world view that shows through, no matter what the world view is or whether the world view is true or false."[24]

Third, when objective and rational standards for aesthetics are aban-doned, postmodernist art can resort to bludgeoning and bullying its au-dience for purely political purposes. Artists often receive state funds for these efforts and dismiss objections as reactionary, hegemonic, ho-mophobic, puritan, fundamentalist and so on. Such politicized displays can even be quite repulsive, and dangerous.

The Walker Art Center in Minneapolis hosted "performance artist" Ron Athey, who had acupuncture needles woven into his scalp by two women assistants while he pierced his arm with thirty hypodermic nee-dles and carved a design onto the back of Darryl Carlton, a fellow per-former. Bloodstained towels were hoisted over the audience on clotheslines, accompanied by Athey's drumming and the dancing of two women who danced until bells sewn into their bodies detached

---

[23]E. Ann Kaplin, *Rocking Around the Clock* (New York: Methuen, 1987), p. 34; quoted in Kenneth Gergen, *The Saturated Self* (New York: Basic Books, 1991), p. 133.
[24]Schaeffer, *Art and the Bible*, p. 38.

and caused bleeding. The audience did not know that Athey's dripping blood was HIV-positive. This "art" was partially funded by the National Endowment for the Arts. The NEA's then chairperson, Jane Alexander, dismissed protests by saying, "Not all art is for everybody."[25] This is aesthetic nihilism: art is uprooted from moral and aesthetic standards. As Corduan notes, when art becomes "nothing more than the function of human whim," it "is laid open to the whim of whoever is in power."[26] Under such circumstances, art can become an antinomian arm of the State for propaganda purposes. Postmodernist art has consequences.[27]

Christians rightly condemn such overt ugliness and immorality, especially when it receives government funding. But many Christians have capitulated to some postmodernist sensibilities regarding artistic truth. A respect for beauty and aesthetic excellence have been eclipsed. Christians should esteem art as a medium for truth and beauty, and so resist postmodernist seductions. A thoroughly Christian understanding of art and the practice of art makes for a strong weapon of resistance against postmodernist erosions of true beauty and the beauty of truth.

Countering Postmodernism: A Christian View of Art
Schaeffer provides an image to inspire a theology of art in his booklet *Art and the Bible* (1973). He speaks of a mural in the art museum at Neuchatel, Switzerland, painted by the Christian artist Paul Robert. The mural depicts the town of Neuchatel and its surroundings. The foreground, near the bottom, shows a dragon fatally wounded. Underneath it are depictions of the vile, ugly and pornographic. Near the top Jesus is depicted as descending with the heavenly hosts. To the left are beautiful women and men on a stairway who are carrying the symbols of different kinds of art. They are carrying them away from the dragon in order to present them to Christ. "Paul Robert understood Scripture a lot

---

[25]Nat Hentoff, "Unsuspecting Patrons Assaulted in the Name of Art," *Rocky Mountain News*, May 30, 1994.
[26]Winfried Corduan, *No Doubt About It: Basic Christian Apologetics* (Nashville: Broadman & Holman, 1997), p. 266.
[27]See ibid., pp. 264-67.

better than many of us. He saw that at the Second Coming the Lordship of Christ will include everything."[28] Because the mural shows the town of Neuchatel and the museum in it, Robert was showing that "works of art should be to the praise of Christ now. The reality of the future has meaning for the present!"[29]

Those who aspire to honor the cosmic lordship of Christ have compelling reasons to accept, recognize, savor and manifest objective aesthetic truths. This is not a snobbish imposition upon the Scripture but a truth that richly resonates at the core of holy Writ. Let me build this case.

First, God created the world according to his will and design. Surveying the work, God deemed it "good"—even before humans were created. There existed an intrinsic goodness that was not specifically moral goodness, since no moral agents yet existed on earth. God brought forth and blessed his creation as *aesthetically* good. It was beautiful, pure and brim full of potential. It was good through and through.

Second, the Creator made the man and woman as the pinnacle of creation, created in the "image and likeness of God." These humans, though of the dust of earth, also came from the Spirit; their sinless feet were planted on the earth, while their imaginations could soar beyond the stars. The task assigned to each of them—as subcreators and stewards under God—was to have equal dominion over creation and to cultivate it within God's wisdom. Much discussion has centered on how humans express the image of God, but, as Dorothy Sayers rightly observed, when we

> turn back to see what [the author of Genesis] says about the original upon which the "image of God" was modeled, we find only the single assertion, "God created." The characteristic common to God and man is apparently that: the desire and the ability to make things.[30]

As God's image-bearers, women and men make things of all kinds, for both functional and artistic purposes. They chop wood for fire and

---

[28]Schaeffer, *Art and the Bible*, pp. 30-31.
[29]Ibid., p. 31.
[30]Dorothy L. Sayers, *The Mind of the Maker* (New York: Harper & Row, 1979), p. 22.

carve wood for decoration; they harvest crops for food and practice cui-
sine for taste; they shovel snow for safety and make snowmen for fun.
Artistic expression is a natural part of God's good creation.

Third, we have reason to believe that God aesthetically enjoys many
aspects of the creation. God made it and knows it in all its multifaceted
being. Philosopher and devotional writer Dallas Willard recounts an
overwhelming experience on the beaches of South Africa when he
"stood in stunned silence and then slowly walked toward the waves.
Words cannot capture the view confronting me. I saw space and light
and texture and color and power . . . that seemed hardly of this earth."
Willard gradually realized that

> God sees this all the time. He sees it, experiences it, knows it from every
> possible point of view, this and billions of other scenes like and unlike it,
> in this and billions of other worlds. Great tidal waves of joy must con-
> stantly wash through his being.[31]

The Creator's recognition and enjoyment of this value is aesthetic
delight. The created beauty delights its Maker. This is reminiscent of the
Wisdom of God that delighted in the things that were made, as re-
counted by the writer of Proverbs (8:22-31).

Fourth, tragedy invaded creation when God's creatures turned against
their Lord, sided with the seductions of the serpent, experienced death in
their beings and then found sin poisoning their once-pristine planet (Gen
3). From then on, all human culture became a thick and complex admix-
ture of good and evil. Human creators—both redeemed and unredeemed—still serve as instruments of God's beauty and truth through
their artistic endeavors, but the very gifts of God given to his image-bearers can be turned against the Creator and the creation itself through sin.
Patterns of good and evil, beauty and ugliness, truth and falsity dye everything east of Eden. Such conditions demand moral and aesthetic discernment. Our world is cursed, and our world is blessed; we must divine
the difference between the two lest we bless what is cursed or curse what
is blessed. As Isaiah said, "Woe to those who call evil good and good evil,

---

[31]Dallas Willard, *The Divine Conspiracy* (New York: HarperSanFrancisco, 1998), pp.
62-63.

who put darkness for light and light for darkness, who put bitter for sweet and sweet for bitter" (Is 5:20).

Yet, fifth, spiritual transcendence may peek or even shine through nature and culture, because creation can express aesthetic excellence far beyond the brute possibilities of mere evolving matter. As Kreeft and Tacelli tersely and humorously put it in their aesthetic argument for the existence of God:

> There is the music of Johann Sebastian Bach.
> Therefore there must be a God.
> You either see this one or you don't.[32]

The authors do not develop this point, but unless there is objective aesthetic value, this brand of argument falls flat. Nevertheless, the Artist does leave traces and clues waiting to be found by his attentive creatures. One Russian Ph.D. student was so impressed with the beauty of some mathematical equations about the universe that he was moved from atheism to theism—even though he was religiously constrained under the old atheistic establishment of the USSR. In the late 1980s, the student exclaimed to a visiting Christian professor of physics:

> I was in Siberia and I met God there while I was working on my equations. I suddenly realized that the beauty of these equations had to have a purpose and design behind them, and I felt deep in my spirit that God was speaking to me through these equations. But I don't know much about Him. Could you tell me about Him?

The American professor gladly obliged, and the student was converted and baptized.[33] Objective beauty is part of God's general revelation (Ps 19:1-6; Acts 14:17; Rom 1—2). For the Russian scientist, God was revealed through both the beauty of the universe and the beauty of the equations that attempted to describe it. These are both objective re-

---

[32]Peter Kreeft and Ronald K. Tacelli, *Handbook of Christian Apologetics* (Downers Grove, Ill.: InterVarsity Press, 1994), p. 81.

[33]"Soviets, Scientists, and Salvation," *Tentmaking Today*, winter 1988, p. 6. The names of the professor and student were withheld in the article because it was published before the fall of communism, when evangelism and conversion were more dangerous. However, Rebecca Merrill Groothuis was the editor of the piece and can vouch for its authenticity.

alities, cases of aesthetic truth seen for what they are.

Sixth, God's concern for beauty is amply documented in the specifi-cations for Israel's ancient temple, which, as Christian architect Daniel Lee notes, "was one of the finest works of art in its day. It combined fig-urative sculpture, exquisite materials, and beautiful proportions, all cre-ated by God's explicit design." The public worship commanded by God "included musical instruments of all kinds, and a trained choir with thousands of voices."[34] Precious stones were placed in the temple for the purpose of displaying beauty (2 Chron 3:6). As Schaeffer notes, "There was no pragmatic reason for the stones. They had no utilitarian purpose. . . . God is interested in beauty."[35] Angels were depicted, as well as objects from the natural world. The temple, the place for wor-shiping the Creator of all beauty, was itself objectively beautiful. It pos-sessed aesthetic value that was not attributable to mere function, cultural trend or subjective preference.

Objective artistic value is also rooted in God's inspiration of artistic work. When God instructed Moses concerning the building of the tab-ernacle, he said that Bezalel was "filled . . . with the Spirit of God, with skill, ability and knowledge in all kinds of crafts" in order to do the ar-tistic work needed (see Ex 31:1-11). Other skilled workers were also given abilities by God for their aesthetic tasks.[36]

Seventh, in contrast to the postmodernist disregard of objective beauty and lasting aesthetic value, a biblical understanding of culture recognizes real properties of artistic goodness in cultural artifacts and looks forward to their being purified and transformed in the world to come. This gives the aesthetic enterprise a hope for meaning and significance beyond the dreams of any of those who deconstruct art into merely cultural, political, linguistic and psychological elements. God's gifts are not limited to natu-ral beauty or the salvation of human souls but incorporate the objective good that is present in diverse aspects of human culture.

---

[34]Duncan G. Stroik, "Is There a Christian Architecture? An Interview with Daniel Lee," *Re:Generation Quarterly* 4, no. 1 (1998): 20.

[35]Schaeffer, *Art and the Bible*, p. 15.

[36]Many of the same points can be found in the nature of the tabernacle described in Exodus 25. See Schaeffer, *Art and the Bible*, pp. 11-14.

Richard Mouw, developing themes from theologian Abraham Kuyper, makes this case in *When the Kings Come Marching In* (1983). Mouw's treatment of the subject is a potent antidote to postmodernist nihilism, as well as to Christian misconceptions about the arts.

Certain evangelical clichés engender a kind of narrow-mindedness and hinder a deeper theological appreciation of aesthetics. We hear it said that "only God and people are eternal" or, concerning culture, "It's all going to burn anyway." Some think that any artistic endeavor unrelated to evangelism or worship is unimportant to God. Culture has only an instrumental value for more important things—things of eternity. We use it to win people to Christ or to express worship. But eternity is no place for earthly artifacts; they will be long forgotten. People are saved; earthly culture is terminated. It is replaced by a heavenly arrangement wholly different from the sin-stained past, besides a few harps and white robes.

Although the world is now under sin and will one day be brought kicking and screaming before God's eternal judgment to account for its rebellion, God will not obliterate every aspect of human culture or only use it as the furniture of hell. Isaiah 60 speaks of the heavenly city—or the perfected end-time kingdom—as a place that will receive "the riches of the nations" (v. 5). Even while describing God's sentence against human pride and arrogance, Isaiah speaks of a future restoration. Similarly, after the narrative of cosmic conflict in the book of Revelation, John tells of "the glory and honour of the nations" that shall be ushered into the heavenly city (Rev 21:26), even though the wickedness of Babylonian wealth has been laid waste (Rev 18:15-17).

These texts do not imply that the unrepentant will be redeemed in spite of their rebellion against God (see Mt 25:31-46; Rev 21:8). Punishment on the evildoers will be enacted, but some of the works of their hands may endure as blessings—although to the praise of God. The key to solving this puzzle of damned souls and redeemed culture may be found in comparing references in Isaiah 2 and 60. Isaiah 2 speaks of a day when the Lord of hosts will turn against "all the proud and lofty, for all that is exalted," such as costly lumber from Lebanon, commercial vessels, beautiful crafts and even the means of military protection. Yet these same items appear in chapter 60 as transformed and radiating God's goodness in the world to come! How can this be?

We must consider the "ships of Tarshish" (Is 60:9). These vessels are rather mysterious in Scripture. Tarshish may have been a region near ancient Palestine, or it may simply be a shorthand term for "the farther regions," but we need not settle that. The crux is that they were impressive ships capable of carrying large loads for long distances. Unredeemed, they symbolized hubris and autonomy.[37] Or as Habakkuk put it in another context, they exemplified a view that made human strength into a god (Hab 1:11). Mouw argues that the idolatrous uses of these artifacts will be rejected in the heavenly city, but their intrinsic goodness will be retained because "I [God] am making everything new!" (Rev 21:5). Unrepentant people, however, will be consigned to the lake of fire and experience the second death (Rev 21:8). Yet according to Mouw:

> God will not destroy the things which they have put to their own rebellious uses. The New Jerusalem will be bedecked with jewels and metals gathered from the nations of the earth; and "the glory and the honor of the nations" will be brought into the transformed City (Revelation 21:26).

This perspective is alien to many American evangelicals because of a lack of theological reflection on the broader vistas of culture in relation to God's kingdom. Yet it makes good sense theologically. The earth and everything in it belongs to God (Ps 24:1). He commissioned humans to fill it with their cultural creations (Gen 1:26-28; Ps 8). God is the bestower of every gift, both to the pagan and the Christian, by his common grace (Mt 5:48; Jas 1:17). The lordship of Christ implicates all things, for he has preeminence over all creation (Mt 28:18; Col 1:15-19). The imperfection of a fallen creation demands purgation, judgment and restoration. Mouw states it well:

> The "stuff" of human cultural rebellion will nonetheless be gathered into the Holy City. God still owns the "filling." The earth—including the American military and French art and Chinese medicine and Nigerian

---

[37]Richard Mouw, *When the Kings Come Marching In: Isaiah and the New Jerusalem* (Grand Rapids, Mich.: Eerdmans, 1983), p. 12.

agriculture—belongs to the Lord. And he will reclaim all of these things, harnessing them for service in the City.[38]

Mouw observes that no military weapon serves as a weapon in the restored creation but is transformed, because the Lord will "beat their swords into plowshares and their spears into pruning hooks" (Is 2:4). Nevertheless, even armaments may bespeak something of human creativity and intelligence, despite their being premised on the sinful realities of a violent world. I believe that in the eschatological kingdom aesthetic goodness of all kinds will be recognized, conserved and (where necessary) transformed as part of the furniture of heaven. In his commentary on the book of Revelation, Jacques Ellul emphasizes that unlike the Tower of Babel (Gen 11), which aspires to work toward heaven from earth, the New Jerusalem comes down from heaven as God's gift of cosmic restoration and not as the culmination of human progress.[39] Nevertheless, it is a glorious *city*—not a restored *garden*—which bears the uniquely human touch.

> All that which had been the cultural, scientific, technical, aesthetic, intellectual work, all the music and sculpture, all the poetry and mathematics, all philosophy and knowledge of all orders, all enter into this Jerusalem, used by God to build up his final perfect work. . . . It is not a museum but an integration into a living whole.[40]

Believing this, the follower of Christ has reason to respect and create works of lasting aesthetic value in every dimension of life. Mouw brings this all together. We must "allow this knowledge to shape the basic attitude and expectations that we bring to our wrestling with the practical questions" of life.

> We must train ourselves to look at the worlds of commerce and art and recreation and education and technology, and confess that all of this "filling" belongs to God. And then we must engage in the difficult business of

---

[38]Ibid., p. 19.

[39]Jacques Ellul, *Apocalypse: The Book of Revelation* (New York: Seabury, 1977), pp. 222-24. David Werther pointed out this reference to me. Although Ellul's insights in this chapter are sometimes profound, I do not follow his tendency toward universalism.

[40]Ibid., p. 225.

finding patterns of cultural involvement which are consistent with that confession. If, in a fundamental and profound sense, God has not given up on human culture, then neither must we.[41]

Developing Aesthetic Discernment

Despite the nihilistic mood of much postmodernist culture, and despite the rejection of objective aesthetic goodness and the displays of ugliness, Christians should remember God's dominion and demands as well as earth's final destiny. Nothing truly good will ever be lost, and nothing evil will triumph over the good—artistic ventures included. Therefore, we should learn to appreciate the aesthetic goodness of nature and culture, to be discerning and develop "disciplined taste," as T. S. Eliot put it,[42] which recognizes objective value beyond our subjective preferences and beyond cultural and marketing trends. While postmodernism terminates meaning and value in the self or society, the Christian worldview widens our horizons, floods our world with divine light and sharpens our focus. This transforming vision allows us to gaze outside of ourselves and to align ourselves rightly with all manner of value—ethical and aesthetic.

A strong theology of creation and objective goodness—both moral and artistic—informs Paul's famous imperatives:

> Finally, brothers and sisters, whatever is true, whatever is noble, whatever is right, whatever is pure, whatever is lovely, whatever is admirable—if anything is excellent or praiseworthy—think about such things. (Phil 4:8)

As Kenneth Myers observes, "Paul does not say that we should reflect on what we *think* is lovely, or whatever we *feel* is admirable. We are to give sustained attention to whatever is *objectively* true and noble and right."[43] The recognition of objective value—whether moral, aesthetic or intellectual—is a discipline of the mind and spirit. Art may uniquely serve this end, as art educator Alexandra York comments:

[41]Mouw, *When the Kings Come*, p. 21.
[42]T. S. Eliot, *Notes Towards the Definition of Culture* (New York: Harcourt, Brace, 1949), p. 29.
[43]Kenneth Myers, *All God's Children and Blue Suede Shoes: Christians and Popular Culture* (Wheaton, Ill.: Crossway, 1989), p. 98; emphasis in the original.

At its apotheosis—aesthetically, philosophically, and psychologically—art provides a spiritual summation by integrating mind and matter. It allows abstract value to be perceived by the senses. And when form and content are exquisitely united in art, they are capable of communicating universal truths.[44]

How we respond to aesthetic value is equally a mark of our maturity, because it requires that we respond properly to God's reality. C. S. Lewis captured this when arguing for objective value:

> The doctrine of objective value [is] the belief that certain attitudes are really true, and others really false, to the kind of thing the universe is and the kind of things we are. . . . Because our approvals and disapprovals are thus recognitions of objective value or responses to an objective order, therefore emotional states can be in harmony with reason (when we feel liking for what ought to be approved) or out of harmony with reason (when we perceive that liking is due but cannot feel it). No emotion is, in itself, a judgement: in that sense all emotions and sentiments are alogical. But they can be reasonable or unreasonable as they conform to Reason or fail to conform.[45]

Lewis's argument addresses both moral and aesthetic value. Aesthetic evaluation should involve the emotions of the perceiver, but the emotions ought to be calibrated to the nature of the object apprehended. It makes no sense to translate the statement "The waterfall is sublime" to mean "I have sublime feelings." The emotions appropriate before the sublime may be awe or humility or thanksgiving or reverence, but the emotions themselves do not possess the properties of that which is being perceived.

Just as my experience of roundness when I see an orange is not itself round, my experience of aesthetic excellence has an objective reference beyond the experience itself. To think otherwise is to fundamentally confuse the perceiving subject with the perceived object.[46] Beauty *is* in the eye (or ear or imagination) of the beholder in that one identifies it and (ideally) responds to it in a particular way that is fit-

[44]Alexandra York, "The Fourth 'R' in Education: Reading, Writing, Arithmetic and Art," *Imprimus* 27, no. 6 (1998): 5.
[45]Lewis, *Abolition of Man*, pp. 31-32.
[46]Ibid.

ting. But beauty is not *only* in the eye of beholder. The act of aesthetic judgment is a judgment of something outside myself, which I take to possess certain qualities, whether it be a painting, a sculpture or a musical performance.[47] My aural experience of the elegance of a particular Pat Metheny jazz guitar solo is uniquely mine, and it produces a subjective response. But Metheny's playing is, in itself, excellent and "worthy of praise," because he has mastered a difficult medium with a style entirely his own, yet still rooted deeply in jazz history. D. Elton Trueblood captures this truth of objective aesthetic value, which bears on our discussion of the nature of truth in chapter four:

> It is reasonable to conclude that the truth about beauty is similar, in logical structure, to any other truth about the world; judgments are true only when they are independent of each observer. The essence of truth is that it is potentially public, even though it might, for a time, be recognized by only one or two persons.[48]

The reception of art often—but not always—evokes emotions, but art is not reducible to emotions or any form of subjectivity. As Lewis argued, our emotional reactions are either congruous or incongruous with the objective facts of the universe. Objects, whether of nature or culture, do not merely *receive* our approval or disapproval, but can and should *merit* certain responses.

Veith nicely illustrates this by responding to the often-heard remark, "I don't know much about art, but I know what I like"—which means that what we "like" is all there is to it. But if a person says he "liked" a blockbuster slasher film, one should ask, "What was good, the cinematography, the acting, the plot development . . . ?" The answer will be "No." The film evoked a strong sensual reaction, but this is not the same as aesthetic goodness. One may be intensely entertained by the mediocre, the tasteless, the trite and the bad.[49] This is a function of bad taste and psychology; it says nothing about the objective aesthetic

---

[47]See C. E. M. Joad, *Philosophy for our Times* (New York: Thomas Nelson, 1940), pp. 178-89.

[48]D. Elton Trueblood, *General Philosophy* (New York: Harper & Row, 1963), p. 246.

[49]Gene Edward Veith Jr., *State of the Arts: From Bezalel to Mapplethorpe* (Wheaton, Ill.: Crossway, 1991), p. 39.

worth of the film.

Take another case. The saxophonist Kenny G is today far more popular than the late jazz saxophonist John Coltrane (d. 1967). Despite Kenny G's immense notoriety (over twenty million recordings sold), his light and customized music is, I believe, intrinsically inferior to that of Coltrane's. A person may "really like" Kenny G's "emaciated pseudo-jazz,"[50] yet still be objectively wrong if she thinks G's playing and composing is of higher aesthetic value than Coltrane's. Kenny G *receives* much praise but fails to *merit* it. This is because Coltrane's passion and endless creativity as a soloist and composer, his pursuance of new forms of expression, his extensive knowledge of many forms of music and his nearly telepathic improvisational skill with his other musicians, put him in a category that utterly transcends Kenny G.

Moreover, Coltrane's philosophy of music, although not explicitly Christian, expressed a yearning to represent objective realities musically, while Kenny G only speaks of expressing *himself*: "I just play for myself, the way I play, and it comes out sounding like me."[51] Compare this statement with Coltrane's reflections:

> Overall, I think the main thing a musician would like to do is to give a picture to the listener of the many wonderful things he knows and senses in the universe. That's what music is to me—it's just another way of saying this is a big, beautiful universe we live in, that's been given to us, and here's an example of just how magnificent and encompassing it is. That's what I would like to do. I think that's one of the greatest things you can do in life, and we all try to do it in some way. The musician's is through his music.[52]

Coltrane's philosophy of music is worthy of contemplation and imitation in the arts. He strove to represent our magnificent cosmos through music, a cosmos saturated with objective beauty bestowed as a gift. Coltrane's music expresses a spiritual quest, which may or may

---

[50]Ted Gioia, *A History of Jazz* (New York: Oxford University Press, 1997), p. 371.

[51]Interview with Kenny G in *BMG Jazz Club Magazine*, summer 1998, p. 4.

[52]John Coltrane interview in Eric Nisenson, *Ascension: John Coltrane and His Quest* (New York: De Cappo, 1993), p. 121.

not have been fulfilled, but his music sometimes evokes transcendence. After a uniquely inspired performance of his piece, "A Love Supreme," an extended jazz prayer, Coltrane stepped from the stage, put down his saxophone and intoned, "*Nunc dimittius.*" These are opening words in Latin for the prayer of the biblical character Simeon, which are traditionally sung during evening prayers. After beholding the infant Messiah, Simeon prayed, "Sovereign Lord, as you have promised, you now dismiss your servant in peace" (Lk 2:29). Coltrane may not have been ready for eternity himself, but his actions revealed that he had received and achieved excellence. He rendered praise where it was due.[53]

Some readers may blanch at my insistence that there are objective aesthetic values rooted in creation and evidenced in human creativity. Evangelicals tend to view art according to simple moral concerns (it ought not be pornographic, attack God or be otherwise immoral). They also deem it pragmatic (it serves evangelistic or moral ends), sentimental (God looks at the heart, not at the art) and as unrelated to objective aesthetic standards (there is no accounting for taste). While these views are not uniquely postmodernist, they dangerously overlap postmodernist philosophies and sensibilities. Christians who hold these views cannot mount a strong counterinsurgency to postmodernism in the arts, a realm that touches us all so deeply and repeatedly.

Beyond Postmodernism: Art in Architecture

For example, the architecture of many churches today shows little respect for objective beauty or the sense of transcendence. Rather, the churches reflect common tastes for mass consumption and resemble shopping malls and theaters. Christian architect Daniel Lee laments,

---

[53]This account is given by Os Guinness in *The Call* (Waco, Tex.: Word, 1998), p. 45. For more on Coltrane's philosophy of life and music, see Nisenson, *Ascension*. For the most thorough musical and biographical analysis of Coltrane, see John Porter, *John Coltrane: His Life and Music* (Ann Arbor: University of Michigan Press, 1998). For an excellent explanation of jazz as a musical art form, see Jonny King, *What Jazz Is: An Insider's Guide to Understanding and Listening to Jazz* (New York: Walker, 1997); and Ted Gioia, *The Imperfect Art: Reflections of Jazz and Modern Culture* (New York: Oxford University Press, 1987).

"When people go to these churches, what they see are forms of commu-nication and imagery they are already comfortable with, and a freedom to consume, to come and go, like in a shopping mall."[54] Yet if the mall is "the T.V. you can walk through,"[55] how can this ambiance alert us to the transcendent, the sacred, the unchanging and unchangeable verities of the God of truth? Lee's vision counters postmodernist whimsy, superfi-ciality and artificiality:

> Paul spoke of the beauty of holiness. I want to capture something of holiness in my work. I seek to design buildings [churches] that in their beauty reveal something of the spectacular beauty of God. My goal is to create architecture that connects to generations past, across centuries of time.[56]

Lee rejects the formalism of modernism and the kitsch of postmod-ernism, and aspires to appropriate the best of the classical tradition of architecture without simply aping the past. Rather than immersing worshipers in present consumer styles, Lee wants his buildings to be conduits that connect the people of God with their spiritual ancestors as well as to God's holiness.

Similar insights should be applied to the church's worship, where a postmodern pastiche of popular and traditional often eclipses the sense of the sacred. Many worship services exhibit eclecticism without an aes-thetic center of gravity; they are a grab bag of choruses, skits, announce-ments and light, entertaining "messages" (not sermons). There is little room for rumination on truth through appropriate artistic forms in worship. It may even distract us from worshiping God "in spirit and in truth" (Jn 4:24).[57] Truth decay often strikes here as well.[58]

---

[54]Stroik, "Is There a Christian Architecture?" p. 21.
[55]Carole Rifkind, "America's Fantasy Urbanism: The Waxing of the Mall and the Waning of Civility," in *Dumbing Down: Essays on the Strip-Mining of American Cul-ture*, ed. Katherine Washburn and John F. Thornton (New York: W. W. Norton, 1996), p. 263. She is quoting William Kowinski but gives no reference.
[56]Ibid.
[57]See Rebecca Merrill Groothuis, "Putting Worship into the Worship Service," in Douglas Groothuis, *Christianity That Counts* (Grand Rapids, Mich.: Baker, 1994), pp. 72-84; on postmodern religion in general, see Veith, *Postmodern Times*, pp. 191-234.
[58]For more on worship in relation to postmodernism, see chapter eleven.

This chapter has not tackled in depth the difficult question of identifying or applying objective standards to works of art (such as complexity, unity, creativity, inevitability), outside of noting some violations of these standards in postmodernist art.[59] My emphatic point is that one who honors Scripture has good reason to believe in real aesthetic value and to reject postmodern relativism as strongly in art as in ethics or theology. Some Christians dismiss this project of honoring objective artistic value because it is alien to their worldview and because they are little acquainted with this kind of judgment. Nevertheless, an "obedient aesthetic life" demands such discernment.[60] The alternative is a cultural capitulation—either implicitly or explicitly—to postmodernist decline. Such surrender only furthers the truth decay already so rampant in our culture.

---

[59]See Schaeffer, *Art and the Bible*, pp. 33-63; Trueblood, *General Philosophy*, pp. 249-53; Myers, *All God's Children*, pp. 75-88; Gaebelein, *Christian, the Arts*, pp. 61-114.
[60]Calvin Seerveld, *Rainbows for Fallen World: Aesthetic Life and Artistic Task* (Beaver Falls, Penn.: Radix, 1980), pp. 42-77.

11

THE FIXED POINT IN A POSTMODERN WORLD

By the time you read this book, postmodernism may be regarded by some as passé or outmoded. Some are already discussing what might emerge after postmodernism (post-postmodernism?), and at least one academic conference has addressed this theme. Nevertheless, the issues I have taken up concerning the nature of truth and its defense and application in our day will remain pertinent and inescapable for some time to come. It may well be that the way in which Christians orient themselves to postmodernism will become the great theological and philosophical watershed for the third millennium.

The Next Watershed

From roughly 1900 to 1930, American Protestants in every denomination were engaged in what historians call the fundamentalist-modernist controversy, a cultural contest that continues to affect Christians. At issue was the authority of Scripture in light of some modern scholarship. The theological modernists (also known as theological liberals) wanted to accommodate the critics who saw biblical supernaturalism as irrational and out of step with the times. The Bible, they argued, must be reinterpreted in ways that downplay or eliminate miracles and other supposedly superstitious claims. Belief in God, the importance—although not the plenary inspiration and inerrancy—of the Bible and the ethical teachings of Jesus were retained, but doctrines such as the virgin birth of Christ, his deity, his literal resurrection and his second coming were deemed mythological and inessential to Christian faith.

Those affirming historical orthodoxy, such as the stalwart apologist J. Gresham Machen (1881-1937), argued that this liberal scholarship was overrated. The Christian can and must affirm a thoroughly supernatural faith without sacrificing one's God-given intellect. In his classic work *Christianity and Liberalism* (1923), Machen affirmed that liberalism was not another version of Christianity but an entirely different religion. He was correct. A Christianity shorn of the miraculous elements that offend some scholars or nominal Christians is not what Jesus and the apostles taught at all. Denominations and churches within denominations today still divide on this essential matter. Is the Bible, properly interpreted, the final authority on whatever it addresses, or can it be revised and updated as we clever, clever people gain further insights into reality?

But note that this watershed debate focused primarily on what biblical claims were *true*, not on the nature of *truth* itself. Both modernists and fundamentalists held to the view that a statement was true if it matched reality. Fundamentalists believed that Jesus was born of a virgin and modernists denied this; fundamentalists believed in a literal second coming and modernists denied this. And so on.

Although the issues addressed by the fundamentalist-modernist debate still affect us, I believe the real watershed today is found at a different place—in some ways, a deeper place: the nature of truth itself. Many outside the Christian orbit reject the notion that truth is what corresponds to reality. Instead of looking for objective, absolute and universal truths, they deconstruct these kinds of imperious metanarratives into merely personal and cultural statements that have no necessary connection with external reality. Sadly, just as modernists gravitated toward ideas that undermined biblical authority and basic doctrine in an attempt to reach secular people and staying in the cultural mainstream, some Christians are hailing postmodernism as the trend that will make the church interesting and exciting to postmoderns. We are told that Christians must shift their emphasis from objective truth to communal experience, from rational argument to subjective appeal, from doctrinal orthodoxy to "relevant" practices. I have reasoned throughout this book that this move is nothing less than fatal to Christian integrity and biblical witness. It is also illogical philosophically. We have something far better to offer.

The Fixed Point
Pascal's arresting insights put the watershed issue of truth into sharper focus:

> Those who lead disorderly lives tell those who are normal that that is they who deviate from nature, and think they are following nature themselves; just as those who are on board ship think that the people on shore are moving away. Language is the same everywhere: we need a fixed point to judge it. The harbour is the judge of those aboard ship, but where are we going to find a harbour in morals?[1]
>
> When everything is moving at once, nothing appears to be moving, as on board ship. When everyone is moving towards depravity, no one seems to be moving, but if someone stops, he shows up the others who are rushing on by acting as a fixed point.[2]

The fixed point in a shifting world is biblical truth and all that agrees with it, for "all truth is God's truth." Truth is rooted in God, who is "a mighty fortress, . . . a bulwark never failing" (Martin Luther). Those who betray truth have joined the multitude that is moving toward depravity morally, intellectually and spiritually—however contented and relevant these postmoderns may seem. By betraying truth, they lose their voice, their authority, their endorsement by reality and their integrity. Humans, as finite and fallible beings, require a knowledge of reality outside of their cultures, languages and preferences in order to have

---

[1]Blaise Pascal, *Pensees*, ed. Alban Krailsheimer (New York: Viking, 1966), 697/383, p. 247.
[2]Pascal, *Pensees* 699/382, p. 247.

any hope for moral, spiritual and intellectual repentance, restoration and renewal. We must be true to the truth, developing the art and discipline of truthfulness in a world of untruth. The realities we autonomously construct are only unrealities, built on sand. In the end, God himself will deconstruct all sham deities. "Do people make their own gods? Yes, but they are not gods!" (Jer 16:20).

How can the church serve as a witness to the "fixed point" for those drifting and bouncing on the choppy seas of incessant cultural change? How can the church be "the pillar and foundation of the truth" (1 Tim 3:15) in postmodern times? Rather than summarizing my earlier arguments, I will conclude with several suggestions that I take to be crucial for this mandate.

Be Seekers of Truth

Those who follow Christ, who is the truth (Jn 14:6), must never take truth for granted, be satisfied with a meager helping of it, refuse to test their truth claims against objective reality or fail to work out the implications of their beliefs in all of life. If we are to resist truth decay, the truth must be our most prized possession. As Proverbs says, "Buy the truth and do not sell it" (23:23). Sadly some Christians believe without being able or even willing to fathom the depths of their faith. But as Machen said:

> The Christian religion flourishes not in the darkness but in the light. Intellectual slothfulness is but a quack remedy for unbelief; the true remedy is consecration of intellectual power to the service of the Lord Jesus Christ.[3]

For many Christians this would mean a radical rearrangement of one's priorities. Making the search for truth pivotal means cutting against the grain of postmodern culture as well as postmodernist philosophy. It entails being countercultural for Christ, who commanded us to love him with all of our minds (Mt 22:37-39). J. P. Moreland's excellent book *Love Your God with All Your Mind* (1997) addresses in depth the

---

[3]J. Gresham Machen, *Education, Christianity, and the State: Essays by J. Gresham Machen*, ed. John W. Robbins (Jefferson, Md.: Trinity Foundation, 1987), p. 34.

matter of developing one's mind for God. It should be carefully studied by any Christian who wants to resist the postmodernist spirit of the age.[4]

Although he was an atheist who hated Christianity and a precursor of postmodernism, Friedrich Nietzsche's life can in some ways challenge or even shame intellectually slothful Christians. Bernard Ramm's excellent chapter on Nietzsche concludes with this rousing (if somewhat hyperbolic) provocation, which I often read aloud to my philosophy students after discussing Nietzsche's work.

> What is the devil's due Evangelicals can glean from Nietzsche? It is the willingness to be driven like Nietzsche. It is the willingness to spare no pains in the search for truth. It is the willingness . . . to work into the late hours of the night or to start in the earliest hours of the day; to pick up a new project as soon as we have finished an older one; to grow weary and exhausted in our quest for truth; to have . . . our eyes watery from too much reading, and our bodies bent over from long, weary hours at the study desk.
>
> No Evangelical whose reading habits are a disgrace to the seriousness of the Christian ministry, or who spends more time before a television set than he does in serious reading in his study has the right to damn Nietzsche from the pulpit to some gruesome place in the Inferno.[5]

Ramm grants that Nietzsche was "a devil's hack" and a vicious and unfair critic of Christianity.[6] But if this brilliant but deceived man could expend so much cognitive energy without God's direction and power, what is possible—and necessary—for those who believe the truth of the gospel?

Truth Means Loving Confrontation

When we reach solid conclusions about what is true, especially on core

---

[4]J. P. Moreland, *Love Your God with All Your Mind: The Role of Reason in the Life of the Soul* (Colorado Springs, Colo.: NavPress, 1997). See also Os Guinness, *Fit Bodies, Fat Minds* (Grand Rapids, Mich.: Baker, 1994).
[5]Bernard Ramm, *The Devil, Seven Wormwoods, and God* (Waco, Tex.: Word, 1977), pp. 61-62.
[6]Ibid., p. 62.

matters of theology and ethics, we must be willing to put these ideas to the test of public debate and dialogue, rather than hide our light under a bowl (Mt 5:15-16). In a culture where tolerance is considered by some the only remaining virtue, we must be willing to take a stand that will be labeled as intolerant, although we strive to remain humble before God. As Schaeffer put it, "Truth *demands* confrontation; loving confrontation, but confrontation nevertheless. If our reflex action is always accommodation regardless of the centrality of the truth involved, there is something wrong."[7] As Jesus warned, "Woe to you when everyone speaks well of you, for that is how their ancestors treated the false prophets" (Lk 6:26).

Truth decays in large part because those who should be truth-tellers and truth-bearers are too frequently shirking their divinely appointed duties, through cowardice or ignorance or both. Consider Pascal's exhortations:

> And is it not obvious that, just as it is a crime to disturb the peace when truth reigns, it is also a crime to remain at peace when the truth is being destroyed? There is therefore a time when peace is just and a time when it is unjust.[8]
>
> Weaklings are those who know the truth, but maintain it only as far as it is in their interest to do so, and apart from that forsake it.[9]

We should be heartened by the words of Jesus, who admonishes us to not fear speaking the truth, even at the expense of ridicule, for he will give us the strength to do so. Eugene Peterson's modern paraphrase of this section of the beatitudes captures this tellingly:

> You're blessed when your commitment to God provokes persecution. The persecution drives you even deeper into God's kingdom.
>
> Not only that—count yourselves blessed every time people put you down or throw you out or speak lies about you to discredit me. What it means is that the truth is too close for comfort and they are uncomfort-

---

[7]Francis A. Schaeffer, *The Great Evangelical Disaster* (Westchester, Ill.: Crossway, 1984), p. 64.

[8]Pascal, *Pensees* 973/949, p. 346.

[9]Ibid., 739/864, p. 256.

able. You can be glad when that happens—give a cheer even!—for though
they don't like it, I do! And all heaven applauds. And know that you are
in good company. My prophets and witnesses have always gotten into
this kind of trouble. (Mt 5:11-12 The Message)

Teach and Preach with a Holy Sobriety

Preaching and teaching in the church should concentrate on great (but
presently neglected) Christian truths of divine authority, God's holiness
and law, our sinfulness, the fear of God, the eternal realities of hell and
heaven, Christ's supremacy and lordship, godly repentance and the
responsibilities of Christian character and community in a compromised world. Public communication must also target apologetics and
ethics in order to reverse truth decay in the pews. Pollster George Barna
and others have shown that the beliefs of many so-called evangelicals
are unbiblical or even antibiblical and that biblical illiteracy is shame-
fully common.[10]

Pastor and author Douglas Webster illustrates this scandal by noting
a conversation with a non-Christian who was seriously interested in the
Christian claim to truth. His wife, a regular churchgoer, claimed that
the problem with their marriage was her husband's unbelief. The man
asked Pastor Webster, "Do you believe it is right for my teenage daughter to invite her boyfriend home to spend the night in the same bed?"
Before he could answer, the man continued, "My wife does. She believes that Jesus desires intimacy in relationships, so it's okay for my
daughter to sleep with her boyfriend. I'm sorry, but I think that is
wrong."[11] The unbeliever had a better grasp of Christian ethics than the
churchgoer, who had been affected by postmodernist sentimentality
and relativism. As Webster expresses it:

> Her feeling toward the moral law is not unusual in the American church.
> By claiming that the unconditional love of Jesus approves immorality in
> the name of intimacy, she divorced law and gospel, forgiveness and obe-

---

[10]See George Barna, *Index of Leading Spiritual Indicators* (Dallas: Word, 1996).
[11]Douglas Webster, "Evangelizing the Church," in *Christian Apologetics in the Postmodern World*, ed. Timothy R. Phillips and Dennis L. Okholm (Downers Grove, Ill.:
InterVarsity Press, 1995), p. 206.

dience. For others, the excuse is diversity or tolerance, justifying sin in the name of Jesus.[12]

To counter this kind of abject aberration, preaching should be word-oriented as opposed to image-oriented, rational as opposed to merely emotional, transformational as opposed to trivial and intellectually stimulating as opposed to merely entertaining or amusing. In other words, it must be countercultural and must not bow to postmodernist trends. The God of Scripture, not the trends of postmodernity, must set the agenda of the church. Rather than focusing on being relevant to a culture that has largely lost the very concept of truth, we must engage that culture truthfully. However much postmodernism affects any-one—whether Gen Xers, Baby Boomers or others—certain basic theo-logical facts have not changed; they are not generation specific. There is no God but God; idols must be unseated and destroyed; hearts and minds and lives must be modified according to God's standards. The consumers of postmodernity need most what they desire least—the perfect righteousness of Christ applied to their lives for the forgiveness of sins and their adoption into God's eternal family.

Women and men called to the high office of teaching and preaching (Jas 3:1) must not shy away from the hard truths of Scripture but em-brace them and declare them with fire and light, borne of prayer and trembling before a holy God. As the apostle Paul instructed young Ti-tus, "In your teaching show integrity, seriousness and soundness of speech that cannot be condemned" (Tit 2:7). A God-centered and truth-intensive ministry of the Word is indispensable in a postmodern time when many would dispense with or marginalize both. Paul's testimony should summon us to fidelity to God's truth, in the face of the tempta-tion to accommodate to the moods and fads of the day.

> With the help of our God we dared to tell you his gospel in spite of strong opposition. For the appeal we make does not spring from error or impure motives, nor are we trying to trick you. On the contrary, we speak as those approved by God to be entrusted with the gospel. We are not trying to please people but God, who tests our hearts. You know we never used

---

[12]Ibid.

flattery, nor did we put on a mask to cover up greed—God is our witness. We were not looking for human praise, not from you or anyone else. (1 Thess 2:2-6)

Evangelicals are easily excited by new technologies and innovative measures, which they are eager to use in teaching, preaching and evangelism. But they often fail to reflect on the reality that these tools are not neutral. They forget (or never knew) that "the medium is the message" (Marshall McLuhan). Many of these technologies may reinforce truth decay unintentionally. An example of this phenomenon is found in a recent *Leadership Journal* article on how to use video in church services. The author gives technical tips and stories to illustrate how to do this but never raises the crucial question of whether or not the media images from popular culture (typically from motion pictures) are appropriate for communicating the message of the gospel. Popular culture, steeped as it is in postmodernist sensibilities, is typically not the medium for expressing the eternal truths of God.

This article ends with a reference to the author's church showing "a visual overview of Revelation."[13] The mind boggles at this. That kind of highly symbolic literature cannot be presented in a visual format without severe distortion. The book of Revelation is not a Stephen King movie starring Jesus. Given the dominance of video in our culture and the numberless "vidiots" who view anything on a screen as mindless entertainment, the employment of video in preaching or worship is very likely to distract people from the gravity and sobriety of the biblical message. This point is debatable, but the author of the *Leadership* article never even raised the question. His greatest concern was that churches should be sure to end the movie clip at the right spot in order to avoid showing scenes containing offensive words.[14] This is to strain a gnat and swallow a camel.

This accommodation to postmodern cultural dynamics illustrates the observation by the astute social critic James Twitchell that many evangelical churches are "programmed from below, from the audience,

---

[13]Wayne Schmidt, "The Value of Video," *Leadership*, spring 1999, p. 46.
[14]For an insightful critique of popular culture from a Christian viewpoint, see Kenneth A. Myers, *All God's Children and Blue Suede Shoes: Christians and Popular Culture* (Westchester, Ill.: Crossway, 1989).

just as with other media."[15] When the people in the pews are soaked in postmodernist assumptions and sensibilities that erode the biblical view of truth, they are in no position to program the life of God's church—for teaching, evangelism or anything else. The church meets real spiritual needs by serving the true God, not by catering to consumer preferences and reacting to the most recent polling data. We are stewards of a revelation from beyond ourselves, to which we are accountable (2 Tim 3:15-17).[16] Paul captures this: "I want you to know, brothers and sisters, that the gospel I preached is not of human origin. I did not receive it from any human source, nor was I taught it; rather, I received it by revelation from Jesus Christ" (Gal 1:11-12).

Worship in Spirit and in Truth
The very idea of worshiping God "in spirit and truth" (Jn 4:23-24) is lost on most postmoderns, given their predilection for image over reality, feeling over truth and entertainment over edification. The notion of God's authority and holiness eliciting honor, praise, worship and adoration must be restored to churches by intentional teaching and repeated practice. This means rethinking the nature of our worship music. Able theologian and social critic David Wells analyzed hundreds of modern hymns and praise songs in relation to classic hymns. He concluded that recent worship lyrics express a "postmodernist spirituality" that emphasizes the individual over the church, felt needs over God's requirements and power over truth. He begins his chapter "A Tale of Two Spiritualities," from *Losing Our Virtue* (1998), with this telling comparison:

> Long my imprisoned spirit lay
> Fast bound in sin and nature's night
> Thine eye diffused a quickening ray;
> I woke—the dungeon flamed with light!

---

[15]James B. Twitchell, *For Shame: The Loss of Common Decency in American Culture* (New York: Saint Martin's Press, 1997), p. 152.
[16]See Twitchell's whole discussion of seeker-sensitive churches in this regard, pp. 142-54. See also Os Guinness, *Dining with the Devil: The Megachurch Movement Flirts with Modernity* (Grand Rapids, Mich.: Baker, 1993); and Douglas Webster, *Selling Jesus: What's Wrong with Marketing the Church* (Downers Grove, Ill.: InterVarsity Press, 1992).

My chains fell off, my heart was free,
I rose, went forth, and followed thee.
                                    Charles Wesley

I need you to hold me
Like my daddy never could,
And I need you to show me
How resting in your arms can be so good.
I need you to walk with me
Hand in hand we'll run and play
And I need you to talk to me
Tell me again you'll stay.
                                    Brenda Lefavre[17]

Besides the vast artistic discrepancy between the majestic Wesley
hymn ("And Can it Be?") and the banality of the Lefavre chorus, they illustrate the great divide between what Wells calls "Reformed or classic
spirituality" and the postmodern perversion.[18] Wesley emphasizes freedom from sin wrought by God's grace. Lefavre emphasizes emotional
need. Wesley, while provoking strong emotion, roots his ringing words in
theological truth. Lefavre sentimentally invokes God to meet emotional
cravings, all theology aside. Sadly, much postmodernist spirituality expressed in music never addresses God as God at all, let alone reveling in
his attributes and praising his person. It simply recites feelings and asks
God to bestow certain psychological or social benefits to meet the felt
needs of the singer ("worshiper" is not the appropriate term here at all).

This must change if truth decay is to be reversed in our churches and
in our souls. A. W. Tozer's words still ring true. "What comes into our
minds when we think about God is the most important thing about us.
. . . Worship is pure or base as the worshiper entertains high or low
thoughts of God."[19] Worship must lift one out of oneself into the objec-

---

[17]David Wells, *Losing Our Virtue: Why the Church Must Recover Its Moral Vision* (Grand
  Rapids, Mich.: Eerdmans, 1998), p. 21.
[18]Wells should not be taken to mean only the Calvinistic tradition, especially since the
  hymn he cites is by Charles Wesley, an Arminian!
[19]A. W. Tozer, *The Knowledge of the Holy: The Attributes of God: Their Meaning in the
  Christian Life* (New York: Harper & Brothers, 1961), p. 9.

tive and eternal realities of God. As Rebecca Merrill Groothuis explains, God's truth must drive all worship.

> It is all too easy, especially in churches that emphasize personal experience, for our worship of God to degenerate into an idolizing of our mental state during the "worship service." When a person constructs a god out of his own imagination, his god is his imagination, and he is guilty of self-worship, which is idolatry. The worshipping Christian must remember that God is an objective reality, not a subjective mental state. God exists independently of anyone's imagination, and to worship him necessarily requires that one turn one's attention away from contemplation of his own subjective experience and toward the God who is objectively "there."[20]

Presenting Truth in Evangelism

Given the postmodernist rejection of the Christian view of truth, Christian evangelism must not assume that unbelievers come to the table with any understanding of the nature of God, Christ, sin, eternity or of their own souls. In our attempts to rationally and lovingly persuade people to embrace Jesus Christ as the only way of spiritual liberation, we must be sure to accurately explain and illustrate our terms. In other words, a great deal of pre-evangelism is usually needed at the level of the nature of truth and its implications on life, since postmodernist thought is so confused on these matters. Postmodernists may be willing to "accept Jesus into their heart" with little or no understanding of the meaning or implications of the gospel of Christ. To them, "accepting Jesus" may be taken to mean trying out a new spiritual exercise or experimenting with a new lifestyle or even simply buying a new product!

A cultural and theological incongruity of titanic proportions was evidenced by a 1999 campaign to "market God." Ten thousand white-on-black billboards were installed around the country, featuring cute messages that included "Let's meet at my house Sunday before the game," "Keep using my name in vain and I'll make rush hour longer" and

---

[20]Rebecca Merrill Groothuis, "Putting Worship in the Worship Service," in Douglas Groothuis, *Christianity That Counts: Being a Christian in a Non-Christian World* (Grand Rapids, Mich.: Baker, 1994), p. 76.

"Don't Make Me Come Down Here," all signed by "God." An anonymous client enlisted the Smith Agency in Fort Lauderdale, Florida, to
"get people thinking about God." Agency president Andy Smith says,
"We thought it would be interesting to make God a regular guy—someone you can talk to, relate to, be comfortable with."[21]

A commentator in the secular magazine *Civilization* showed far more
wisdom than the sponsors of the program by saying, "One wonders,
though, if God the product would stand up against truth-in-packaging
laws."[22] One further wonders how God the product stands up against
the God revealed at Sinai, in Holy Scripture and in Jesus Christ—the
God who is the real and all-knowing Audience of one. Taking trite advertising slogans and affixing the word *God* to them on billboards
across the country (at great expense), in fact, breaks the commandment
of God not to take his name in vain (Ex 20:7). We are to hallow the name
of God, not market it (Mt 6:9). God is not a consumer item but rather "a
consuming fire" (Heb 12:29). Audience-driven marketing will not cause
people to "start thinking about God"; it will simply erect bigger and
better golden calves. It will also give them but another mindless
chuckle, this time with a religious reference. The laugh track is always
running in postmodern America, where nothing has any weight beyond its fluctuating market value.[23]

Given the impoverished views of evangelism and biblical truth in
the church, one great danger of postmodernity is false conversions and
the consequently hollow praise offered to God for saved souls that, in
fact, are not saved. Those holding to a postmodernist view of truth may
appear very "spiritual," and to go along with Christian belief to a point,
just so long as religion meets their felt needs. Nevertheless, unless one
knows Jesus Christ and his gospel to be true, one cannot be a Christian
at all. One remains entrapped in the kingdom of darkness. Unless one

---

[21]Naila-Jean Myers, "Who Needs a Burning Bush?" *Civilization*, June-July 1999, p. 31.
[22]Ibid.
[23]On the omnipresence of the laugh track in American culture, see Jean Baudrillard,
    America, trans. Chris Turner (New York: Verso, 1988), p. 49. On the dangers of inap-
    propriate humor see letter 11 in C. S. Lewis, *The Screwtape Letters*, rev. ed. (New
    York: Macmillan, 1982), pp. 49-52.

accepts God's unrivaled authority and holiness—a holy authority that transcends the preferences of self and the conditioning of culture—one cannot repent, believe and accept the things of God on God's terms alone. Kierkegaard put it well to the complacent religionists of his age: "As a sinner man is separated from God by a yawning qualitative abyss. And obviously God is separated from man by the same yawning qualitative abyss when He forgives sins."[24] These concepts are not easily assimilated by postmodernist sensibilities, but they are true, and they must be made known, not diluted.

Evangelism cannot either be effective or authentic in an intellectual climate in which the general tenor of the non-Christian mind is oblivious or hostile to the very idea of truth. What the great apologist and theologian Machen said many years ago deserves quotation:

> It would be a great mistake to suppose that all men are equally well prepared to receive the gospel. It is true that the decisive thing is the regenerative power of God. That can overcome all lack of [intellectual] preparation, and the absence of that makes even the best preparation useless. But as a matter of fact God usually exerts that power in connection with certain prior conditions of the human mind, and it should be ours to create, so far as we can with the help of God, those favorable conditions for the reception of the gospel. We may preach with all the fervor of a reformer and yet succeed only in winning a straggler here and there, if we permit the whole collective thought of the nation or of the world to be controlled by ideas which, by the resistless force of logic, prevent Christianity from being regarded as anything more than a harmless delusion. Under such circumstances, what God desires us to do is to destroy the obstacle at its root.[25]

The root of the obstacle today is the postmodernist redefinition and degradation of truth. Without exposing and destroying this prevalent and fashionable falsehood about truth itself, evangelism—and all of Christian endeavor for that matter—is nothing but a vain religious exercise, a pointless flailing against the chilling winds of untruth.

---

[24]Søren Kierkegaard, *Fear and Trembling* and *The Sickness unto Death*, trans. Walter Lowrie (Princeton, N.J.: Princeton University Press, 1954), p. 253.
[25]Machen, *Education, Christianity, and the State*, p. 51.

Rediscover the Doctrine of Calling

One potent dynamo of postmodernist instability—intellectually, morally and spiritually—is the rootlessness and restlessness of many postmoderns concerning the meaning of their identities. The self becomes saturated, sated with possibilities, options and preferences—yet without an inner gyroscope for direction, correction and inspiration. When all values are constructed, no hierarchy of objective values is possible, no guiding ideal is available and no taboos intrude; there are only experiments, amusements and diversions. The postmodern self is protean and dynamic but also fragmented and ultimately empty of objective meaning. The self was made for better things.

In this toxic cultural environment, Christians need to know who they are and who they serve. They should be crystal clear on what they are summoned to know, who they are summoned to be and what they are summoned to do before the face of God. As postmodernists vainly pose and preen for effect, experience and power, Christians can and must lodge their identities firmly in the transcendent reality of the triune God.

As their primary calling, all Christians are enjoined to love God with all of their beings (Mt 22:37-39), to exemplify virtue in the Holy Spirit (Mt 5:1-12; Gal 5:22-26) and to obey God's commands (Ex 20:1-17). But followers of Christ are also called to find their unique life purpose in order to use their particular gifts and abilities to their utmost for God's glory.

The doctrine of calling has fallen on hard times in the postmodern world. People speak of their "religious preferences" and "spiritual lifestyles" instead of their God-ordained duties, responsibilities and privileges. I cannot adequately broach this weighty subject, but I will offer a few ideas that might assist us to better represent "the fixed point" of truth today. On this matter, Os Guinness's excellent work *The Call* is pivotal.[26]

First, Christian calling brooks no separation between the secular and the sacred. All of life is to be lived under the comprehensive lordship of

---

[26]Os Guinness, *The Call* (Nashville: Word, 1998). See also Gary D. Badcok, *The Way of Life: A Theology of Christian Vocation* (Grand Rapids, Mich.: Eerdmans, 1998); and John Stott, *The Contemporary Christian: Applying God's Word to Today's World* (Downers Grove, Ill.: InterVarsity Press, 1992), pp. 128-45.

Christ (Mt 28:18). One does not don a spiritual self for religious activities and another self for entertainment or one's profession. All of our actions should be unified in obedience to God and for God's glory (1 Cor 10:31; Col 3:17). Similarly, neither are church-related work nor missions more spiritual than other professions such as law, business, education, journalism or politics. The kingdom of God bears on every dimension of life, and agents of that kingdom serve as salt and light wherever the Spirit leads them. As Christians incarnate their worldview in public life, they help reverse truth decay in myriad ways. In the midst of the fragmentation of postmodern pluralism, the Christian sees all things as unified in God's overarching plan for the universe, summed up in the supremacy of Christ. All has meaning in reference to that fixed—and living—point (Col 1:15-20; Heb 13:6).

Second, the discovery of an individual's particular calling involves aligning at least three key elements. A person should focus his or her life on (1) what he or she is good at doing, (2) what needs to be done for the common good and (3) what gives the person deep satisfaction and meaning.

1. Christians have natural and spiritual gifts that ought to be identified and utilized to the utmost. In a fallen world, we cannot always employ our talents to the fullest, but we should strive to find our areas of excellence and develop them for God. We identify the truth about our gifts best through the dynamics of personal Bible study, prayer, Christian friendship and in the matrix of the church community—not through psychological testing, which tends to be impersonal and mechanical, not to mention unreliable.[27] In this way, we model what biblical community should be, a community where we should be "speaking the truth in love" (Eph 4:15) to one another, stimulating each other to love and good deeds (Heb 10:24). It should be noted that this is not the postmodernist sense of community or lifestyle, which is self-contained and horizontal, without a stable, vertical reference outside of itself.

2. However, our gifts need to be coordinated with those who stand to

---

[27]On the inadequacies of modern intelligence and other testing, see Neil Postman, *Technopoly: The Surrender of Culture to Technology* (New York: Alfred A. Knopf, 1992), pp. 123-43.

benefit from them. Howard Hendricks reportedly once said that if you think you have the gift of teaching, you had better be able to find a good number of people who have the gift of listening to you! What does the church and world lack that we can uniquely provide? We are gifted to serve, not to glorify our gifts or to duplicate what others have already done well in their place of service. Just as Paul's ambition was to preach the gospel where Christ was not known so that he would not be building on someone else's foundation (Rom 15:20), so should we employ our gifts where they are truly needed.

3. Last, if we are employing our real gifts for worthy purposes, this should give us a rich sense of joy and even adventure in knowing that we are moving in God's will for our lives (Rom 12:1-2). "The joy of the LORD is your strength" (Neh 8:10). This is not a superficial titillation or (heaven forbid) a postmodern diversion but a purpose and practice that orients one's fundamental identity toward specific ends. As Frederick Buechner wonderfully phrases it, "The place God calls you to is the place where your deep gladness and the world's deep hunger meet."[28] The soul should celebrate its contribution to others' well being.

As followers of Jesus refuse the false seductions of style, hype and spiritual consumerism, they regain and retain a resonating sense of what it means to hear and heed the call of God, come what may. While postmodernists madly "reinvent" themselves (to no ultimate end) ever more rapidly, radically and frantically, the Christian can rest in his or her identity in Jesus Christ, his kingdom and his calling. As we "seek first his kingdom and his righteousness" (Mt 6:33), our lives are brought into greater harmony with God's truth and, therefore, into greater disharmony with all untruth, postmodernist or otherwise. In so doing, we serve as signs, clues and rumors of God's objective reality in a world moving toward depravity in nearly every direction.

The Final Word from the Fixed Point
Although originally written to a premodern culture, the words of Jesus

---

[28]Frederick Buechner, *Wishful Thinking: A Theological ABC* (New York: Harper & Row, 1973), p. 95.

in the book of Revelation still prove riveting to those who yearn to stay true to him today. As our Fixed Point, the First and the Last, Jesus deserves the final word:

> To the angel of the church in Laodicea write:
>
> These are the words of the Amen, the faithful and true witness, the ruler of God's creation. I know your deeds, that you are neither cold nor hot. I wish you were either one or the other! So, because you are luke-warm—neither cold nor hot—I am about to spit you out of my mouth. You say, "I am rich; I have acquired wealth and do not need a thing." But you do not realize that you are wretched, pitiful, poor, blind and naked. I counsel you to buy from me gold refined in the fire, so that you can become rich; and white clothes to wear, so that you can cover your shameful nakedness; and salve for your eyes, so that you can see.
>
> Those whom I love I rebuke and discipline. So be earnest, and repent. Here I am! I stand at the door and knock. If anyone hears my voice and opens the door, I will come in and eat with them, and they with me.
>
> To those who overcome, I will give the right to sit with me on my throne, just as I overcame and sat down with my Father on his throne. Those who have ears, let them hear what the Spirit says to the churches. (Rev 3:14-22)

Appendix

TELEVISION
Agent of Truth Decay

TV Guide *published a short manifesto—actually, an advertisement by ABC—* on the goodness of television, just in case anyone doubted it.

> For years the pundits, moralists and self-righteous, self-appointed preservers of our culture have told us that television is bad. They've stood high on their soapbox and looked condescendingly on our innocuous pleasure. . . . Well, television is not the evil destroyer of all that is right in this world. In fact, and we say this with all the disdain we can muster for the elitists who purport otherwise—TV is good.
>
> TV binds us together. It makes us laugh. Makes us cry. Why, in the span of ten years, TV brought us the downfall of an American president, one giant step for mankind and the introduction of Farrah Fawcett as one of "Charlie's Angels." Can any other medium match TV for its immediacy, its impact, its capacity to entertain?[1]

Indeed, no one can dispute television's unrivaled immediacy, impact and entertainment capabilities. But it is exactly these features that make it a potent agent of truth decay in postmodernity. Television is an unre-

---

[1]"TV Is Good," *TV Guide*, August 9-15, 1997. No author is listed.

ality appliance that dominates our mentality. We then take this unreality mentality and impose it on the rest of the real world. That is, we (mis)understand the world in terms of the mentality inherent to the form of communication that is television.

Throughout this book, I have distinguished between postmodernity as a truth-decaying social condition and postmodernism as a truth-decaying philosophy, as well as emphasizing that these reinforce each other in various ways. One primary engine or dynamo for truth decay is the cultural system of television. I will highlight five ways in which television contributes to the loss of truth, and then give three practical suggestions for overcoming these effects.

Television seldom, if ever, directly addresses postmodernist philosophy (or any other philosophy). However, its very nature contributes to a loss of truth by reinforcing certain crucial themes in postmodernism. Television has become a commercial and cultural institution in American life; as such, it is unproblematic to the vast majority of Americans and, therefore, highly influential. Jacques Ellul is right that "television acts less by the creation of clear notions and precise opinions and more by enveloping us in a haze."[2] Neil Postman captures our sad situation: "Television has achieved the status of a 'meta-medium'—an institution that directs not only our knowledge of the world, but our knowledge of the *ways of knowing* as well."[3] While many have noticed and object to the content of television fare (too much sex, violence, anti-Christian material, etc.), television's nature as a medium is largely ignored, thereby granting it a kind of epistemological immunity from criticism. Yet Scripture calls us to "test everything. Hold on to the good. Avoid every kind of evil" (1 Thess 5:21-22).

The medium of communication matters since it always shapes the messages it carries, and these mediated messages shape us. A novel and

---

[2]Jacques Ellul, *The Technological Bluff*, trans. Geoffrey W. Bromiley (Grand Rapids, Mich.: Eerdmans, 1990), p. 336.

[3]Neil Postman, *Amusing Ourselves to Death* (New York: Penguin, 1985), pp. 78-79. The dominance of television as a medium in American culture also fits into the category of what Ivan Illich calls a "radical monopoly." See Ivan Illich, *Tools for Conviviality* (New York: Harper & Row, 1973), pp. 54-61.

a television series based on a novel differ in crucial ways, for example. Therefore, any medium should be exegeted to determine its nature, function and structure. Only in this way can we ascertain what it does well, what it cannot do and what it does poorly. This is what Marshall McLuhan meant by his hyperbolic slogan, "the medium is the message."[4] Taking his cue from the discussion of idolatry in Psalm 115, McLuhan also remarked that, "We become what we behold"[5] (see also Ps 1). When we become habituated to a particular form of communication, our mentalities and sensibilities bear its mark.

A raft of studies from several decades indicate that Americans consume vast quantities of television—an average of about four to five hours per day, with many taking in much more. Televisions are also becoming nearly omnipresent, imperialistically colonizing automobiles, airports, restaurants, classrooms, bars, daycare centers and computers.[6] They are even being placed on some gasoline pumps. Once, while attempting to explain a family member's strokelike symptoms in the triage area of a hospital emergency room, I found myself competing with a blaring television. After I turned it off (without asking permission), the attendant behind the check-in desk huffily turned it back on. Nearly 100 percent of American homes have at least one television, and three out of four have more than one. Eighty-four percent of households have at least one VCR. Many have elaborate home-theater systems costing thousands of dollars. And half of all Americans say they watch too much television![7]

The Image over the Word: Discourse in Distress

What is there about the nature of the television medium that shapes its message? First, television emphasizes the moving image over written

---

[4]Marshall McLuhan, *Understanding Media: The Extensions of Man* (Cambridge, Mass.: MIT Press, reprint 1994), pp. 7-21.

[5]Ibid., p. 45.

[6]George Guilder believes the days of old fashioned television are numbered, because its basic functions will be absorbed by computers. See George Guilder, *Life After Television* (New York: W. W. Norton, 1994).

[7]For these and more disturbing statistics about television watching, consult "Television Statistics," on the TV-Free American Web page <www.tvfa.org>.

and spoken language. It is image-driven, image-saturated and image-controlled. This is precisely what television does that books, recordings and pictures cannot do; it brings us visual action. However, when the image dominates the word, rational discourse ebbs. We are attracted to the incandescent screen just as medievals were attracted to stained glass windows. As McLuhan noted, the light comes through them as opposed to light being shown on them (as with books and photographs and other objects in the physical world). These technologically animated images move and combine in ways unknown only a few decades ago, thus increasing their power to mesmerize.

Ellul observes that the "visionary reality of connected images cannot tolerate critical discourse, explanation, duplication, or reflection"—all rational activities required for separating truth from error. Cognitive pursuits "presuppose a certain distance and withdrawal from the action, whereas images require that I continually be involved in the action." The images must keep the word in check, keep it humiliated, since "the word produces disenchantment with the image; the word strips it of its hypnotic and magical power."[8] Words can expose an image as false or misleading, as when we read in a magazine that a television program "re-created" an event that never occurred. Novelist Larry Woiwode further develops the implications:

> The mechanics of the English language have been tortured to pieces by TV. Visual, moving images—which are the venue of television—can't be held in the net of careful language. They want to break out. They really have nothing to do with language. So language, grammar and rhetoric have become fractured.[9]

When the image overwhelms and subjugates the word, the ability to think, write and communicate in a linear and logical fashion is undermined. Television's images have their immediate effect on us, but that effect is seldom to cause us to pursue their truth or falsity. Television's

---

[8]Jacques Ellul, *The Humiliation of the Word*, trans. Joyce Main Hanks (Grand Rapids, Mich.: Eerdmans, 1985), p. 142.

[9]Larry Woiwode, "Television: The Cyclops That Eats Books," *Imprimus*, February 1992, p. 1.

images are usually shorn of their overall context and meaning, and are reduced to factoids (at best). Ideas located within a historical and logical setting are replaced by impressions, emotions and stimulations. While images communicate narrative stories and quantitative information well (such as graphs and charts), words are required for more linear and logical communication. Propositions and beliefs can be true or false; images in themselves do not have truth value. The persuasiveness of the image on television led media theorist Tony Schwartz to claim that truth is now an outmoded concept, since it belongs to a time when print communication was dominant.[10]

Media critic Malcolm Muggeridge understood this well:

> The one thing television can't do is express ideas. . . . There is a danger in translating life into an image, and that is what television is doing. In doing it, it is falsifying life. Far from the camera's being an accurate recorder of what is going on, it is the exact opposite. It cannot convey reality nor does it even want to.[11]

The images of television may be arresting, alluring and entrancing, but they are prefabricated presentations that shrink events into factoids or outright falsehoods. This is a feature of the very nature of television, as Francis Schaeffer pointed out:

> TV manipulates viewers by its normal way of operating. Many viewers seem to assume that when they have seen something on TV, they have seen it with their own eyes. . . .
>
> But this is not so, for one must never forget that every television minute has been edited. The viewer does not see the event. He sees . . . an *edited symbol* or an *edited image* of that event. An aura and illusion of objectivity and truth is built up, which could not be totally the case even if the people shooting the film were completely neutral.[12]

---

[10]Tony Schwartz, *The Responsive Chord* (Garden City, N.Y.: Anchor, 1973), pp. 18-22, cited in Kenneth Myers, *All God's Children and Blue Suede Shoes: Christians and Popular Culture* (Westchester, Ill.: Crossway, 1989), p. 162.

[11]Malcolm Muggeridge, cited in Woiwode, "Television: The Cyclops That Eats Books," p. 3.

[12]Francis Schaeffer, *How Should We Then Live? The Rise and Decline of Western Thought and Culture* (Old Tappan, N.J.: Revell, 1976), p. 240; see also Ellul, *Humiliation*, p. 140.

The triumph of the televised image over the word contributes to the depthlessness of postmodern sensibilities. Reality becomes the image, whether or not that image corresponds to any objective state of affairs—and we are not challenged to engage in this analysis. The above-quoted ABC piece of propaganda advises us to "celebrate our cerebral-free non activity."[13] As a consequence of such nonactivity, truth suffers and truthfulness is downplayed, if not ignored. Joshua Meyrowitch, a professor of communication, complains that his students "tend to have an image-based standard of truth. If I ask, 'What evidence supports your view or contradicts it?' they look at me as if I came from another planet." This is because "It's very foreign to them to think in terms of truth, logic, consistency and evidence."[14] Such oblivion exists not only in the case with media students but is true of culture at large, as Kenneth Myers stresses: "A culture that is rooted more in images than in words will find it increasingly difficult to sustain *any* broad commitment to any truth, since truth is an abstraction requiring language."[15] In postmodernism, truth and logic are mere social constructions, which can be deconstructed and reconstructed at whim. Television gives a powerful object lesson in these notions of truth and so furthers truth decay in the souls of millions for hours every day.

Muggeridge commented that when the Israelites worshiped the golden calf instead of waiting for the Word from Moses, they attempted to televise (or make visible) God.[16] Biblically speaking, God commands that we not make graven images nor attempt to televise the invisible. In the beginning was the Word, not the image (Jn 1:1). God gave us a book, not a video. When, in any culture, written language is marginalized by television, biblical truth begins to lose its vibrancy. Christians must restore the primacy and power of the Word as an antidote to truth decay by television.

---

[13]"TV Is Good."
[14]Quoted in John Leo, "Spicing Up the (Ho-Hum) Truth," *U.S. News & World Report*, March 8, 1993, p. 24.
[15]Myers, *All God's Children and Blue Suede Shoes*, 164.
[16]Muggerridge, *Christ and the Media* (Grand Rapids, Mich.: Eerdmans, 1977), p. 59.

The Loss of Self: Truth Removed

Second, along with the displacing of the word by the flickering television image comes a loss of authentic selfhood, whereby the self is deemed as a moral agent inexorably enmeshed in a moral and spiritual universe. Instead the self is filled with a welter of images and factoids and sound bites lacking moral and intellectual adhesion. The self becomes ungrounded and fragmented by its experiences of television. This matches the postmodernist abandonment of a unified and normative self that is disciplined and directed by transcendent truths.

By contrast, a love of serious reading orients the self toward grand narratives and abstract truths—such as the holiness and mysteries of God, moral truth, the pursuit of virtue, the dangers of vice, immortality—and these truths place the self in a position of rectitude before them. People whose sensibilities and worldviews are adjusted through serious reading tend to live by what they have read. They live in conversation with great minds, even when they are not reading.[17] As William Ellery Channing noted, "It is chiefly through books that we enjoy intercourse with superior minds." Watchers of television, on the contrary, simply engage in the imitation of proliferating images and multiple personae. Barry Sanders sounds this grim theme: "With the disappearance of the book goes that most precious instrument for holding modern society together, the internalized text on which is inscribed conscience and remorse, and, most significant of all, the self."[18] Postmodern illiterates live their lives through a series of television characters (better: shadows of characters), and changing channels becomes a model for the self's manner of experience and its mode of being. Moral and spiritual anchorage is lost. The self is left to try on a pastiche of designer personae in no particular order and for no particular reason.

The reading of great literature immerses us in realities beyond ourselves, although not unrelated to our selves. But this life of reading requires an existential participation not permitted by television, which

---

[17]On this theme, see Sven Birkerts, *The Gutenberg Elegies: The Fate of Reading in an Electronic Age* (New York: Faber & Faber, 1994). This book is highly recommended.

[18]Barry Sanders, *A Is for Ox: The Collapse of Literacy and the Rise of Violence in an Electronic Age* (New York: Vintage, 1995), pp. 77-78.

simply sweeps us along at its own pace. One cannot muse over a television program the way one ponders a character in Shakespeare or in C. S. Lewis, or a Pascal parable, or a line from a T. S. Eliot poem such as "But our lot crawls between dry ribs/to keep its metaphysics warm."[19] No one on television could utter such a line seriously. It would be "bad television"—too abstract, too poetic, too deep, just not entertaining. As such, a serious selfhood—in which the self knows itself as a unique actor in a great cosmic drama that is larger than one's self—is rendered impossible. Inwardness and self-reflection are replaced by an outward compulsion for increasingly more mediated experiences that draw one increasingly further away from the essence of one's soul and its ultimate, eternal fulfillment. As fallen beings, we have always been mysterious to ourselves, but television can only exacerbate our sad stupidity. Kierkegaard perceived that the self is quite easy to lose in the ways of the world:

> About such a thing as [the self] not much fuss is made in the world; for a self is the thing the world is least apt to inquire about, and the thing of all things the most dangerous for man to let people notice that he has it. The greatest danger, that of losing one's own self, may pass off as quietly as if it were nothing; every other loss, that of an arm, a leg, five dollars, a wife, etc., is sure to be noticed.[20]

Through television, oblivion to self is amplified and broadcast globally and ceaselessly. As a consequence, the self is destabilized, uprooted and hollowed out; it becomes ungrounded, weightless, truthless, opaque to itself—and it likes it that way, because no alternative is available (on television). Postmodernism prevails; the loss of the self in relation to truth is celebrated, not mourned, for "TV is good." But, as Jesus intoned, what is it worth if we gain the whole world (televised for all to see) and forfeit our souls (Mt 16:26)?

A Peek-a-Boo World: Discontinuity and Fragmentation
Third, television relentlessly displays a pseudoworld of discontinuity

---

[19]T.S. Eliot, "Whispers of Immortality."
[20]Søren Kierkegaard, *Fear and Trembling* and *The Sickness unto Death*, trans. Walter Lowrie (Princeton, N.J.: Princeton University Press, 1954), p. 165.

and fragmentation. Its images are not only intrinsically inferior to spoken and written discourse in communicating matters of meaning and substance, but the images appear and disappear and reappear without a proper rational context. An attempt at a sobering news story about slavery in the Sudan is followed by a lively advertisement for Disneyland, followed by an appeal to purchase pantyhose that will make any woman irresistible and so on, ad nauseum. This is what Postman aptly calls the "peek-a-boo world"—a visual environment lacking coherence, consisting of ever-shifting, artificially linked images. In order to detect a logical contradiction, "statements and events [must] be perceived as interrelated aspects of a continuous and coherent context." When the context is one of no context, when fragmentation rules, the very idea of contradiction vanishes.[21] Without any historical or logical context, the very notion of intellectual or moral coherence becomes unsustainable on television.[22]

In reflecting on an essay by Walter Benjamin, social critic Jerry Mander discusses the implications of the detachment of image from context with respect to artistic values.

> The disconnection from inherent meaning, which would be visible if image, object and context were still merged, leads to a similarly disconnected aesthetics in which all uses for images are equal. All meaning in art and also human acts becomes only what is invested in to them. There is no inherent meaning in anything. Everything, even war, is capable of becoming art.[23]

Since postmodernism thrives on fragmentation, incoherence and, ultimately, meaninglessness as modes of being and acting (since there is no God, no objective reality and no universal rationality to provide unity to anything), this facet of television serves postmodernist ends quite well.

The biblical conception of truth contradicts this surrender to incoher-

---

[21]Postman, *Amusing Ourselves to Death*, p. 109.
[22]Ibid., p. 110.
[23]Jerry Mander, *Four Arguments for the Elimination of Television* (New York: Morrow Quill Paperbacks, 1977), p. 288. Mander is discussing Walter Benjamin's essay, "The Work of Art in the Age of Mechanical Reproduction," from the collection *Illuminations*. See also Birkerts, *Gutenberg Elegies*, pp. 224-29.

ence, since truth is a noncontradictory, unified whole, and because God's universal plan proceeds in a linear (if often mysterious and unpredictable) fashion. The prologue to Luke's Gospel would have made bad television, since Luke claims that he "carefully investigated everything from the beginning," such that he could "write an orderly account" of Jesus' life, so his original reader, Theophilus, might "know the certainty of the things [he had] been taught" (Lk 1:3-4).

Pathologies of Velocity: No Time for Truth

Fourth, the increasingly rapid pace of television's images makes careful evaluation impossible and undesirable for the viewer, thus rendering determinations of truth and falsity difficult if not impossible. With sophisticated video technologies, scenes change at hypervelocities and become the visual equivalent of caffeine or amphetamines. The human mind was not designed by its Creator to accommodate to these visual speeds, and so the sensorium suffers from the pathologies of velocity. This means that one simply absorbs hundreds and thousands of rapidly changing images, with little notion of what they mean or whether they correspond to any reality outside of themselves. The pace of this assault of images is entirely imposed upon us; it bears little if any resemblance to reality. As Ellul notes, "The person who puts the images in sequences chooses for you; he condenses or stretches what becomes reality itself for us. We are utterly obliged to follow this rhythm."[24] This, of course, is the exact opposite of what happens in reading.

Habituation to such imposed velocities tends to make people intellectually impatient and easily bored with anything that is slow moving and undramatic—such as reading books (particularly thoughtful ones), experiencing nature in the raw and engaging in face-to-face conversations with fellow human beings. Hence, the apprehension of difficult and demanding truths suffers and withers. The pace of television's agenda disallows edification, understanding and reflection. Boredom

---

[24]Ellul, *Humiliation of the Word*, p. 141. Ellul is right to point out in a footnote on page 141 that this can be overcome to some degree if one videotapes a program and stops and starts it when one chooses. But this is only a small measure of control overall, and most people fail to use this function critically.

always threatens and must be defended against at all costs. The over-stuffed and over-stimulated soul becomes out-of-sync with God, nature, others and itself. It cannot discern truth; it does not want to. This apathetic attitude makes the apprehension and application of truth totally irrelevant.

On the other hand, the godly art of truthfulness requires a sense of pacing one's senses and thoughts according to the subject matter before one. As Augustine said, "The peace . . . of the rational soul [is] the harmony of knowledge and action."[25] The acquisition of knowledge (warranted belief in what is true), requires intellectual patience and fortitude. One must linger on perplexing notions, work them through, compare them to other ideas and attempt to reach conclusions that imply wise and rational actions. Before God, one must shut up, listen and be willing to revolutionize one's life accordingly (see Eccles 5:1-7). God's word—"Be still and know that I am God" (Ps 46:10)—simply cannot be experienced through television, where stillness and silence are only technical mistakes called "dead air." Television thus becomes a strategic weapon in the arsenal of postmodernist cynicism and apathy.[26]

The Entertainment Imperative: Amusement Triumphant

Television promotes truth decay by its incessant entertainment imperative. Amusement trumps all other values and takes captive every topic. Every subject—whether war, religion, business, law or education—must be presented in a lively, amusing or stimulating manner. The best way to receive information interpersonally—through the "talking head"—is the worst way according to television values; it simply fails to entertain (unless a comedy routine is in process). If it fails to entertain, boredom results, and the yawning watcher switches channels to something more captivating. The upshot is that any truth that cannot be

---

[25]Augustine *The City of God* 19.13.
[26]For more on the problems of speed in postmodern culture, see Mark Kingwell, "Fast Forward: Our High-Speed Chase to Nowhere," *Harper's Magazine* (May 1998): 37-48; Stephen Bertman, *Hyperculture: The Human Cost of Speed* (Westport, Conn.: Praeger, 1998); and James Gleick, *Faster: The Acceleration of Just About Everything* (New York: Pantheon, 1999).

transposed into entertainment is discarded by television. Moreover, even off the air, people now think that life (and even Christian ministry) must be entertaining at all costs. One pastor of a megachurch advises preachers that sermons should be roughly twenty minutes in length and must be "light and informal," with liberal sprinklings of "humor and anecdotes."[27] Just like television, isn't it?

The truth is that truth, and the most important truths, is often not entertaining. An entertainment mentality will insulate us from many hard but necessary truths. The concepts of sin, repentance and hell, for instance, cannot be presented as entertaining without robbing them of their intrinsic meaning.[28] Jesus, the prophets and the apostles held the interest of their audience not by being amusing but by their zeal for God's truth, however unpopular or uncomfortable it may have been. They refused to entertain but instead edified and convicted. It was nothing like television.

Becoming Untelevized: The People of Truth

As Postman, Ellul and other critics have noted, television is not simply an appliance or a business: it is a way of life and a mentality for approaching reality. As such, it amplifies and reinforces postmodernist themes of truth decay. Ellul is right: People are "being plunged into an artificial world which will cause them to lose their sense of reality and to abandon their search for truth."[29] To thwart television's power, one must refuse its seductions. Television is good at some forms of entertainment but is very bad at helping us develop the habits of being that lead us deeper into truth for God's sake and the sake of our own souls. Mander does not overstate the cause when he claims, "Television effectively produces a new form of human being—less cre-

---

[27]Discussed in Douglas Webster, *Selling Jesus: What's Wrong with Marketing the Church* (Downers Grove, Ill.: InterVarsity Press, 1992), p. 83. This is not Webster's own philosophy of homiletics!

[28]For a satirical treatment of this, see the chapter "Making Repentance Fun," in Tom Raabe, *The Ultimate Church: An Irreverent Look at Church Growth, Megachurches, and Ecclesiastical "Show Biz"* (Grand Rapids, Mich.: Zondervan, 1991), pp. 39-42. This is a neglected classic and a rare piece of thoughtful evangelical satire.

[29]Ellul, *The Technological Bluff*, p. 337.

ative, less able to make subtle distinctions, speedier, and more inter-ested in *things*."[30] Given this dire condition, some very practical steps can be taken to reverse television's truth-decaying effects on the human being.

1. Engage in a TV-free fast for at least one week and note the changes produced in your thoughts and attitudes. Discuss these effects with those closest to you and or record them in a journal. I require students in one of my courses to engage in a media fast of some sort, and most pick television. They almost uniformly report that the fast revealed a level of attachment to the tube they did not expect. They did suffer some withdrawal at first. However, they later experienced a calming ef-fect and a more contemplative attitude to life; they found more time for friends, family and reading. When they went back to watching televi-sion, many were shocked to realize what they had not seen when they were habituated and desensitized to this medium: most television pro-gramming is insipid, illicit and idiotic.[31]

2. If either the will or the ability to go "cold turkey" is lacking, create instead TV-free zones and times. For instance, many watch television when they are physically or emotionally drained. This is the worst time to do so, since television decreases intellectual vigilance and is not truly relaxing.[32] Therefore, one might make the two hours after returning from work a TV-free zone. The same could be done for the two hours before going to bed. Instead of having the television be the focus of the living room or family room (with all chairs drawn in its direction), place the television in another less-frequented room so that one has to go out of the way to watch it. This breaks the television reflex and leaves the way open to better things, truer things.

3. Replace television watching with truth-enhancing activities, par-ticularly reading thoughtful books. The desire to read and the ability to read well suffer under the ruthless regime of television, as do writing

---

[30]Jerry Mander, *In the Absence of the Sacred: The Failure of Technology and the Survival of the Indian Nations* (San Francisco: Sierra Club Books, 1991), p. 96.

[31]Ellul reports the beneficial effects of television depravation in a French study in *Technological Bluff*, pp. 338-39.

[32]See Mander, *Four Arguments for the Elimination of Television*, pp. 192-215.

skills.[33] Therefore, truth suffers. The very act of reading demands a deep level of intellectual engagement and bestows tremendous pleasure and benefit for the faithful. We *watch* television; we *read* books. Few have described the truth-conducive nature of print and reading as well as Postman:

> Whenever language is the principle medium for communication—especially language controlled by the rigors of print—an idea, a fact, a claim is the inevitable result. . . .
>
> Print is serious because meaning demands to be understood. A written sentence calls upon its author to say something, upon its reader to know the import of what is said. And when an author and reader are struggling with semantic meaning, they are engaged in the most serious challenge to the intellect. This is especially the case with the act of reading, for authors are not always trustworthy. They lie, they become confused, they overgeneralize, they abuse logic and, sometimes, common sense. The reader must come armed, in a serious state of intellectual readiness.[34]

The mental act of reading is not passive, but active. It engages the mind and the imagination in wondrous ways not possible through television—in ways that are, in fact, discouraged by television. Through reading, truth becomes possible and knowable. The discipline of wresting meaning from texts and assessing their truth is invaluable for people who aspire to "[speak] the truth in love" (Eph 4:15). Truth is restored by attending to the Good Book—whose authors are trustworthy, but not always easy to understand (2 Pet 3:16)—and to good books, which require the kind of cognitive criticism Postman describes (Phil 4:8).

The author of Hebrews chastised his or her readers because of their slowness and laziness in learning important biblical truths, which resulted in spiritual ignorance and immaturity. In our truth-decayed day when television hinders the acquisition, internalization and application of so much truth, we should transpose this ancient warning to apply to ourselves.

---

[33]See Woiwode, "Television: The Cyclops That Eats Books," p. 1.
[34]Postman, *Amusing Ourselves to Death*, p. 50; see also, Birkerts, *Gutenberg Elegies*, p. 122.

> We have much to say about this [Jesus' priesthood], but it is hard to explain because you are slow to learn. In fact, though by this time you ought to be teachers, you need someone to teach you the elementary truths of God's word all over again. You need milk, not solid food! Anyone who lives on milk, being an infant, is not acquainted with the teaching about righteousness. But solid food is for the mature, who by constant use have trained themselves to distinguish good from evil. (Heb 5:11-14)

Neutralizing the acids of truth decay means refusing the enticements of one of its chief postmodern agents—television.

Douglas Groothuis *is also the author of* The Soul in Cyberspace *(Baker) and* Unmasking the New Age *(IVP). More information about Dr. Groothuis is available at <http://www.gospelcom.net/ivpress/groothuis>.*

Index of Names

Index of Subjects

advertising, 55-56
aesthetic value, 239-62
apologetics
  communicating biblical views to postmoderns, 161-86
  defending against postmodern views, 139-60
  method of, 175-79
  relevance versus engagement, 163-65, 184-86
architecture, 56, 244, 261-62
art, 14, 239-62
beauty, 248-56, 258
beliefs, 93, 100-101, 154
Bloom, Harold, 51-52
Bruce, F. F., 162-63
calling, 277-79
Christendom, 33-35
Christian community, 194-95
church history and race, 220-22
coherence theory of truth, 148
Coltrane, John, 259-60
confrontation, 267-69
constructivism, 38-39
conversions, 274-75
correspondence view of truth, 13, 86-93, 109-10, 130-31, 150-51
Craig, William Lane, 182-83
critical realism, 131-33
cyberspace, 57-58
deism, 35
Deloria, Vine, 50-51

Derrida, Jacques, 230
Eagleton, Terry, 129-30
egalitarian view, 228-36
emotion, 258-59
Enlightenment, 26, 35, 37, 131
Eno, Brian, 240-41
ethics, 14, 168-72, 187-210
ethnocentrism, 224-28
evangelism, 274-76
evolution, 102
foundationalism, 175-76
Foucault, Michel, 14, 49-50, 98-100, 202-4
fundamentalist-modernist controversy, 263-64
Gellner, Ernest, 39-40
gender, 211-38
Gnosticism, 51
God
  as creator, 217-19, 249-50
  as lawgiver, 207-10
  as truth, 61-62, 65-81, 147, 151
"God" billboards, 274-75
"Good Taste," 241-43
Grenz, Stanley, 14, 116-17
Henry, Carl F. H., 116-17, 120-22, 125
Hick, John, 128-29
history, 214-16, 225-28
Hmong culture, 226-27
Holy Spirit, 145
housing project, Pruitt-Igoe, 27
hypergoods, 170-71
human nature, 202-4
human progress, myth of, 40-41
humanism, 34
hymns, 272-73
identity, 28-29, 54-55, 217, 277-79
incarnation, 118, 126-27

integrity, 10-11
Jasper, John, 221
Jencks, Charles, 136-37
Johnson, Phillip, 183
Kenneson, Philip, 14, 145-52
Kenny G, 259-60
King, Martin Luther, Jr., 18-19
Kirkegaard, Søren, 10-11
language
  biblical, 60-65
  functions of, 86-93, 171-72
  as human creation, 29, 41
  minorities' use of, 204-7
  as revelation of God, 66, 112-15
  translation of, 96-97
law (or principle) of excluded middle, 78, 88-89
law (or principle) of noncontradiction, 76-78, 88-89
Lee, Daniel, 261
Leff, Arthur Allen, 208-10
Lindbeck, George, 118-19
logic, 48-49, 76, 120-27, 176-77
  of Christian claims, 179-82
Luther, Martin, 19, 34-35
McGrath, Alister, 14, 116-17, 120-22, 124, 125, 127-28, 130
media, 27-28, 54
Menchu, Rigoberta, 31
metanarratives, 56-57, 74-75, 130, 135-38, 190-91, 204-6, 264
Middleton, J. Richard, 131-33

THE ATHEISM OF MODERNISM 37
FACT/VALUE 43